THE THEORY AND PRINCIPLES OF ENVIRONMENTAL DISPUTE RESOLUTION

hope@edrusa.com

Many actual events are described in this book. Those descriptions convey James Caplan's experiences, conclusions, and opinions about those events. Other participants in or observers of those events may have different experiences, conclusions, or opinions on how those events developed or about their importance. Mr. Caplan urges people with more to add or concerns about the events or his opinions may contact him at www.environdispute.com. He is also preparing a book of environmental dispute resolution case studies and asks all readers to consider submitting examples to him.

Concerning the graphics and photos displayed in this book, unless otherwise noted, James Caplan prepared the visual material, obtained it under contract with Clipart.com, or copied from federal or other public domain sources.

Library of Congress Cataloging-in-Publication Data is available from the Library of Congress

ISBN 978-0-9827537-0-5

Table of Contents

Acknowledgments

Cheryl Elizabeth Caplan, my beloved wife, strongly encourages my work. Her faith in me and in what I have been trying to accomplish simply makes me love her more.

My oldest daughter, Myrrh Caplan, graduated from Western Washington University, Huxley College with a degree in Environmental Policy. She always provides great EDR ideas whether as a student or as a LEED-certified environmental manager. My thanks to her for being a wonderful daughter and source of good ideas.

My youngest daughter, Dr. Eloi J. Hoopman, DO provides excellent advice about the medical model I use as the basis for the "EDR method that works." My thanks to her for being a wonderful daughter and interpreter of medical mysteries. Her husband, Neil Hoopman, an expert webmaster and software engineer, provides fabulous support in building our website www.edrusa.com and in preparing books for web publication. My thanks to him for his expertise, patience, and clear direction.

Hans and Annemarie Bleiker, from the Institute for Participatory Management and Planning in Monterey, CA, www.ipmp-bleiker.com have been my teachers, mentors, colleagues, and friends for many years. Their pioneering work in helping agencies implement controversial projects, and my use of their methods, served as a "launch pad" for this book and its concepts. I couldn't be more grateful to them.

Established by the U.S. Congress, the U.S. Institute for Environmental Conflict Resolution www.ecr.gov of the Morris K. Udall Foundation is breaking new ground for federal agencies and their partners as they attempt to build ECR into environmental decision-making and management. The goals of the U.S. Institute for ECR are to:

Resolve environmental conflicts and improve environmental decision-making through collaborative problem solving approaches (commonly referred to as environmental conflict resolution (ECR))

Increase the capacity of agencies and other affected stakeholders and practitioners to manage and resolve conflicts

Provide leadership within the federal government to improve environmental decision-making and policies through ECR".

Many of the quotes contained in this book came from Dr. Gabriel Robbins' web site: "Good Quotations by Famous People" at www.cs.virginia.edu/~robins/quotes.html.

Dr. Walt Cieko, Ph.D., BCIAC assisted me with understanding and interpreting psychological terms. For more about Walt's practice see www.waltciecko.com.

About the Author

Jim Caplan joined the USDA Forest Service in 1979 as a recent graduate of the University of Wyoming with a Bachelor's Degree in Political Science and a Master's Degree in Community and Regional Planning. Although Jim never entered a doctorate program, he earned enough graduate hours, sixty-four, to meet the basic academic course requirements for a PhD.

In 1980, as Jim helped coach Forest Service managers during and after the Mio Fire in Michigan, Eastern Region Forest Service leaders asked Jim to write up his theories and guidelines for environmental dispute resolution, ideas Jim developed in graduate school. Jim did so and he delivered <u>Conflict Management and Crisis Control: A Manager's Guide</u> (1980) to Eastern Region leadership just before leaving for a permanent assignment in the Forest Service Alaska Region.

In Alaska, Jim assisted regional leadership with public involvement and state relations, eventually becoming Regional Public Affairs Director. In 1987, Jim left Alaska for Wyoming, becoming Supervisory Land Use Planner in charge of completing the Bridger-Teton National Forest Land and Resource Management Plan. Then-Chief of the Forest Service, Max Peterson referred to the plan as "the most controversial in the lower-48." Jim successfully completed the plan and environmental impact statement in 1989 having garnered wide-spread public support and no law suits. Throughout this assignment, Jim used public participation methods taught by the Institute for Participatory Planning and Management and his own concepts embodied in <u>Conflict Management and Crisis Control.</u>

In 1990, he received an assignment with the Forest Service New Perspectives Team as Assistant Director for Communications and Planning in Washington, DC. When that successful assignment ended in 1992, Jim was appointed as national Public Affairs Director and served in that role until 1996 when Chief Jack Ward Thomas appointed him Deputy Regional Forester for Natural Resources in Alaska. Jim served in this role until 2002, including a one-year stint as acting Regional Forester.

Because of the Clinton-Bush administration change and political pressure in Alaska, Jim was reassigned to the Umpqua National Forest as Forest Supervisor in 2002 and served in that role until 2006. At that time, he returned to Washington DC as Special Assistant to the Deputy Chief for National Forest System, before retiring in 2007 to lead a Red Cross county-level organization for two years. While in DC, Jim rewrote <u>Conflict Management and Crisis Control</u> on his own time to incorporate more than 25 years of front-line Forest Service experience in environmental dispute resolution. Eventually two books evolved from that effort, <u>The Theory and Principles of Environmental Dispute Resolution</u> (2007, rev. 2010) and <u>The Practice of Environmental Dispute Resolution</u> (2007, rev. 2010).

Throughout his career, Jim won numerous awards for high-level performance. His list of publications is contained in Appendix C at the end of this book.

Preface by the Author

I began work in the field of environmental dispute resolution (EDR) soon after joining the U.S. Forest Service in 1979. My work actually began during the legendary 1980 Mio Fire that charred more than 50,000 acres across upper Michigan, at one time burning along a fourteen-mile-wide front. A failed attempt to create 110 acres of habitat for the Kirtland's Warbler, a Jack Pine nesting bird, the Mio Fire resulted in two deaths and the loss of more than 50 homes and structures. Because the fire was an "escaped, prescribed" fire, and thus the work of an agency burning crew gone wrong, the Forest Service justifiably bore the full brunt of criticism and blame from people and communities affected by the fire.

Soon after the fire escaped, I was asked to do what I could to help mitigate impacts to the agency and the local people. I offered several actions that, eventually taken, helped mitigate the disaster's social impacts. These actions included fielding government claims adjusters while the fire still burned, hastening investigative results, and quickly offering apologies to the people and communities affected. Other actions followed including reviews of prescribed-fire policies, national and regional.

In the weeks following the Mio Fire demobilization, the Regional Forester and Public Affairs Director asked me to write up my environmental dispute resolution methods. Drawing on conflict studies I had done in graduate school and theories I had developed there, and influenced by the brilliant work of Dr. Hans and Annemarie Bleiker of the Institute for Participatory Management and Planning, I eventually delivered Conflict Management and Crisis Control (1980). Soon after finishing that book, I was transferred to Alaska where my skills were refocused on the environmental conflicts around the Tongass National Forest. Other assignments followed, including completing the Bridger-Teton National Forest Land and Resource Management Plan in 1989 without litigation. At the time, that plan was considered "the most controversial" in America.

And so it went over my years with the agency. Leaders transferred me from one environmental hotspot to another where, with varying degrees of success, I was able to help protect the environment, meet production goals, reduce conflict, heal relationships, and improve the agency's operational flexibility. I rose from a Public Information Specialist in 1980 to the top of the agency's national communications hierarchy in 1992 and, there, served on the agency's core leadership group until 1996. Beginning in late 1996, I lead Forest Service land management for the State of Alaska and, in 2002, in Oregon on the Umpqua National Forest. One of the reasons for this success was my application of environmental dispute resolution practices to the intense "wars in the woods" going on around me.

Now, after more than 30 years of experience in environmental dispute resolution, I have come to believe the world's single greatest environmental threat is not nuclear war, desertification, large-scale stand-replacing wildfires, or global warming and climate change, as formidable as those threats are. Rather, the single greatest ecological threat is the intractability of our environmental disputes and our collective lack of will and skill to resolve them.

Even when faced by compelling needs to act in order to support the health of our planet, and simultaneously in support of our human communities and economic wellbeing, we are paralyzed by intractable environmental disputes. No other species saddles itself with such high-conflict, low-cooperation, maladaptive strategies and behaviors perhaps precisely because the stakes are so high, because the very survival of our economies and our species, and so many other species, is at stake. Because we collectively lack the will and skill to resolve these disputes, developers cannot develop, environmentalists cannot protect, and societies and cultures drift, gridlocked, while, as with the Mio Fire, the world burns.

So, this handbook's main theme is that we can deal with the effects of environmental battles if we can effectively apply EDR practices at appropriate spatial and time scales. In the face of mounting environmental stresses, effective EDR can be defined in its broadest terms as adaptive, saving behavior for the human race and, ultimately for all species that count on us for stewardship.

As presented in this handbook, EDR is not public relations in the classic, creating-a-public- position sense, nor is it agency-action-oriented public involvement. Rather, it is a unique synthesis of ecology, psychology, decision and management sciences, and alternative dispute resolution concepts and tools. It is built on several ideas and processes I developed over time. Thus, the handbook details an effective "expert system," one based on sound science, shaped by extensive experience, and packaged for novices, caring community leaders, and seasoned practitioners alike.

Some of the ideas presented in the handbook may initially strike readers familiar with environmental conflicts as strange. For example, my experience is that environmental disputes tend to move through **stages**, from a basic issue with just one subject and two or few disputants, to a full-blown conflict characterized by a confusing mish-mash of multiple issues and disputants, then to a crisis in which disputants often give up control of outcomes to third parties, and finally into recovery wherein new relationships develop and issues emerge, and some old disputes "recycle."

For many skilled third-party "neutrals" or "interveners," the dispute-stage idea may be foreign. This alien feel is due to the fact that such professionals are often called as a full-blown conflict careens towards crisis. They may never work at the issue stage where abatement often prevents dispute escalation. And they may miss the whole concept of recovery with its "new country" feel and the pressing need to adopt measures to prevent dispute recycling.

In addition to the idea of dispute stages, my experience also tells me that environmental disputes tend to follow one of four principal "**pathways**." The first of these is "distress," a path characterized by strife over disparate values. These values can include the relative importance of jobs and environmental quality or the value of public processes or the use scientific information in decision making.

The second pathway is "scandal." This path gets followed when one disputant alleges that another has violated shared values. The behavior in dispute is often about promises not keep, processes not followed, or relationship expectations not met. In a scandal, the disputant feeling victimized asks society-at-large to enforce social norms against or punish the "offending" disputant.

The third pathway is "anarchy" in which a disputant attempts to impose different values on another. Here, the dispute focuses on the merits and impacts of social change.

The final pathway is "catastrophe" in which natural events or failures of the human-built environmental adversely impact people and natural resources. Catastrophe involves loss to people and environments, often severe, sudden, and irreversible,. Catastrophe shatters shared values about stable communities, lifeways, and natural conditions. This pathway is not about so much about the disastrous event, a cyclone through a village for example, as it is about what human behavior follows.

Another odd element is that I also incorporate ecological concepts into my EDR model. This takes many forms, including descriptions of ecological scale, discussions of the applicability of different EDR methods and tools at different scales, and incorporation of the ecological factors of "structure," "composition," and "function" into my approach.

And, finally, based on holistic-medicine concepts, I offer readers a diagnostic structure, a prescriptive model and methods, and management system with over 150 tools, some well-known like mediation and others, like the "medicine wheel," far less so. This approach permits EDR practitioners at any skill level to assess stage, pathway, factors, and other relevant dispute information and then select the most build a program plan and EDR community to address disputes at hand.

Chapter 1: Introduction and Why Resolving Environmental Disputes Matters

Key Definition

Environmental Dispute: person-to-person, group-to-group, or nature-to-person/group strife marked by power struggles between parties with opposing positions and different desired outcomes[1]

What natural-resource manager, environmental engineer, environmentalist, developer, or elected official has not felt frustration, perhaps despair, at an environmental dispute that has become intractable? A dispute that delays needed action, increases costs, and places resources at risk. A dispute with no apparent end in sight. And how many times have stakeholders seen the same dispute reappear on another project or proposal, and perhaps again and again on many projects or proposals, with no apparent resolution of fundamental disagreements? How many millions of dollars and lost hours of hard work have gone into fighting environmental skirmishes — resources that could have been put to beneficial use?

Perhaps you share this frustration. You wonder how to work your way out of some seemingly intractable disputes that have thus far come back time and again like a pesky virus. Well, this Theory and Principles book and its companion Practices book could be of great use to you. Will Rogers said, *"If stupidity got us into this mess, then why can't it get us out?"* Obviously, Will was poking fun at us in an effort to get us to "smarten up," and that is what the two books are about, "smartening up" our ways of handling environmental disputes.

I will show you how our current American approach to handling environmental disputes leads environmentalists to propel environmental loss, causes developers to derail development opportunities, puts resource-dependent communities striving for prosperity at risk, and strips opportunity and flexibility away from the most highly trained and experienced environmental and natural resource managers in the world!

Throughout the book, this symbol ⟹ indicates an important idea or key concept. Please see Appendix D for a list of **Definitions and Descriptions** used in this book, pages 177-179.

An Opportunity to Make Real Change Exists

Can we do better? Yes! And that is the primary purpose for the two books. My intent is to pass on what I have learned about environmental dispute resolution (EDR), and a bunch of related

---

[1] *The Dictionary of Conflict Resolution* (1999, p.152-3) defines "dispute" as "to argue about, debate; subject matter of debate, CONTROVERSY." *The Dictionary* goes on to point out that there are other definitions in conflict resolution work, including: "When one against whom a complaint is lodged fails to respond satisfactorily to the aggrieved party." My definition, in contrast to *The Dictionary's* more narrow view, which reflects more legalistic claim/counter-claim thinking, broadens these meanings to place them in a larger societal context. "Dispute resolution" is defined as the "study and practice of resolving disputes" (p.154).

"stuff," to present and future generations of conservation leaders and others with a vested interest in environmental quality and successful development.

And why am I qualified to expound on the subject? In over 25 years with the Forest Service, I dealt successfully with one highly controversial project or program after another, sometimes as staff and sometimes as decision maker. Only one of my decisions was ever litigated and few were ever administratively appealed. On all of these assignments, the teams I built instituted valuable environmental protections and moved important development projects forward without giving up resource- or environmental-management flexibility. I got to know hundreds of dedicated people at state and local levels doing similar work with similar results.

How is it possible that some people are successful when others are not? Will the knowledge I provide here work infallibly? No one can guarantee perfection, but if you work rigorously with what you learn here, you will successfully achieve environmental dispute resolution (EDR) *most* of the time. And, if and when you fail, you will understand why you failed so that you can do better the next time.

Some Common Beliefs about Environmental Disputes

Over the years, I have encountered many beliefs held by people involved in environmental disputes. These include:

- "We're right and they're wrong…They're crazy, irrational, unreasonable…"
- "Every time we reach an agreement, they ask for more…."
- "You can't stop progress, so I'm not going to try …"
- "All they care about is making money…"
- "All they care about is hugging trees, taking care of Bambi, not about people…"
- "I work in the woods all day, so I'm a true environmentalist…"
- "I care about nature…I'm a true environmentalist…"
- "Save the planet to save yourself…because it's right…"
- "The courts always rule against us…"
- "The media is always against us, never gets the story right…"
- "The government should do something…politicians should do something…,"
- "Land managers should do something…."
- "Leave management to the professionals…why are the experts so wrong…?"
- "Our community is dying and no one seems to care…"
- "We had a group working together on environmental stuff for awhile but outsiders came in…conflicts occurred…the group fell apart, stopped meeting…"

Some of these sound familiar? If you have been around environmental disputes, you have probably heard many of the same things. You may even have uttered a few of them yourself.

The Importance of Being a Committed Stakeholder and EDR Leader

So, in this face of such negativity and intractability, you'd like to engage with the environmental opponents in your area and make a positive difference. A note of caution is in order, however:

Public/Shareholder Involvement

⬍

Environmental Dispute Resolution

you should attempt to resolve an environmental dispute only if values you really care about may be lost if something is not done.

This caution applies whether you intend to develop and manage an EDR program personally or turn it over to a professional EDR specialist. EDR can be long and trying. You have to be strongly committed to succeed.

So, let's say you are a committed stakeholder, dedicated to developing and leading an EDR program. In that case, you have to be ready to step back from the dispute specifics. You'll have to focus on "fixing the [EDR] problem, not the blame.[2]" You'll have to work for community, not agency, interest group, or business. Failing to achieve this kind of objectivity and perspective may mean you will fail to address critical problems or to seize opportunities that should not be allowed to slip away.

If you do have something at stake and are willing to act with clear-headed, positive intentions, you are invited to get going and make a difference! To paraphrase Henry Ford (1863-1947), "*Whether you think that you can, or that you can't, you are probably right.*"

Is There A Difference Between EDR and Public Involvement?

The aim of public involvement by public agencies is to gain citizen consent for program or project implementation. For businesses, board and shareholder relations have similar goals—gaining investor consent for management actions.

Although consent building and EDR can be complimentary, **EDR specifically focuses on resolving disputes rather than gaining consent**. You implement EDR because you realize that an intractable environmental dispute exists, one that likely transcends a specific program or proposal being disputed—one that threatens values you consider important such as the continued health of your industry or your community. Looking at it a different way, EDR aims to eliminate unwanted, unnecessary costs to people and communities, including the effects of issue gridlock and loss of community economic opportunity and social vitality. So, **while EDR can be a part of public or shareholder involvement, EDR leaders may also choose to conduct EDR separately and sometimes delay or stop an involvement effort to focus on EDR.**

Through EDR, historically intractable disagreements move from being frequently litigious to being rarely so. Long-term disputes stop recycling and may become dormant or extinct. Communities can rediscover a sense of common purpose achieved through the intense competition of ideas supported by the successful application of EDR principles and practices.

---

[2] Japanese proverb

Satisfaction

Cost

Peer Talk   Negotiate   Litigate

Mediate   Arbitrate   Appeal Lit.

Techniques

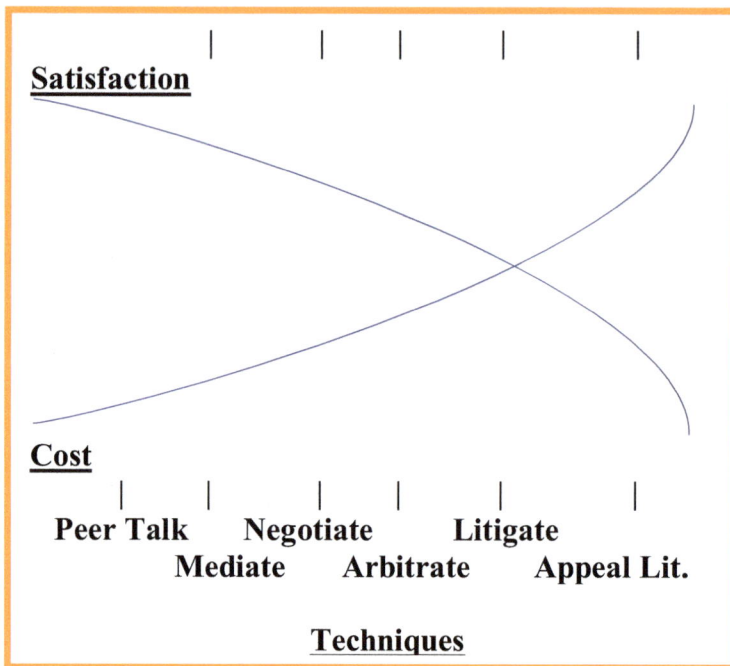

Community leaders and advocates often have a similar experience when it comes to using the legitimate institutions of dispute resolution. The more formal the means selected to gain desired results, the higher the costs and often the lower the satisfaction. This is one reason why people sometimes resort to illegitimate, even violent means to try to achieve their goals — the means seem more direct, less likely to require compromise, and fit their limited financial capability.

The authors of *Contemporary Conflict Resolution*[3] state that, in international circles, people acknowledge that dispute resolution at the early stages is most cost effective. Based on empirical evidence, they estimate that late-stage interventions cost as much as four times more than the early-stage interventions. Moreover, these costs represent only direct expenses for the interveners and do not represent direct, indirect, and opportunity costs for the opponents, all other participants, and communities at large.

So, one of the contextural ironies of EDR is that **the higher cost, seemingly higher-payoff techniques often yield reduced satisfaction**. The following figure, which I've used for years in training and orientation sessions, shows the general relationship of satisfaction to cost by technique.

EDR practitioners, public servants, and advocates should understand this relationship: well-done EDR can minimize costs and increase likely satisfaction. In their 2003 report, the United States Institute for Environmental Conflict Resolution reports dollar costs for these various intervention techniques range from a low of $9,537 for mediation to $60,557 for a trial verdict.[4] Similarly, I estimate that National Environmental Policy Act analytic and decision documents can be prepared using consent-building public involvement and effective EDR techniques for about one-eighth to one-quarter the cost of similar documents prepared with pro forma public involvement and no EDR efforts.

Alternative Dispute Resolution (ADR) is similar to EDR, except that the former focuses for the most part on labor-management relations and inter-personal disputes. ADR has become the tool for settling disputes short of litigation, at lower cost, greater effectiveness, and reduced effort than formal lawsuits. The American Bar Association reports that "*nearly 80 percent of all*

---

[3] *Contemporary Conflict Resolution: The prevention, management, and transformation of deadly conflicts, Second Edition.* Ramsbotham, Oliver, Woodhouse, Tom, and Miall, Hugh. Polity Press, Malden, MA. 2005. p.125.
[4] "ECR Cost-Effectiveness: Evidence From the Field." April 2003. United States Institute for Environmental Conflict Resolution of the Morris K. Udall Foundation. Tucson, AZ.

responding lawyers recommend ADR to their clients.[5]*"* The report also states that "...*the use of mediation in environmental and natural resource cases is becoming a standard part of the litigation and dispute resolution processes.*"

Based on scope and variables, ADR is the most prominent and best-understood subcategory of EDR (as economics is a subset of sociology and human ecology). ADR is largely limited in scope to personal and small-group conflicts. Still, a steering committee of federal agencies has been attempting to extend ADR to environmental disputes, focusing on mediation and collaboration,[6] and on control of variables so disputes can be managed more effectively and efficiently. Although the ADR model includes valuable ideas, methods, and conclusions for EDR, after years of working in the field, I conclude that there is **not sufficient efficacy and scope in present ADR techniques and models to deal with disputes for ecosystems above "sub-river-basin" scale, let alone nation- or worldwide**.

This Book

Government is often the entity to which we turn to deal with environmental disputes. The authors of *Contemporary Conflict Resolution*[7] make the point that, nationally or internationally, government and sovereign states remain the principal means for creating balance between forces, whether balancing globalization versus local economies and institutions or mediating among competing interests at any geographic scale.

However, The Theory and Principles of Environmental Dispute Resolution is not just for government officials and employees, but also for everyone who wishes to understand and conduct EDR. With its companion Practices book, this book represents "one-stop shopping" for elected officials, advocates for development and the environment, and common folks who wish to make progress on environmental challenges and gridlock — which currently bedevil us all. These caring folks can look to these pages for paths "out of the woods."

The purpose of the two books is simple enough, but the subject matter is complex. So, I've organized the books according to the ways I have come to think of environmental disputes after more than 25 years of dealing with them as a federal official and concerned private citizen.

I use a basic "typology" that separates disputes into distinct and understandable categories. The typology is briefly presented and discussed in this book and then extensively developed and applied in Practices. Practices follows a prescriptive approach to build an EDR program which can display considerable complexity, consistent with the nature of the disputes themselves and as varied as the people who are party to them.

By using this method, relatively inexperienced EDR practitioners can tap into an "expert system" and be guided to effective EDR methods that are likely to work most of the time.

---

[5] *Environmental Dispute Resolution: An Anthology of Practical Solutions.* Eds., McNaughton, Ann L. and Martin, Jay G., American Bar Association. 2002. p.20-21.

[6] *Interagency Initiative to Foster Collaborative Problem Solving and Environmental Conflict Resolution: Briefing Report for Federal Department Leadership.* June 2004 (rev. May 2005). U.S. Institute for Environmental Conflict Resolution of the Morris K. Udall Foundation. Tucson, AZ.

[7] *Contemporary Conflict Resolution: The prevention, management, and transformation of deadly conflicts, Second Edition.* Ramsbotham, Oliver, Woodhouse, Tom, and Miall, Hugh. Polity Press, Malden, MA. 2005. p.100.

Practitioners will gain greater precision over time as they experience the nuances of this system and develop their own ideas and understand through trial and error.

Contents and Organization

This book is organized into four principal sections:

Chapters 1-3	Build an historic and cultural understanding of environmental disputes
Chapters 4-6	Build knowledge of ecosystems and dispute psychology
Chapters 7-8	Build knowledge of dispute-resolution models and choices
Chapters 9-13	Explore ethical, leadership, and future potentials for EDR

So the reader may skip chapters to focus on subjects of greatest interest, each chapter begins with a content summary.

My intent for this book is that it be a catalyst for positive change and support for people wanting the best for their communities. As Anais Nin wrote, *"And the day came when the risk to remain tight in a bud was more painful than the risk it took to blossom."* Go ahead—blossom! Good reading!

Chapter 2: The American Way, Personal Sovereignty, and the Environmental Movement as Important Parts of the EDR "Landscape"

America celebrates the individual; protection for individual rights is the cornerstone of the Declaration of Independence and the U.S. Constitution. Therefore, each person has the right to seek redress of any grievance through legal means

Environmentalism began in America just after the Civil war and evolved from philosophy to a set of land- and resource-management practices and resource reserves

Over time, the philosophers and idealists of the early environmental movement gave way to legalists and managers and the scope changed from addressing local issues to saving the planet;

As with many "personal sovereignty" movements, progress on some environmental issues could only be made at the cost of violence against property and sometimes against people

Chapter 1 provided an introduction, some background, and an overview of the contents and definitions used in this book and the companion <u>Practices</u> book. The reader should now understand that I believe our failure to resolve our environmental disputes results in both threats to our society and also to nature. In addition, I assert that the tools to deal effectively with conflict and disputes are fairly well understood, at least in human systems and at local scale, although how to apply them to large-scale ecological situations and environmental disputes is less well understood.

So, if environmental disputes that threaten our society and humanity itself are all too common, how did Americans come to create conditions that enable these stubborn disputes? More importantly, how is it that we tolerate these conditions rather than changing them? Why do environmentalists propel environmental destruction? Why do developers undermine their ability to provide the goods and services Americans want and need? For some answers, we might first examine some of our country's legal and cultural foundations of our society. Good places to start are the Mayflower Compact (1620), the Declaration of Independence (1776), and the U.S. Constitution (1790).

Mayflower Compact

The Mayflower Compact established a New World colonial government as the servant of the common people. It conceived of people directly subject to the Will of God with no intermediary hereditary rulers. In this, the framers of the Compact made a revolutionary departure from contemporaneous European thinking in which hereditary, feudal rulers served as church leaders and their earthly authority derived directly from God. In a small, significant way, the Compact ended western feudal-derived governments and ushered in democracy based on citizen sovereignty.

Declaration of Independence and U.S. Constitution

The writers of the Declaration of Independence and the Constitution were influenced by the Compact, by American Indian government forms based on the rights and responsibilities of individuals (such as those governing the Iroquois Confederacy), and by the progressive political thinking of the day from Europe which was itself influenced by ancient Greek philosophers, the governments of Greek antiquity, Biblical concepts, and Renaissance-era experiments in self-rule.

I first read the Constitution about 45 years ago. It was in the back of a high school textbook—twenty-six pages with lots of white space. I read it, and then I re-read it. I have read it many times since, and it is always an emotional experience for me. It is perhaps less a treatise about law than it is one about noble social intention. So, for me, it is a profoundly spiritual or "essence" document.

The Constitution is all the more remarkable when you consider that the collection of visionaries who wrote it resided in a few far-flung and poorly connected former colonies of the British Empire. They had hostile neighbors in every direction, but instead of creating a warlike state bent on conquest, they fashioned a government dedicated to the benefit of all and the sovereignty of individual citizens.

The Constitution is complex in its intentions, but the story it tells is straightforward enough: the purpose of American government is to **protect the American People, their property, and their rights.** In other words, the government's role in the lives of citizens is to bring about peace and justice subject to the will and consent of the governed. Our government must reflect what the people value. In America, government is the servant of the people and thus, by definition, government officials and employees are public servants—people charged with making, interpreting, and enforcing the laws that are themselves "mutually arrived at and mutually binding."

The United States as a whole is a sovereign nation, meaning it can determine its own fate and exert control within and near its boundaries. The Constitution vests various powers and authorities in the federal government and allocates the remainder to the various states and Indian tribes. In turn, the states vest various powers and authorities in the counties, boroughs, parishes, cities, towns, and other local governments.

However, although tribes, states, and local governments hold power, the federal government power "trumps" any powers asserted by subordinate jurisdictions. Another way of saying this is that everyone has to conform to federal laws, but people in one state or tribe do not have to abide by the laws of adjacent and equal states or tribes.

Conversely, it is also true that **"We the People," and the people we elect to represent us, are accountable to <u>seek peace and justice</u> for our society**. We can ignore laws that do not apply to us but **we cannot ignore our personal responsibilities to one another that extend across all government jurisdictions**.

18

Personal Sovereignty — the American Way

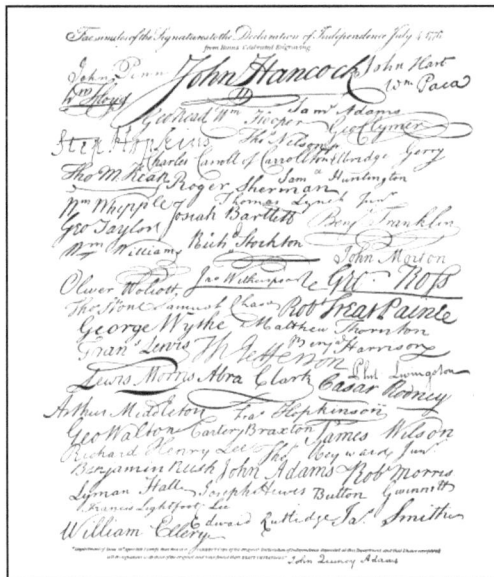

To match personal accountability, American citizens are vested with sovereign powers. These powers regard our persons, not the state. The Founders carefully articulated these powers in the "Bill of Rights" amended to the Constitution and designed to protect the American people from government oppression and to establish a nation based on personal freedoms. The Bill of Rights defines specific elements of personal sovereignty (the Right to Free Speech, for example).

Our individual rights under the Constitution echo the Declaration of Independence (1776). The Declaration clearly states that the governments of the United States "derive their just powers from the consent of the governed." The sovereign power of the United States flows from the people, not from other sources such as "the divine right of kings," God Himself, or an aristocracy (those with the most wealth or property). Governments may act only with citizens' consent. Government actions must be taken for citizens' benefit.

Over the course of American history, a recurrent theme has been the struggle to balance personal sovereignty against the collective need for a prosperous, secure, and successful society. With personal sovereignty comes personal responsibility and, just like nations, the requirement to personally respect the sovereignty of other people—in practice, a dynamic balance complex and difficult to achieve.

For example, as Oliver Wendell Holmes (1841-1935) wrote in a Supreme Court opinion, "*The right to swing my fist ends where the other man's nose begins.*" In a similar way, your right to free speech does not permit you to maliciously yell "Fire!" in a crowded theater when no fire is present. At the same time, as a reflection of personal accountability for the common good, you must cry "Fire!" if fire **is** present. These simple instances are instructive but do not reflect the complicated nature of balancing individual rights and the public good when dealing with the environment over an entire nation or the world.

In the past, these Americans felt sanctions and censorship from the majority culture, including the enactment of laws preventing their enjoyment of personal choice. For example, until the 1990's in some states, people who married outside their color faced prison or had to abandon their property and relocate. Now, seventy percent of Americans support the right to so-called "inter-racial" marriage and states have repealed "miscegenation" statutes.

In short, past personal sovereignty movement successes teach us that our society's sense of "commonwealth" and "social order" can be altered by the actions of individuals seeking to have their personal rights honored. In fact, under the Constitution, the forces of personal sovereignty are very strong, and any sufficiently mobilized minority population with legitimate complaints can eventually prevail on Constitutional-rights issues. The "untouchables" in our society have as many sovereign rights as anyone else. But to enjoy them, they have to assert their political, economic, and legal strength and show ultimately that they will accept responsibility and accountability as citizens.

So, over the last 150 years, minorities and women have struggled through the process of achieving personal sovereignty. And, after many generations of struggle, homosexuals, bi-racial couples, and pornographers now enjoy the rights and security taken for granted by other Americans.

U.S. Courts have continuously affirmed citizen sovereignty. Regarding rights of citizen privacy versus federal surveillance of potential terrorists, Federal District Judge Anna Diggs Taylor wrote in 2006, "*There are no hereditary kings in America and no powers not created by the Constitution.*" In other words, the judge deemed the right of individuals to privacy as inherent to the Constitution and thus undeniable by any leader regardless of their reasoning (i.e., even the public good, as was the Bush Administration's argument in this case).

Under federal and state constitutions, personal sovereignty is protected and individuals are allowed mechanisms to seek redress of their grievances. Any citizen may pursue resolution by:

- Asking executive-branch officials for new regulations or new interpretations of law
- Suing opponents or governments in the courts
- Changing or passing new laws through legislative bodies
- Creating citizen-motivated law using legal authorities such as referenda or initiatives
- Creating enforceable agreements through means such as EDR
- Seeking public office
- Supporting like-minded change agents for public office
- Using recall elections to remove elected officials with non-conforming views
- Engaging in non-violent anarchy intended to influence public opinion and, eventually, public policies (such as tree-sitting or environmental marches, sit-ins, and other protests)
- Fomenting violent anarchy and revolution (this mechanism was the basis for the founding of the nation but carries severe consequences if revolution fails)

In response to the nearly continuous pressure for the redress of citizen grievances and for increasing or better-defined personal sovereignty, the United States has followed a **"pulse-evolution" culture and change process**. This permits the gradual accommodation of minority interests through the means mentioned above without a wholesale tearing of the social fabric. We self-regulate our pace of change through government institutions and the informal enforcement of social norms.

Put in the context of Peter Senge's *Fifth Discipline*[8] thinking, the initiating and reinforcing force of personal sovereignty is opposed by the balancing forces of the status quo. These system dynamics of force and counter-force are another way of analyzing moves toward personal sovereignty. Senge also speaks to connected but "time-discontinuous" events.

---

[8] *The Fifth Discipline: The Art and Practice of the Learning Organization.* Senge, Peter M. Doubleday. NY, NY. 1990.

Reflecting Senge's ideas, personal-sovereignty issues initially emerge, create dialogue, and evoke public responses. The responses are usually attempts at censorship, minimization, and suppression. Under pressure, the movements may go quiet for prolonged periods before they re-emerge into the public consciousness. Then, perhaps because of a specific illustrative event, they move forward with greater energy and urgency. For people trying to achieve personal sovereignty, timing and opportunity are frequently everything.

This pattern has proved **as true for environmental activists as it has been for any other people seeking individual sovereignty**. The U.S. Constitution does not yet mention the word "environmental." But concepts from the Constitution motivate environmental activism and permeate environmental disputes.

The Environmental Movement

Movements towards personal sovereignty can be viewed as dispute "pulses" that begin with one or a few issues, develop into full-blown conflicts, reach a crisis, and then move into recovery and the creation of a new status quo. The environmental movement has followed this pulse pattern, and indeed its evolution has been described as coming in "waves[9]" that represent changing citizen preferences and societal affluence.

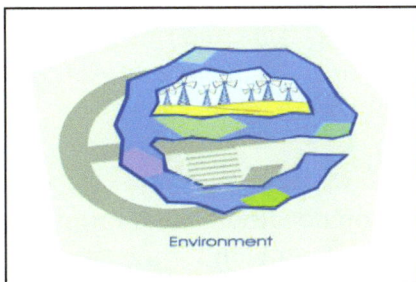
Environment

The environmental movement represents a personal-sovereignty pulse born of recognition of the need for enlightened self-interest in the care and sustainable use of nature. The ideas may be presented as utopian preservationism aimed at restoring Eden-like conditions. Or they may represent pragmatic utilitarianism aimed at delivering renewable ecosystem services and commodities to humans.

Regardless of the philosophical underpinnings, **the overall intention is control of natural resources to support a certain, desired quality of life**. "Saving the Planet" is ultimately about "saving me," and "caring for the land" is about "serving the people." This basic notion has been expressed in different ways over the history of environmental conservation.

The First Wave, which began in about 1865 with the publication of George Perkins Marsh' *Man and Nature,* established the American conservation movement and the physical basis for environmental action. Later in the 19th century, the movement evolved into **two broad views: "preservation" championed by John Muir and "beneficial use" championed by Gifford Pinchot**. The two men cooperated for a long time, but eventually they differed more and more over preservation and development issues. As a result of the First Wave, legislation and executive designations established reserves such as parks, refuges, and forests with different management approaches depending on whether the reserves were focused on preservation or beneficial public use.

---

[9] *The Death of Environmentalism: Global warming politics in a post-environmental world.* Shellenberger, Michael and Nordhaus. Grist. 2005.

Early conservation actions were often based on perceptions that public land and resource set-asides were needed to protect key resources, such as water flows and water quality, to provide timber, mineral and other resources for the long-term development of the nation, or to protect America's rare and beautiful natural features and frontier heritage. For example, some of the lands and resources reserved in the 19th century were intended to prevent a perceived, but non-existent, "timber famine." The establishment of these reserves was one of the first "brinksmanship" strategies used in resource debates.

Management of these resources, and similar resources in state, local, or private ownership, was generally "custodial" and with few acknowledged effects caused by people during the First Wave. Today, America's reserved-land system does not grow very much spatially, but it grows ever more valuable to the increasing American population.

The First Wave reserved many of the physical, biological, and ecological resources that are the subject of some environmental disputes today. As reserves were created, strong functional and relationship elements developed among organizations such as the Sierra Club and the Forest and Park Services. Environmental disputes were relatively uncommon at this time.

During the Second Wave, which began in the 1950s, Congress and state legislatures **passed foundational laws establishing environmental protection, management agencies to enforce those protections, and regulations governing the agencies' performance**. These laws included the federal National Environmental Policy Act, the Wilderness Acts, the Endangered Species Act, the Clean Air Act, the Clean Water Act, the National Forest Management Act, the Alaska National Interest Lands Conservation Act, and the Federal Land Planning and Management Act.

Second Wave actions by legislative bodies and executives focused on developing and refining rules for managing reserved lands and waters, and also on resources of concern for the nation as a whole (as in the Clean Air and Clean Water Acts). Issues and conflicts were addressed by establishing regulatory and enforcement structures that allowed for both government enforcement and for litigation against the government by Non-Governmental Organizations (NGOs).

This movement toward environmental legislation went so far that NGOs were paid by the federal government to sue the federal government in the public interest as provided for by the Equal Access to Justice Act, an act that has served many modern sovereignty pulses, including the civil and women's rights movements. During the Second Wave, people also saw the rise of "not-in-my-back-yard" (NIMBY) and "locally unacceptable land use" (LULU) politics and advocacy. The American courts became very busy trying to handle land use and environmental disputes.

The Second Wave expanded **beyond the physical, biological, and ecological features** reserved in the First Wave, adding rules and regulations governing environmental quality nationwide on all land ownerships. Procedural requirements in some of the acts, such as the National Environmental Policy Act, helped focus disputes on procedural compliance rather than resource condition, protection, or values.

During the Second Wave, environmental advocates such as the Sierra Club abandoned their long-standing close relationships with government agencies and developed strong political and litigation strategies. In pursuing their goals, environmental groups often followed social and political brinksmanship strategies concerning vanishing species and resources, such as whooping cranes and wetlands.

In the Third Wave, which began in the 1960s, long-established and newer NGOs (such as the Trust for Public Lands, the Nature Conservancy, Ducks Unlimited and others) **expanded** their conservation role. They accomplished this by forging partnerships. They looked for ways to combine investments by private industry with the land and resource commitments of private landowners and governments to create pragmatic solutions to environmental problems, an approach often called "sustainable development."

Since the 1980s, these groups have become ever more prominent as non-litigious advocates, mediators, dealmakers, and role models. Congress created the National Forest Foundation to join organizations like the National Parks Conservation Association to support reserved lands and resources. Private industry is increasingly seeing Third Wave market opportunities to respond to buyer preferences and to respond to incentives or legal requirements that create the impetus for them to have a "green portfolio."

In one sense, Third Wave cooperation and collaboration efforts might seem to **return the conservation movement to its First Wave days**, a time marked by relatively convivial relationships among opponents. However, **this is illusory** because Third Wave collaborative efforts occur within the context of litigation and strife so common in the still-surging Second Wave. It is good to note that the waves are not mutually exclusive, but rather, the impetus from each continues even as a new environmental wave is becoming primary.

Today, power is relatively balanced, or "symmetrical," between use and protection advocates and effective dispute-resolution methods are limited. Third Wave disputes tend to result in impasse. Consequently, Third Wave collaborative efforts may have significant EDR value, particularly as regards small spatial and time scales. But applying collaborative techniques to national scale disputes is unlikely to be successful without significant legal and regulatory, even perhaps Constitutional, changes.

The First through Third Wave actions were successful in so many things, including stemming the loss of species and blunting the effects of development on resources. However, the inevitable effect of creating and protecting reserves, and then fighting acre-by-acre over use and condition, has been to create a kind of "eco-reserve apartheid," an intense consciousness of boundaries and constraints and intense disputes over protections and management prerogatives.

And we have a crazy quilt of conservation resources. Small urban reserves surrounded by housing developments or neighboring airports; rural others under incredible pressure such as water fowl wetlands ringed by goose-hunter gun pits. And we have large reserves managed prone to loss by catastrophic fire, or insect and disease infestations— phenomenon that threaten private lands and resources and infrastructure nearby as well.

As I have suggested, this **"eco-reserve apartheid"** extends beyond physical and biological resources

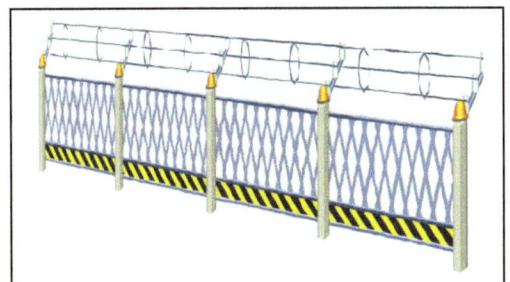

confined within boundaries. The concept also speaks to how people have chosen to express their values and preferences and how those strong expressions have organized nature to permit or exclude human uses. Thus, emotionally, intellectually, politically, and spiritually, people have committed to this apartheid and dispute changes to ubiquitous environmental laws and resource reserves.

The Fourth Wave of Environmentalism will have to struggle with and conquer these eco-reserve apartheid issues and many more. I believe the Fourth Wave began in the1990s. Fourth Wave environmentalism **reflects increasing interconnectivity, the "One World" or Gaian concept, and is enabled by internationally shared media and the World Wide Web, and high-speed, high-volume international transportation**.

As an example of Fourth Wave advocacy, in 2007, Al Gore launched a three-year "Global warming" public-relations and information campaign using around-the-world, sequential band performances, a global event called "Live Earth" The organizers of this event and the three-year campaign hope to generate world-wide environmental-protection advocacy in every country and culture.

In one sense, the Fourth Wave reflects the elements of the first three waves folded into large-scale, international ecological concepts, including the ideas and values derived from diverse

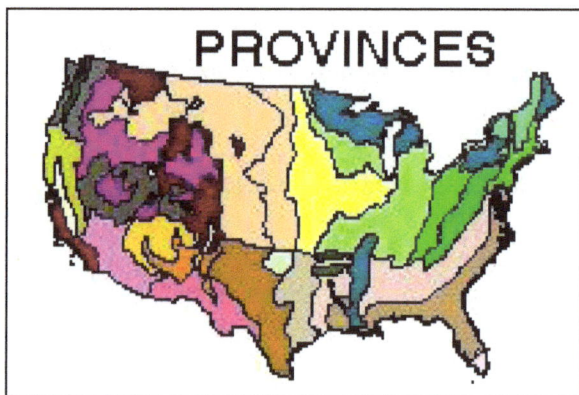

cultures. Around the globe and potentially across national boundaries, large-scale aboriginal and ecological reserves are likely to result from Fourth Wave advocacy.

Ecosystems are made up of physical and biological elements, including people, and the relationships among those elements. Depending on spatial and time scales, ecosystems get different classifications — from continental at a large scale to land-type phases at the smallest scale (see Chapter 4 and Appendix A for more discussion of this subject). Ecologists look at these different ecosystem categories as "nested hierarchies" of ecosystems that run from the microscopic scale to the planetary scale. Certain ecosystem phenomena, particularly physical ones, seem to occur only at certain scales. Natural complexity and chaos have different meanings at different scales as well.

Fourth Wave environmentalism reflects this ecological focus on scale and on nested categorizations by calling upon advocates of all kinds to look at any policy, decision, or action in terms of effects and values at many time and spatial scales. Successful Fourth Wave environmental policy and management will mean looking at global effects for local actions and at human-nature relationships on multiple scales.

Fourth Wave environmentalism will also mean we must develop EDR strategies and methods that are effective at many spatial and time scales. This work will entail greater emphasis on cooperation and collaboration and much larger land units and events. New methods for fair and just accommodation of people and their culture and interests will also need to be developed. Some of these possibilities are discussed in Chapter 12.

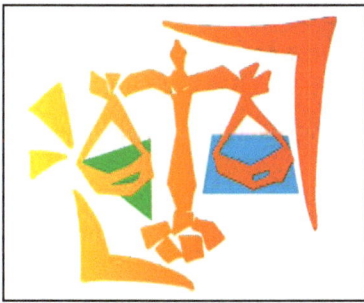

Adding "Peace" to the Concepts of "Environmental Justice"

"Environmental justice" refers to situations in which the bad environmental effects of civilization, such as air or water pollution, fall disproportionately on the politically or economically weak and disadvantaged, and that those effects, and people's grievances regarding these effects, should be redressed. I provide a definition for "environmental justice" in Chapter 1. The "environmental justice" movement has developed over the past 20 years as a combined environmental and personal-sovereignty initiative.

The creation of classes of environmental "haves" and "have-nots" is an instance of the environmental-justice movement mimicking other sovereignty movements, such as women's and civil rights, to gain power and control. While respecting the issues and the need to resolve them if appropriate to the dispute, EDR leaders must recognize the potential for the emergence of victim behavior and advocacy around these issues.

Because victimization is a theme of the environmental-justice movement, and because people feeling victimized often resort to confrontation and counter-tyrannical behaviors, EDR practitioners have good reason to insert the concept of "environmental peace" into any discussion of "environmental justice." Environmental peace means creating harmony between people and nature and among the people who live with nature.

EDR practitioners have an obligation to confront issues about peace and justice as they select techniques, plan programs, invite participation, and help form dispute-resolution communities. For example, justice may not be served if disputants reach a settlement outside existing laws, or peace may not be found if the economically disadvantaged people most impacted by the settlement are not in the room when it is reached.

Like "law" and "order", "peace" and "justice" are concepts that must ultimately be used together, "Law" alone is mere words--rules without enforcement. "Order" alone may exist without law—as in a dictatorship. But together, "law and order" provide behavioral standards and objectives to achieve a civil and prosperous society. Likewise, "peace" may exist without justice as in a "peaceful" village depopulated by genocide. Justice may exist without peace as in the execution of "rebels"—killing that then leads to more rebellion.

Together, "peace and justice" provide a hierarchy of mutual goals: justice aimed at achieving peace and peace focused on ensuring justice.

Likewise, achieving environmental justice alone is no antidote for bad environmental conditions imposed disproportionately on the poor and politically disadvantaged. Environmental justice without peace as its goal can only be punitive for some, the societal equivalent of a firing squad for environmental "criminals."

Environmental peace alone is also no antidote for societal ills because it may require the elimination of dissent and abandonment of whole industries or programs important to a prosperous society. Environmental peace without justice as its goal can only be exclusive, an environmental caste system with elites, pariahs, and "untouchables."

25

Rather, the concepts of **"environmental peace and justice" have to be used together** as mutual goals to promote a civil, prosperous society. Chapter 9 discusses the importance of a focus on environmental peace and justice as one element of EDR's ethical foundations.

Case Example: Why Habitat Conservation and Other Reserve Plans Must Eventually Fail

The Pacific Northwest Forest Plan calls for significant habitat set-asides for old-growth dependent species, including the Spotted Owl. Several years ago, Clinton Administration officials drew boundaries on maps for Late Successional Reserves and other habitat set-asides intended to ensure the survival of the Owl and other species.

In 2002, while I was Forest Supervisor of the Umpqua National Forest, fires burned about 9% of that national forest, including small amounts of Spotted Owl "core" areas and more significant amounts of Late Successional Reserves. At the same time, vaster acreages were burning to the south on the Rogue and Siskiyou National Forests (site of the Biscuit Fire) that affected owl cores and reserves even more greatly. The following year, major fires disturbed the Deschutes National Forest to the east and again burned acres on the Umpqua National Forest.

Early in 2003, my staff and I convened a Disturbance Ecology Workshop in Roseburg, Oregon. The Workshop examined whether the Northwest Forest Plan could provide adequate protection for old-growth dependent species if large-scale disturbance events such as fire, disease, wind, insect infestations, and non-native invasive species were taken into consideration.

We asked the builders of the Northwest Plan, such as Dr. Jack Ward Thomas and Dr. Gordon Reeves, to participate. We also asked Dr. Daniel Botkin, a world-renowned expert on disturbance ecology, to give his views. We included the public, asking them, given the knowledge we had gained together, what they thought and how we should act in response to the fires.

As to whether reserves could work long-term, the answer was a simple "no." At the geographic and ecological scales represented by the Northwest Forest Plan, it was **not possible to remove uncertainty and eliminate significant risks to old-growth-dependent species** using a set-aside approach. The Northwest Forest Plan reserve system was not adequate to protect the species at targeted levels, or perhaps any level of biological viability, over time. It was a "best-we-can-do-for-now" stop-gap measure that would work with varying degrees of effectiveness to reduce losses of different old-growth-dependent species short-term. It was chaotic plan, subject to chaos (see Chapters 12 and 13 for more discussion on how humans impose chaos on nature).

What went mostly unstated was that the reliance on reserves for protection is actually likely to endanger the species over time because of the broad-scale impacts of chaotic events such as fire, disease, climate variation, and invasive exotic species. An even greater insight is that people's assumption that the reserves will be adequate is an even greater threat to the species within because people do not understand the risks over time.

At the workshop, the answers about what to do with this knowledge were not clear. The development interests were worried that the answer was to expand the reserves or incorporate other land ownerships into species protections, thus limiting their future pragmatic uses, industry employment, and financial expectations. The environmental interests were worried that the answer was to eliminate the reserves; thus, environmental interests advocated expanding the reserves into a utopian global-scale network of reserves or increasing conservation requirements within.

Faced with the clear knowledge that the whole reserve "business" was and would be ultimately a failure, no one knew what to do next, other than defend past thinking and the status quo. Opponents loudly reinforced their positions and eagerly restated their commitment to recycling the disputes that had sparked the Northwest Forest Plan to begin with.

I held three public follow-up meetings to explore possible rethinking options, and I gave up after each one ended in loud confrontations. I wanted to resolve the disputes, not reinforce and recycle them. So I moved on to using techniques other than meetings.

The reserves meet the definition of a chaotic system--brittle and mal-adaptive. Yet, reserves give short-term stability. And they provided the illusion of permanence and long-term stability, of protection for vulnerable species. Like rocks opposing the flow of a river, they will fail as a direct result of their boundaries, ecological disturbances from outside, and, most importantly, because of the rigidity with which they are treated and defended by agencies and opposing publics.

The "Second-wave" laws, regulations, societal values, and communications that have created a reductionist "reserve system" mentality and boundary-designation pattern are the stuff of much commentary and reflect the history of American conservation for the last 150 years. Certainly, **Congress did not set out to create a rigid, failure-prone system** when they created the Endangered Species Act and other laws. In light of apparent risk and uncertainty, and prevailing wisdom about resource management, Congress' intentions were visionary, rational, understandable, and ultimately well-intended.

Yet, the practices that can protect a physical resource, such as a mountain in a National Park, from negative human impacts cannot protect the biological and biophysical aspects of ecosystems from change. If Congress were to reassess the approach to managing resources to sustain complex ecosystems, they would likely create laws that would allow for broad, perhaps national or international-scale considerations with high risk and uncertainty at local levels but adaptive approaches that bring human interests and actions into sustainable-ecosystem concepts. We must agree on goals but allow for multiple means to get the goals accomplished across all landscapes, working and natural. See Chapter 12 for more discussion of these ideas.

The framers of the Northwest Forest Plan had a strong Presidential mandate and little time. They brought together the best scientific and resource-management minds available and produced a comprehensive plan in astonishing time. It was, and remains, a technical masterpiece.

Yet, their approach was much like centralized planning as practiced by the former Soviet Union — done with a guard at the door to keep the public out. Their plan was to be technically objective and perfect within the time available, but to exclude the emotional, advocacy-prone, uneducated, and unsophisticated masses.

When they revealed their plan, all Hell broke loose. Intense disputes became "do or die" full-blown conflicts. Rapid accumulation tactics led to crisis and political decisions, which were heavily influenced by environmental interest groups, and brought about "watershed" changes. In pursuit of environmental justice, environmental peace became the casualty.

Business Responses to Environmentalism

In Gifford Pinchot and the Making of Modern Environmentalism,[10] Char Miller points out that in the late 19th and early 20th centuries the environmental movement took two paths. John Muir's views propelled the preservation movement. Gifford Pinchot's views propelled the wise-use or renewable-resource-management movement.

The business-environmentalism relationships of the 20th century show that **natural resource-based industrial capitalism could not embrace preservationism** for otherwise productive resources. Those businesses could accept wise-use at least the extent that renewable and non-renewable resources were made available to serve as feedstock for industrial operations.

In the same period, **other businesses learned to coexist well with both environmental views**, including recreation, tourism, fishing and hunting guides, outdoor photography and art, skiing, boating, and driving for pleasure. In fact, as lands and waters received environmental protection, businesses generally sprang up to take advantage of the opportunities. Whole communities that had been born to support mining or logging businesses grew to support recreation and retirement or to serve as bedrooms for growing cities.

Lands and waters once fought over, in a struggle of natural beauty against industrial beast, are now being viewed as important elements in an emerging "green economy." The green economy attempts to marry environmental protectionism and market consumerism. Energy production from the sun and biofuels from vegetation are just two examples of business responses to green-economy concepts. In addition, carbon storage and sequestration to reduce the unacceptable effects of climate change may best be done on public lands generally and on private lands under specific conservation easements or contract, potential income sources for landowners.

---

[10] Gifford Pinchot and the Making of Modern Environmentalism. Miller, Char. Island Press. 2001.

The Gifford Pinchot Maxims

The fact that we have entered the Fourth Wave of Environmentalism should not obscure EDR understanding from the First Wave and the value of that understanding today. Gifford Pinchot founded the U.S. Forest Service. After leaving the agency, he delivered a series of lectures at Yale in the early 1900s that contained maxims that bear on environmental dispute resolution. Most of these can be found hanging in Forest Service offices around the country:

The Constitutional Mandate for Public Service

"A public official is there to serve the public and not run them."

Dealing with Public Opinion

"Find out in advance what the public will stand for; if it is right and they won't stand for it, postpone action and educate them."

Dealing with Scandal

"Don't be a knocker; use persuasion rather than force, when possible; plenty of knockers are to be had; your job is to promote unity."

Communications, Consent, and Collaboration

"Use the press first, last and all the time if you want to reach the public."

"Public support of acts affecting public rights is absolutely required."

"It is more trouble to consult the public than to ignore them, but that is what you are hired for."

Commitment to Dispute Resolution

"Learn tact simply by being honest and sincere, and by learning to recognize the Point of view of the other man and meet him with arguments he will understand."

"Don't make enemies unnecessarily and for trivial reasons; if you are any good you will make plenty of them on matters of straight honesty and public policy, and you need all the support you can get."

Gifford Pinchot was a gifted leader and practical politician. His maxims for dispute resolution are as true today as they were 100 years ago. A final word,

"Our responsibility to the Nation is to be more than careful stewards of the land; we must be constant catalysts for positive change."

Disputes Leading to Crisis and Violence

Americans are wise to remember that our 19th century Civil War had many roots in sovereignty issues, including those concerning slavery and the right of citizens to support their state's secession from the Union. In fact, after the Civil War in a show of deep cultural commitment, Americans rejected violent revolution as an acceptable dispute-resolution option. While other sovereign nations fell into repeating patterns of civil war and insurgencies, America committed herself to domestic peace. Even personal duels, common enough in the 19th Century, were outlawed by the 20th Century, replaced with modern legalistic practices such as law suits and arbitration.

Even so, looking back, most of the major sovereignty movements of the late 19th and 20th centuries **exhibited violence** in the later stages of full-blown conflict, in crisis, and sometimes in the early stages of recovery. These included the labor movement, civil rights movement, women's rights movement, Sagebrush Rebellion, and the environmental movement. Some violence associated with these movements continues today, such as the bombing of abortion clinics, which is a manifestation of the continuing crisis over women and their personal sovereignty. Similarly, in the case of the environmental movement, Earth First! and the Earth Liberation Front/Animal Liberation Front have been responsible for violent property crimes. Sagebrush rebels have conducted civil disobedience and threatened harm to federal officials while the rebels illegally occupied public lands.

As regrettable and unacceptable as these criminal acts are, the presence of sovereignty-motivated, violent, criminal acts is a sign of a full-blown conflict that is reaching the crisis stage. EDR practitioners should recognize the symptoms for what they are and be able to plan and act accordingly.

As I mentioned in the Fourth Wave environmental movement discussion, a relatively new sovereignty pulse concerns interconnectivity in a postmodern worldwide community. This pulse is less about a specific ethnic or lifestyle minority than it is about a search for the freedom to move and communicate in an unrestricted manner across political and international boundaries.

In the early stages of this pulse, some issues have escalated to full-blown conflicts with censorship, repression, and reprisal, but as of yet, there have been few major national- or global-scale crises. The exception seems to be the violent war between religious fundamentalists and Western nations, which is in part based on the effects of Western culture on culturally and theologically conservative populations — effects brought about and stimulated by satellite TV and the Internet.

Unfortunately, there has been violent criminal behavior also associated with interconnectivity, including murderers and rapists locating victims "on line." Some criminal acts with political motivation, such as the riots resisting the World Trade Organization and Al Qaeda terrorist plots, were partially hatched, researched, scheduled, and coordinated over the Internet.

These disputes and the sovereignty pulses that accompany them are dependent on the convergence of several factors, including technology, political awareness, leisure time and financial capacity to devote to the dispute, sometimes a perception of economic disparity, media to spread the word, and commitment by those people who expect to gain from the change. Organizers of groups seeking to advance personal sovereignty often use reprisals or repression by their opponents as a motivator and flashpoint for action. The more vigorous the balancing or counter-force effort, the more it presents an opportunity for action, violent or non-violent.

Respect for Personal Sovereignty and Environmental History As One Basis for EDR

In Chapter 1, I explored some often-held and –expressed perceptions about environmental disputes. As evidenced by these statements and perceptions and the intractability of many disputes, many people clearly do not understand the implications of the American Way of handling environmental disputes.

A stakeholder committed to resolving an environmental dispute must understand the importance of acknowledging and respecting personal sovereignty as the basis for any meaningful and lasting resolution. This may mean:

- Reviewing American concepts of "peace and justice" from the U.S. Constitution and then explaining their meaning in terms of "environmental peace and justice" from Chapters 1 and 2
- Explaining and emphasizing the history of American personal sovereignty, people's rights, and the resulting actions of the legislative and judicial branches to opponents and on-lookers
- Explaining and exploring the roles of other institutions such as the media and advocacy groups in informing citizens and shaping opportunities and outcomes
- Helping people develop and implement processes that allow for the intense competition of ideas while assuring just, peaceful, and lasting outcomes

While assisting groups and communities do develop effective processes, the committed stakeholder may also want to:

- Educate opponents, participants, media, and on-lookers about the American history of environmental movements, policies, and practices
- Lead values-based discussions about the impact and importance of this history
- Move into natural settings for discussions so that the impacts of policies can be perceived and understood
- Model probable conditions that may occur if actions are taken

If the committed stakeholder feels unprepared to tackle the subjects, the stakeholder may want assistance. Most communities have excellent resources available through schools or professional groups.

Chapter 3: Some Basic Drivers, Factors, and Progression in Environmental Disputes

---

Competition is an essential component of ecosystems including the human component wherein people often define their conflicts with others in terms of winning and losing

Equally important is cooperation--from cellular to planetary scales

Environmental disputes often escalate predictably from an issue, to a full-blown conflict, to a crisis, to a recovery in the aftermath of crisis; crises often "cascade" as well with natural phenomenon effecting social ones, for example

---

If environmental disputes are a manifestation of American society and our commitment to personal sovereignty, what more specific aspects of environmental disputes should people concerned about EDR keep in mind? After all, aren't environmental disputes and EDR really complicated?

The answer is both "yes" and "no." Environmental disputes can be bewilderingly complex unless causes or "drivers" are understood. Resolution can be very difficult to achieve unless curative means and methods are also understood and applied.

This chapter will build a better, but not complete, knowledge of environmental dispute drivers, factors, and progression for the reader. The companion Practices book looks at these topics in diagnostic and prescriptive ways, moving the reader from the theories and insights presented here to more thorough analytical and practical approaches.

Competition

One source of energy fueling environmental disputes is competition. Reflecting our ecological context, and species characteristics and evolution, humans vie with one another for scarce resources — for such things as gold, sunshine, clean water, clean air, affection, mates, and jobs. Humans also vie with one another to control the outcomes of events, competing not only for sports scores and championships but for better results in contract negotiations. Humans vie with their natural environment as well, turning hills into plains and escaping gravity in spacecraft.

In fact, **we would not be human without competition**. Competition defines us as individuals, communities, cultures, societies, and nations. That we exist on Earth means we have to use natural resources and ecological services. People have competing views and attitudes on how resources and services should be used, including:

- Full utilization and consumption
- Wise use and sustainable development
- Eco-feminism and One World
- Reverence for all life

- Transcendentalism
- Pragmatic self-interest
- Intergenerational stewardship
- Environmental justice

These and other differing values ensure fierce competition, particularly for resources we hold in common, such as public lands and waters.

Cooperation and Collaboration

At the same time, people **and societies would not exist if humans were not highly cooperative with one another.** Just as most sports would not happen without teamwork, civilization would not exist without cooperation. We would not share languages or technologies or create great public works. Without intense cooperation and collaboration, there would be no great symphonies or theatric productions, no National Parks and Forests, no Fortune 500 corporations.

Some people view disputes as competitions that can be won, thereby creating a winner and a loser and usually suppressing cooperation. Chapter 8 explores the effects of win-lose approaches in greater detail.

Other people view disputes as opportunities to cooperate or collaborate and, thereby, to create many winners.

In *Getting to Yes,*[11] authors Roger Fisher and William Ury describe the **methods and means to perform what they call "interest-based" bargaining**, an approach endorsed by the U.S. Institute of Environmental Conflict Resolution. The method they espouse involves

- separating the people from the problem
- focusing on interests held by people rather than the positions they take
- inventing options that represent mutual gains, and
- using objective criteria to evaluate success

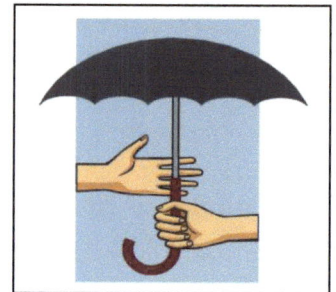

They try to move people away from arguing about their rights and past positions and towards stating their interests and desired outcomes.

To implement this method, they develop the idea that the disparate values humans hold allow any dispute (at least prior to the crisis stage) to be guided in order to achieve much (perhaps most, or even all) of what individuals want. What is not obvious to most disputants is that the means exist to restructure or revise relationships, or to change the composition of the dispute, in order to bring about mutual wins.

The story of the busy mom with two kids fighting over the last orange in the house is a good example. The busy mom witnesses the conflict, grabs the orange, and cuts it in two. She hands each child one half. The mom is surprised when both kids cry in protest. One girl actually wanted to zest the orange rind and add it to frosting for a cake. The other girl wanted the orange sections to eat because she had missed her after-school snack.

---

[11] *Getting to Yes: Negotiating Agreement Without Giving In.* Fisher, Roger and Ury, William. Penguin Books USA Inc., NY, NY. 1991.

The mom's action is an example of "Solomon's Solution," a tactic often employed by the courts in civil suits. In the case of a divorce, for example, a 50-50 division of financial assets is often considered to be "just." This is "bottom-line justice" wherein a balance sheet is prepared and the economic values for both disputants are carefully calculated, compared, and adjusted to be equal. Under this method, the judge imposes compromise and takes control of the outcome away from the opponents. Most times, upon being handed the verdict, the divorcing disputants will admit that it is passably equitable but declare that it's not just.

Like the mom, if the judge cares at all after years of handling marital strife, she may also be surprised and frustrated when both plaintiff and defendant are disappointed by and disparage the court's decision. **Because each party has different values and interests, "bottom-line justice" often does not satisfy either party**. This is why divorce mediation involving interest-based dialogue is the fastest-growing segment of the divorce-conflict industry because it can and does incorporate people's values and interests into court decisions.

When it comes to natural resources, some competing parties in the dispute may, for example, value gold more than productive ranchland, and other parties may value productive ranchland more than gold. Interest- or values-based cooperation may permit both parties to get all they want of both land and gold. Or, if cooperation fails, one party may "win" all of both resources. Then both parties may "lose" things or relationships they value highly or forego core interests.

In prolonged disputes that emphasize wins and losses, **blame usually becomes embedded in the communications and dispute cultures of the combatants**. The longer the conflict goes on mired in tit-for-tat tactics, the deeper the disputants are likely to embrace blame. This is may be accompanied by disputants diminishing, dehumanizing, and vilifying others, verbal and perhaps physical violence, and cultic and isolationist behaviors by the various "camps." Both sides may demand that nonaligned people join their cause and, if they don't, declare the nonaligned to be "in bed" with their opponents.

Over the years, I was declared "in bed" with so many opposing factions that the "bed" surely could have filled the Superdome. That I managed disputes and conflicts well without joining any opposing group was also true, and so, after completing the Bridger-Teton Land and Resource Management Plan, both my environmental and development interest "bedfellows" offered me a job.

The prolonged conflict between environmental interests and the timber industry in the Pacific Northwest and Alaska has all of these characteristics. It took four years of work by my staff on the Umpqua to get the opposing groups to be generally civil to one another in public settings.

However, our work had previously created a cautious breakthrough wherein both groups supported a three-fold increase in our timber program—a program that had been re-aimed, mainly to restore ecosystem function while greatly increasing wood and biomass supplies to local mills. To attain this end, we had restructured, changed a few components, and renegotiated some aspects of Forest Service/timber industry/environmental group relationships.

When cooperation is introduced into competitive disputes, a wide array of benefits can appear. In the *Getting to Yes* model, people's disparate interests can be met. The dispute may start over the ownership of land and gold or the preservation of spotted owl habitat, but the cooperation born out of the dispute can lead to personal wealth, growth and development, social innovation, community improvements, technological advances, better environmental safeguards, and stronger social agreements about schools, roads, and other infrastructure. People hold values far beyond the immediate source of dispute, and when these values are understood by all parties and brought into a cooperative model, good outcomes for all can result.

But is this approach sufficient to deal with all environmental disputes. My answer is, "No" and the reason is geographic scale. *Getting to Yes* **works well for small-scale disputes but breaks down quickly at larger-scales**. EDR practitioners have to use well-scaled and more robust models to be successful.

Common Topics and Drivers

EDR practitioners find that environmental disputes have a diverse set topics and drivers that get cited in many, sometimes unrelated disputes. Some of these include:

- Environmental factors
    - Scarcity of species, habitats, and physical resources (such as pure water)
    - Vulnerabilities such as resources being prone to fire, insects, or disease
    - Trends leading to potential losses of desired conditions, including human effects and environmental changes such as climate change
    - Invasive species displacing natives and reducing diversity or viability
    - Conditions in the aftermath of human consumption such as logging, mining, or diversion of water for agriculture
    - Ecological and geographic scales and inter-related resource conditions

- Human factors
    - Freedoms and opportunities for prosperity and wealth
    - Rights, roles, responsibilities, and connection to other people
    - Ethics, morals, and spiritual relationships to nature
    - Radicalism
    - Traditions, culture, connections to place
    - Consumptive uses of resources
    - Non-consumptive uses
    - Jobs and community economics
    - Communications content, patterns, and impacts
    - Environmental and inter-generational justice
    - Government and its effects and values on environmental protections and developments

An abbreviated, "hip-pocket" set of common problems or opportunities might look like this:

Human Factors

> 1) Consumptive uses
>   Renewable [plants, animals, protozoa]
>   Non-renewable [minerals, gases]
> 2) Non-consumptive uses
>   Recreational
>   Essence [impressionistic, intuitive, spiritual, ritual, religious uses]

Environmental Factors

> 3) Rare, threatened, endangered, or unique environmental conditions
>   Species
>   Habitats
>   Phenomenon
> 4) Understanding, prevention, and mitigation of unwanted impacts
>   Natural events
>   Human uses

These and other factors are explored in later chapters (for example, the psychology of environmental disputes is explored more in depth in Chapter 5 of this book). **These factors and others are also used in the "Practices" book to help build an effective EDR program at any geographic scale**.

Dispute Progression and Escalation

When cooperation fails, people adopt win-lose tactics, competition for control becomes ascendant, and disputes grow. Environmental and human factors get talked about and become the basis for opponents' positions and communications. Disputes escalate from issue to full-blown conflict, to crisis, and then recovery.

Here are the dispute definitions again from Chapter 1:

> **Issue** — a topic about which there is more than one opinion or position; usually a narrow, values-based dispute among two (or a few) parties leading, if unmanaged, to full-blown conflict. Abatement at this stage is the most cost-efficient option, although abatement usually does not usually attempt to mitigate or eliminate the basic values conflict among parties.

> **Full-blown Conflict** — a dispute with many issues and participants as well as complex interactions and communications; some conflicts exhibit rapid accumulation of issues and participants that lead to crisis.

> **Crisis** — an event (or series of events) that results in a permanent, significant change in the structure, composition, or functions and relationships associated with a conflict; picture reaching a ridge between two watersheds: by crossing over, you enter a new

watershed — a crisis is a "watershed" event. Loss of control by conflict participants is a characteristic of a crisis.

Recovery — the new structure, composition, and functions or relationships that exist after a crisis; if recovery is handled effectively, long-standing and recycling disputes may be reduced or eliminated.

If a dispute grows from an issue into a full-blown conflict, and if a conflict reaches sufficient intensity over a short enough period of time, a crisis occurs. For example, a border war may be a series of skirmishes for years, but once large armies mobilize and one side is defeated in battle, the border conflict is resolved by a long-term, perhaps permanent change in the border.

Dispute escalation can lead to dramatic changes in leaders and participants. The authors of Contemporary Conflict Resolution note that, "**It is a characteristic of conflicts that they intensify and widen, power passes from moderate to more extreme leaders, violence intensifies and restraint and moderation wither**[12]." If radicalization occurs and intensity increases rapidly, crisis and a "watershed" change are very likely.

Issues

As the definition suggests, issues represent **the first stage of dispute progression**. They form the building blocks of more complex and intense disputes, full-blown conflicts. Issues are relatively simple disputes usually with few disputants and topics. Issues are often defined in terms of topic, participants and their opinions, intensity, duration, scope, and location. Issues usually concern small geographic areas or projects.

Full-Blown Conflicts

Full-blown conflicts usually involve many issues, disputants, and participants. They tend to be **complex and confusing** to uninvolved on-lookers and may be characterized by **intense position-taking, propagandizing, and supporter-recruitment**.

Sometimes forces and counter-forces involved in full-blown conflicts accumulate gradually. Other times, one disputant may try the "**rapid accumulation" of force, persuasion, or political pressure to attempt dispute-resolution in their favor**. The so called "preemptive strike" in war or litigation illustrates rapid accumulation. The use of the internet to create "flash mobs" that create social disruption and catch authorities off guard is another form of rapid accumulation. Businesses see similar tactics in proxy fights and manipulation designed to seat or unseat board members.

The "War in the Woods" in the Pacific Northwest and Alaska was characterized by full-blown conflicts dating back to the 1970's. Disputants sought legal and political remedies to their issues, varying their tactics depending on the political party in office or the current status of court rulings. The full-blown conflicts were punctuated by a few EDR efforts and resulting crises, most notably President Clinton's efforts to meet with disputants which then resulted in the

[12] *Contemporary Conflict Resolution: The prevention, management, and transformation of deadly conflicts, Second Edition.* Ramsbotham, Oliver, Woodhouse, Tom, and Miall, Hugh. Polity Press, Malden, MA. 2005., 164.

Northwest Forest Plan for spotted owl areas of WA, OR, ID, and CA. Subsequent efforts to roll back NW Forest Plan provisions by the George W. Bush Administration largely failed along with the timber industry's "sue-and-settle" litigation strategy during the Bush years. Economic mitigation efforts supported by state and county governments and funded by Congress have been partially successful at stabilizing institutions such as schools but generally failed to create new economic drivers for the region.

Crisis

Unfortunately, the frequent result of not handling conflict well is a prolonged and debilitating, full-blown conflict that will eventually be **punctuated by a crisis or a series of crises**. A crisis takes the form of a turning point in a course of events, the structure of an industry or community, the functions or relationships among people/interests or people and the land, or the short- or long-term condition of the land. After the crisis, a significant, often disastrous, and sometimes permanent alteration has occurred. Often crises mean fundamental changes in the structure, composition, and functions or relationships of the competition, dispute, or conflict, and the changes are often permanent.

For example, after one nation is defeated in a war and border changes between two nations; one nation may be absorbed into another. Now the structure has changed and there is one nation instead of two. The functions and relationships have changed because the victor rules the loser rather than being an opponent; two economies are now one. If the conflict continues, the loser is now an insurgent or terrorist force subject to immediate execution rather than an army with soldiers who will get treated relatively well if captured.

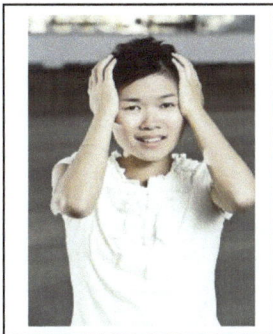

Similarly, a large-scale fire eliminates a timber stand. It cannot be replaced because, due to changing climatic conditions, the site is no longer wet enough to support the reestablishment of the historic forest. The structure of the vegetation on the site has changed. The site no longer functions as habitat for dependent critters. Relationships have changed within the plant and animal community and with human users.

A hillside may endure years and years of rain and snow as winter and spring events. But one spring a heavy, melting snow pack may receive heavy warm rains, and the hillside crumbles into a nearby river, dirt, boulders, brush, trees, summer cabin, and all.

During and after crises, people lose resources and opportunities. In many cases, natural catastrophes (e.g., floods, hurricanes, fires, earthquakes, tsunamis, disease pandemics) lead to crises as a result of social unrest, property destruction, and gross alteration of people's quality of life. People acting against other people can be equally devastating. Divorce, murder, theft, arson, conviction for white-collar crime, revolution, recall elections — all are examples of conflicts leading to crises among people. Whether natural or human-caused, all are examples of crises that lead to irrevocable change, so-called "watershed events."

People sometimes refer to **a crisis moment as a "point of no return." Lately, we have come to hear the term "tipping point"** to describe the same or similar concepts when applied to environmental and political phenomenon such as global warming or war. Thus, terms to describe crisis may vary, but they all share a common sense of change and irreversibility.

Sometimes, we decide to precipitate a minor crisis in order to avoid even more debilitating crises in the future. Public land managers initiate fire in ecosystems to prevent fuel buildup that, if left to build, could result in the large-scale loss of valuable or endangered resources, homes, or even communities when later burned.

The George W. Bush administration invaded Iraq on the premise that weapons of mass destruction were in the hands of an unstable dictator. In the aftermath of September 11, 2001, we had already invaded Osama bin Laden's Afghanistan stronghold and driven off the Taliban Islamic fundamentalist militants who were behind the attacks on the World Trade Center and the Pentagon. We could do this with broad-based national and international support because they were an apparent "clear and present danger" to the U.S. and other nations.

In the run-up to the Iraq invasion, the idea that Saddam Hussein was a similar but better-armed threat seemed like a plausible reason for such an invasion. Hussein's own bellicosity and past actions against his own people, Iranians, Kuwaitis, and America gave additional credence to the perceived threat. Most Americans supported the President, many with strong reservations. But once weapons of mass destruction failed to appear and a pathetic Hussein was captured and paraded in public view, much of the rationale for being in Iraq was lost. As more and more American blood was spilled and treasure lost, public support for a crisis precipitated under a false set of premises steadily declined.

The Bush administration actually had many other reasons for invading Iraq, such as securing energy resources and influencing the regional development of Islamic democracies. But these reasons were not publicly vetted and probably would not have been seen as being sufficiently urgent to warrant the precipitation of a crisis and the invasion of a sovereign nation.

As history has often shown, **if parties in power manipulate public perceptions mischievously, deadly crises can result. Later, as public truth replaces perception, blame and mistrust reverberate throughout society, making recovery painfully slow**.

Recovery in the Aftermath of Crisis

After a crisis is over and the changes have occurred, people tend to discuss and reevaluate "what is the state of things now," "why did this happen," "how could this have been prevented," and "what are we doing about it (the changed condition)." People reassess their assumptions about the structure, composition, functions, and relationships surrounding the conflict and the crisis. They question the assumptions held by others who had some interest in or power over the conflict and the course of the crisis.

This is necessary for individuals and communities to develop acceptance of the changed conditions and to decide what to do next. This is the recovery that occurs in the aftermath of crisis. The process is **sometimes called "recovery"** when it refers to a natural event such as hurricane Katrina, and **sometimes termed "reconciliation"** when it refers to the aftermath of an interpersonal or inter-group conflict such as apartheid in South Africa. I use "recovery" to express both.

During recovery, blame may appear and be far more widespread than simple blame assigned by one opponent to another during a pre-crisis dispute. In the early stages of recovery, society and the media often seem to join in the effort to locate a guilty party or parties and assign blame, seeking punishment whether warranted or not.

Blame is frequently assigned to individuals and organizations deemed to have responsibility for, or power over, the disputes, conflicts, or conditions leading up to the crisis. Questioning and reassessment of assumptions and responsibilities and the resulting assignment of blame often lead to losses of credibility and legitimacy, breakdowns in communications, withdrawal of financial support, and reassignment of responsibility for resources, regulations, or provision of services. During recovery, a realignment of power, control, prestige, and confidence often occurs. Jobs are lost. New coalitions of interests form. New leaders with different "recovery" agendas emerge.

After the Katrina hurricane disaster, the Federal Emergency Management Agency (FEMA) was perceived to have done such a poor disaster-response and relief job that a U.S. Senate panel called for its complete dissolution. In essence, they said, "Start over from the ground up." The FEMA Director was forced to resign, even before the panel proffered its advice.

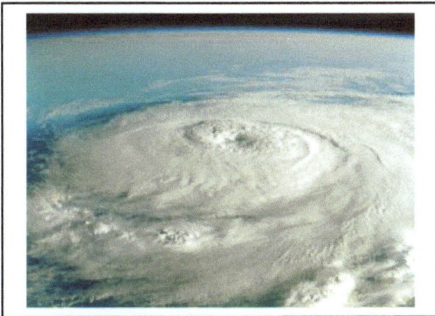

In contrast, Congress showered the agency most responsible for the disaster, the U.S. Corps of Engineers, with money. The Corps was seen to have made a vigorous and good-faith effort over many years to build the best levee and waterway system Congress felt the country could afford. Yet, the system was undersized, designed for Class III hurricanes. When that system failed during the Class V Katrina event, the Corps was asked to reconsider its assumptions about the system and build a better one for the future, one that could handle Class V hurricanes. Unlike FEMA, society and its representatives chose to adopt different assumptions about Corps' performance but not the elimination of the agency.

In terms of political leadership, with the New Orleans electorate dispersed across many states, mayoral candidates for the 2006 election campaigned like Presidential candidates. They were forced to make frequent visits to absentee voters hundreds of miles away, many in other states.

Election issues were vastly different post-Katrina too. Power shifted to those who had balanced ideas for rebuilding communities. Race and economic issues shifted from questions of jobs, crime, and local investment to questions of the survival of neighborhoods and people's basic property rights.

A realignment of power, control, prestige, and confidence is occurring in New Orleans even now. Jobs have been lost and new ones are being created. New coalitions of interests have formed to focus on post-Katrina issues. New leaders with different "recovery" agendas have emerged, and the landscape of New Orleans politics and political infrastructure has changed forever.

Crises Cascades

Crises are often interrelated. One kind of crisis leads to many others and precipitates related, irrevocable changes. I call this a "crisis cascade," similar to a series of drops in a waterfall.

For example, Hurricane Katrina devastated the physical infrastructure and many of the natural resources of the New Orleans area. This resulted in the loss of human life, the dispersal of New Orleans residents all over America, and great disruption to New Orleans' economy and culture, all of which resulted in local political upheaval and change. The political dynamics of recovery resulted in the FEMA Director being fired and a Senate panel recommending complete dissolution of the agency. The massive human need brought about by the storm also resulted in the redirection of a large discretionary component of the federal budget to Katrina relief, reducing spending on natural resource protections and management across America.

Historically, natural-resource based crises arising from a given set of conditions and conflicts have occurred over and over again, cascading in a pattern of human loss and change. For example, the annual seasonal flooding of the Nile River killed people, crops, and livestock for thousands of years until the Aswan Dam was built.

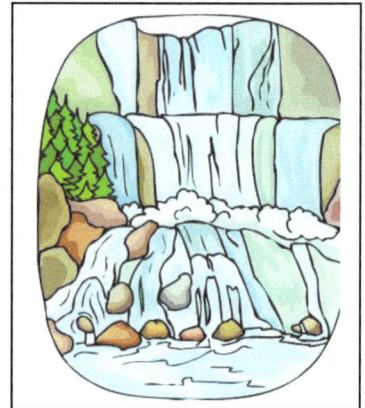

Once built, the dam itself became an ecological "crisis," although not as dramatic as catastrophic annual floods. The flooding historically assured the long-term fertility of the river plain. Now natural fertility is impaired. Certain pests and diseases affecting people and nature alike have become more common. So, a new set of conflicts and a cascade of crises formed when the dam came on line and the river controlled.

Crises Often Foretold

Ironically, most crises are not simply the end result of fate, but rather, many are predictable, and the rate and quality of predictions is improving all the time through technology. **Participants in, and observers of, conditions and conflicts can often forecast the eventual crisis.** This is especially true of natural catastrophes but also applies well to human-caused catastrophes.

It is also true, that the press of day-to-day business as well as stressors such as scandal, anarchy, and personal distress often prevent people who are party to a dispute from perceiving a looming crisis. Often, other people, caring onlookers and dispassionate observers, see crisis coming before the direct participants.

In advance of Katrina, local newspapers had extensively covered potential devastation from a major hurricane. Emergency-management professionals had sounded the warning. A severe hurricane season had been predicted by the National Weather Service experts six months in advance. Local, state, and federal emergency management people had more than a week's advance warning that Katrina was likely to devastate the Gulf Coast. They had more than two days warning that New Orleans would be impacted.

Yet, even with evidence before them as was the case in New Orleans, responsible people often fail to perform. They fail to gather data at all, or they ignore the information and insight that the data or onlookers provide. They reject their own intuition and the intuition of others close to the subject. They resist or discount projections or forecasts.

Other times, they fail to perform because they lack the skills, motivation, confidence, or support from other people, including peers and supervisors. Sometimes, when they try to perform, they cannot get other parties to the conflict to reduce tensions or sufficiently shift priorities to permit action. Frustrated, they may simply let a crisis run its course and try to make a difference during recovery.

EDR Relationship to Hierarchies of Needs

Abraham Maslow studied healthy people in the 1930's and 1940's with the intention of discovering how they ordered their needs, from highest to lowest priority (graphic below from Wikipedia). His classic "Maslow's Hierarchy of Needs" has proven both durable and valuable in helping people understand human response to social and environmental changes. The most basic, "primitive" requirements are displayed at the base of Maslow's triangle and the most "advanced" characteristics at the top.

Maslow's hierarchy has several applications to EDR work:

- Much of the negative energy people bring to an environmental dispute concerns the potential for risk and loss to the environment, communities, families, or themselves

- The intensity of negative energy tends to increase as the topic descends the hierarchy, from self-actualization to physiological needs

- The intensity of negative energy tends to increase with the credibility of the perceived threat; the more credible and imminent the threat, the greater the negative energy

- The intensity of negative energy tends to increase with the apparent proximity of the perceived threat to people and environmental characteristics valued by EDR participants; the closer the perceived threat is geographically, the greater the energy

- Once people's concerns are triggered, facts may play a limited role in reducing negative energy at least until people's fear recedes

- People's acceptance of facts may be source-dependent; if a person does not trust a particular source, whether person, institution, or government, facts from the source may not matter

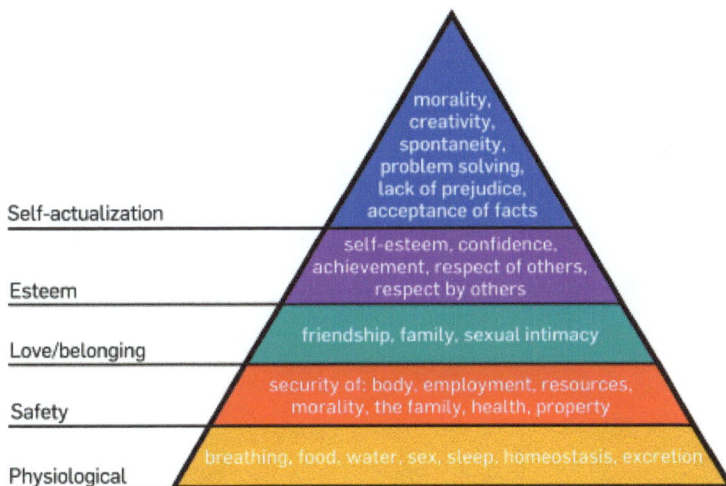

Self-actualization — morality, creativity, spontaneity, problem solving, lack of prejudice, acceptance of facts

Esteem — self-esteem, confidence, achievement, respect of others, respect by others

Love/belonging — friendship, family, sexual intimacy

Safety — security of: body, employment, resources, morality, the family, health, property

Physiological — breathing, food, water, sex, sleep, homeostasis, excretion

Community Needs hierarchy (top pyramid, bottom to top):

- Cohesion/ consent/ resolution
- Community Leadership/ Institutions
- Organizational leadership and commerce
- Safety and infrastructure
- Human population and natural resources

- EDR leaders and practitioners should work to understand people's fear intensities, where they fit on Maslow's hierarchy, and how to craft processes and techniques so that people's fears may be reduced and fact acceptance can happen

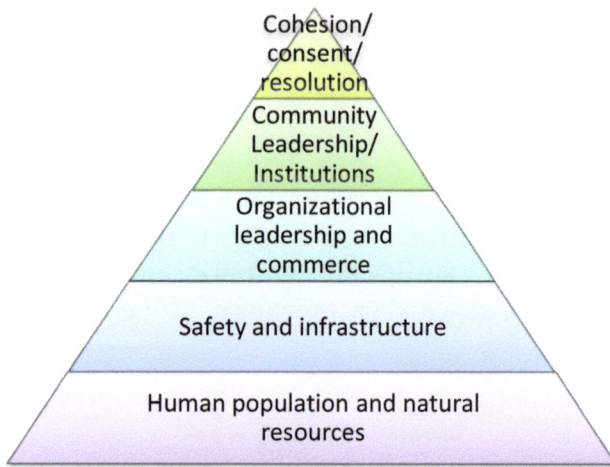

When I was in graduate school at the University of Wyoming in the 1970's, a student team developed a diagram similar to Maslow's for communities. The Community Needs hierarchy above left displays the essential needs of human civilization, from the presence of a human population and natural resources at the base to societal-actualization characteristics of goals cohesion, informed consent, and dispute resolution at the top. Communities meeting their needs at all levels tend to be adaptive, complex and successful over the long term. Communities that do not meet these needs tend to be maladaptive, chaotic, and unsuccessful.

Business Needs hierarchy (bottom pyramid, bottom to top):

- Adapt/ evolve/ expand
- Business institutions/ law/support
- Business leadership and workforce loyalty
- Safe work place/adequate supplies of labor and resources/markets
- Entrepreneur with access to human, financial, and natural resources

I built a similar hierarchy for businesses. My Business Needs hierarchy shows an entrepreneur with an idea and access to human and natural resources at the base. Moving upwards, it displays elements that allow the business to adapt, evolve, and expand, even dominate a business sector.

Like people, communities and businesses will respond to environmental disputes based on potential risk and loss, perceived threat, and fact credibility. For example, losses of nearby timber supplies threaten timber-dependent businesses and communities of place such as a town at the base of the hierarchies. Therefore, their negative energy may be very high coming into an EDR effort intended to resolve timber-supply issues.

Similarly, communities of interest such as environmental groups or communities of tradition such as Indian tribes might view timber harvest as a present threat to old forest species and conditions or traditional resources uses. They may also react with fear driven by needs at the hierarchies' bases. As EDR leaders and practitioners develop dispute-resolution communities and build EDR programs, they will want to help participants turn fears into hopes and actions. Chapter 5 discusses some aspect of this EDR work.

Chapter 4: Environmental Disputes Exist in an Ecological Context

Environmental disputes exist in an ecological context, making them different than social disputes such as a labor-contract dispute

Environmental disputants often are not aware of ecological-scale differences impacting the dispute; for example, a person struggling with salmon-restoration restrictions on a culvert project might be trying to address a land type phase condition and be unaware of ecoregional issues and public policies about salmon

Environmental disputes exhibit ecological elements: structure, composition and function; they are similar to wildfire, requiring people, disparate values, and a trigger and led to unacceptable consequences

EDR structure should be considered the physical, biological, spatial, legal, and regulatory elements involved in an environmental dispute, including legal ownership of resources.

EDR composition should include the physical and biological components present, adding to them cultural (moral, ethical, and traditional) values, the human-built environment, and the means people use for communications.

EDR functions should be considered to include human-to-human and human-to-nature relationships and the content of communications as symbolic of and conducive to human relationships. Functional and relationship elements include human uses of nature (sometimes called ecological services), the flow of solar and other energy, and the effects of human stewardship on ecosystems.

Chapter 3 provided some basic insight into the effects of competition, cooperation, and win-lose approaches to disputes. In addition, I developed further the concept of dispute escalation from issue to full-blown conflict to crisis to recovery that I first introduced in Chapter 1. Chapter 3 pointed out again that dispute resolution is most cost-effective in the earliest issue or full-blown conflict stages, before crisis. Chapter 3 also discussed the phenomenon, common in work with natural resources, of crisis cascades such has hurricane catastrophes that drive scandal and anarchy and personal distress. Crises are often foretold but, many times, people have a hard time accepting the threat's reality because of denial, disbelief, distraction, or distrust of the forecaster.

To understand more about why environmental disputes differ from other human conflicts, this chapter presents a basic understanding of ecological concepts, geographic scale phenomena, and how the subjects might apply to environmental dispute resolution.

Applying Natural Systems Concepts to Human Disputes

I have adapted many ecological definitions and ideas for EDR purposes. Based on years of field experience, **I conclude that environmental disputes can be scaled along with ecology from local micro-sites, such as a dispute over a tree along a property line, up to planetary-scale disputes over carbon dioxide and other greenhouse gas emissions.**

In 1997, Drs. Norm Christensen and Jerry Franklin wrote a chapter titled "Ecosystem Function and Ecosystem Management" to be included in the book, <u>Ecosystem Function & Human Activities</u>.[13] The book examines many aspects of the interaction between people and natural systems with a focus on the Chesapeake Bay and its environs.

In their chapter, Drs. Christensen and Franklin give us valuable insight into human-ecosystem relationships while explaining ecological concepts such as structure, composition, function, spatial and temporal scales, ecological services, and diversity. Many of the concepts I share in this book are adaptations of this piece by Drs. Christensen and Franklin and derived from conversations with systems ecologist Dr. Ann Bartuska, currently Forest Service Deputy Chief for Research and Development. Ann was briefly my boss in the Ecosystem Management staff and a valued colleague for many years.

From "*Ecosystem Function & Human Activities,*" 'ecological structure' refers to the spatial, physical, and biological elements of an ecosystem, for example, whether a given system is a forest, a grassland, a wetland, or a lake, river, or ocean environment. 'Composition' refers to the physical characteristics of a given system, such as weather, mineralization, and soil chemistry; the plant, animal, and protozoan species that are present; and species that may make use of the ecosystem seasonally or opportunistically, such as migratory species. 'Function' refers to the relationships among the physical and biological elements, including energy flow, the passage of nutrition from one component to another, and post-disturbance recovery. Ecosystems can be defined and analyzed from a drop-of-water scale to a planetary scale. At the end of this chapter is a discussion of *Ecological Units* at many scales. Appendix A contains a full paper on the subject.

So, to promote understanding and undergird EDR practices, I propose to add EDR definitions to match the ecological categories of "structure, composition, and function." **EDR structure** should be considered the spatial, legal, and regulatory elements involved in an environmental dispute, including the legal aspects of resource ownership. **EDR composition** should include the physical and biological components present, adding to them cultural (moral, ethical, and traditional) values, the human-built environment, and the <u>means</u> people use for communications. **EDR functions** should include human-to-human and human-to-nature **relationships,** how one uses, works with, or changes another, and the <u>content</u> of communications as symbolic of and conducive to human relationships and desired outcomes. Functional and relationship elements include human uses of nature (sometimes called "ecological services"), the flow of solar and other energy, and the effects of human stewardship of ecosystems.

As displayed and discussed in the <u>Practices </u>book, Chapters 6-13, these definitions work well and efficiently to support EDR diagnoses, prescriptions, direction-setting, and action selection.

Many people "throw their hands up" and despair of understanding ecosystems, let alone resolving long-standing high-intensity environmental disputes over them. Perhaps their despair reflects a similar view from systems ecology. "*The ecosystem is a highly complex phenomenon.*

---

[13] *Ecosystem Function & Human Activities: Reconciling Economics and Ecology.* Simpson, David R. and Christensen, Norman L. Jr., Chapman and Hall, NY, NY. 1997.

It is not only more complex than we think. It is more complex than we can think."[14]

To live with and within these systems, people do not find it necessary to understand them perfectly; however, to live in harmony with them means accepting their diversity and respecting how that diversity leads to long-term ecosystem sustainability. People should also understand that their environmental disputes reflect the larger ecological context and relationships that people live within.

For example, wars over petroleum supplies reflect solar energy from millions of years ago, and the desire to own scarce minerals, such as diamonds, reflects the evolution of the Earth, dating to 5 billion years ago. Dispute resolution communities do not need to have a perfect understanding of the ancient forces that produced these resources to develop effective EDR today. However, EDR leaders will want to understand how such resources are developed and used today as they work towards EDR with disputing interests.

EDR work requires only that we understand these factors only sufficiently, not perfectly. An expectation of perfect understanding and absolute rigor may in fact be a barrier to progress. My experience tells me that, in highly complex EDR situations with many issues at large time and spatial scales, managing disputes hierarchically and "adaptively" will likely prove satisfactory. In less complex EDR situations, disputes may be resolved more definitively and display short-term "closure."

Ecosystem-management work over the past twenty-five years has shown me that natural systems are competitive systems. Along with sometimes fierce competition, because of the functions of the parts and relationships among them, natural systems also exhibit remarkable levels of cooperation and complexity. As mentioned, they have structural, compositional, and functional or relationship characteristics. When all of these characteristics are examined together, a natural system becomes understandable — the whole is equal to the sum of its parts and the relationships among them. To achieve effective EDR, we have to understand similar things about the disputes and disputants.

Chapters 12 and 13 explore the application of ecological concepts to human situations in government, society, and business in much greater depth. In particular, the material looks at how to bring about high-level EDR performance in those institutions and their activities.

The National Hierarchy of Ecological Units and Its Use in EDR

The Forest Service and many other agencies use a hierarchical ecosystem classification system called "ECOMAP[15]". Ecological hierarchies are useful for understanding natural phenomenon and human-ecosystem relationships and interactions. They are also useful for understanding human ecology, economics, and environmental dispute resolution elements. Appendix A of this book contains a full presentation of the National Hierarchical Framework of Ecological Units.

---

[14] Egler, F.E. 1974. Egler, F. 1977. *The nature of vegetation: its management and mismanagement.* Aton Forest, Norfolk, CT.[Thanks to Zane Cornett for finding this quote].

[15] *Forest Service's National Hierarchical Framework of Ecological Units (ECOMAP 1993)*, Dr. Bailey, Robert G.

The primary purpose for delineating ecological units is to identify land and water areas at different levels of resolution that have similar capabilities and potentials for management. Depending on scale, ecological units are designed to exhibit similar patterns in: (1) potential natural communities, (2) soils, (3) hydrologic function, (4) landform and topography, (5) lithology, (6) climate, and (7) natural processes such as nutrient cycling, productivity, succession, and natural disturbance regimes associated with flooding, wind, or fire.

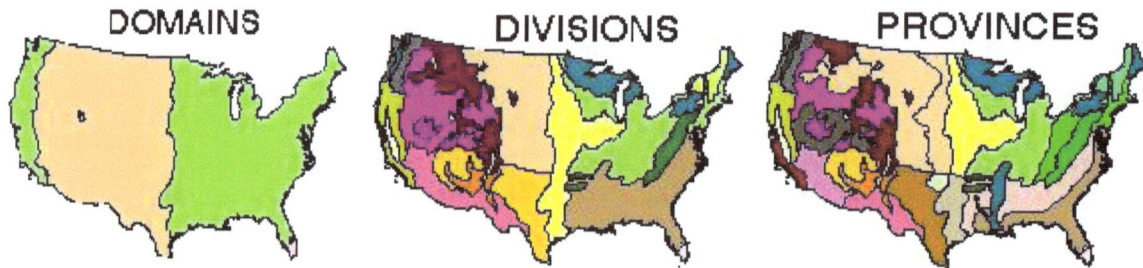

The graphics here illustrate the three geographically largest classifications: Domains, Divisions, and Provinces. There are five additional classifications covering successively smaller geographic areas and ecosystems described below: Section, Subsection, Landtype Association, Landtype, and Landtype Phase.

In addition to the hierarchical elements themselves, the third column in the table displays potential purposes and uses of the ecological units for analysis and land management. I have also included a fourth and fifth column to the table to illustrate some possible EDR components including issues and considerations.

To be effective, EDR practitioners at one ecological scale must be aware, at a minimum, of issues and considerations at the next higher scale and also at the next lower scale. Otherwise, practitioners will likely miss some important contextural elements that may delay or sidetrack their efforts and certainly render the efforts less effective.

So, practitioners working at national or state levels should become aware of international and regional laws, practices, conflicts, and other considerations. They should also become knowledgeable of county and local concerns and intentions.

Planning and analysis scale	Ecological Units	Purpose, Objectives, and General Use	Examples of Issues Likely to be Encountered in EDR Work	EDR Considerations
Ecoregion Global Continental Regional	Domain Division Province	Broad applicability for modeling and sampling National strategic planning and assessment International planning	Global and continental environmental issues such as climate change, warming, invasive species, pollution, desertification Social and economic issues such as human migration, trade barriers, affluence, competition, corruption, war	International and national treaties, laws, regulations, and agreements Individuals and organizations holding broad-scale power in conflict with national or regional interests Communications barriers, including language, time, and distance
Subregion	Section Subsection	Strategic, multi-forest, statewide, and multi-agency analysis and assessment	Species and habitat protection over large areas Wide-area restrictions on human use and development Regional and state economic impacts Wealth and power disparities	National and state laws and regulations Multi-jurisdictional and overlapping authorities (federal, state, county, special districts) Urban/rural division leading to political strife
Landscape	Landtype association	Forest or area-wide planning and watershed analysis	Protection for species and habitat Consumptive human uses such as logging and mining Non-consumptive human uses such as recreation, hunting, fishing Destructive forces such as flood, fire, and wind	Limits on the decision-making discretion of local land managers and owners Long-standing local conflicts over such things as boundaries, management practices, environmental protection Communication barriers and hardened positions
Land unit	Landtype Landtype phase	Project and management area planning and analysis	Fitting broader direction to specific resources and conditions Boundary management including survey and fencing	Resistance to national, regional, and local authority Unwillingness to engage Absent interests from other areas
Hierarchy can be expanded by user to smaller geographical areas and more detailed ecological units if needed.		Very detailed project planning.	Destruction of mitigation measures such as fences or signs Poaching, littering	Law enforcement presence Embedded conflicts or feuds

Wildfires and Disputes Are Ecologically Similar

A simple comparison to wildfire helps put humans and our disputes into an ecological context. In many ways, disputes are like wildfires:

- To have a wildfire, we require fuel, oxygen, and a heat source

- To have a dispute, we require people, disparate values, and a triggering condition, issue, or event

- Under the right conditions, both wildfires and disputes will lead to unnecessary and unacceptable losses

- We intervene in both when we have important values that may be lost

- Fires and disputes are unavoidable, but using good information and skill, we can influence or control their severity

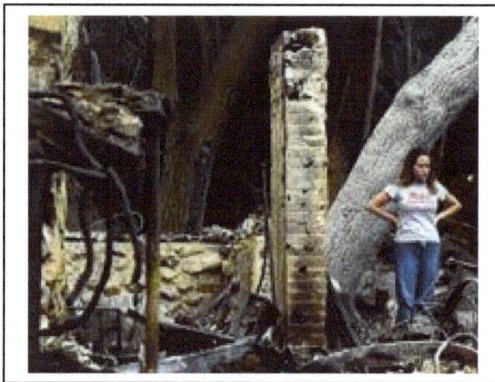

- Wildfires and disputes cost us the least when we control them at their "ignition source"

- Prevention, observation, and suppression are all parts of active firefighting and dispute resolution

- Disputes will not resolve themselves as long as "burning conditions" remain favorable

- Disputes will recycle until people change their values or gain dispute-resolution skills just like fire-prone areas burn and, perhaps many years later, re-burn unless deprived of fuel or a spark

- Only a dispute-resolution community with leaders, teams, and experts can resolve disputes; the wildfire incident-command system is a good model for dispute resolution

- As is true of fire prevention and suppression, dispute resolution means moving towards the dispute and engaging it thoughtfully, respectfully, and safely

- Recovery planning and actions should begin while the dispute is still running its course, which is similar to using best practices in post-wildfire restoration work

"Resistance" refers to a complex mixture of transference, projection, and shaped experience resulting in one party to a conflict adopting the behaviors of another while still disagreeing with them

Blaming plays a big role in dispute escalation going from situational to characteristic to intentional and personal

Values are what people desire or think is important; there are three general types of values in common usage, including personal (individual, psychologically based), social (aggregate, sociologically based), and economic (aggregate, economically based) values that contribute to environmental disputes

Values shape people's experience of life, starting with sensation, interpreted through values, beliefs, and past experiences, then leading to behaviors and actions

As individuals, we behave rationally in disputes, seeking to maximize our personal values; as members of communities of place, interest, tradition, or fate we also may seek to maximize shared social and economic values

In Chapter 4, I presented basic information about ecological concepts, including structure, composition, and function or relationships as well as geographic scale. I then borrowed concepts from ecology and applied them to environmental dispute resolution, and, in a table, showed how environmental dispute resolution factors fit with aspects of ecological scale.

This chapter digs more deeply into psychological and social factors that motivate and drive environmental disputes, including common personal, social, and economic elements.

Dispute Psychology

Some people assert that disputes develop because people do not understand their own values or how their emotions, mentation, and intellect function. These people say that most, if not all, disputes exist because people lack self-awareness of how they perceive and experience others. Other people hold that disputes are inherent in a free, competitive society and disputants should be encouraged to struggle and fight, regardless of their self-awareness or expression skills.

Psychologists use terms such as **"transference," "projection," "externalization," and "resistance"** to describe some of the behaviors I have seen in EDR efforts.[16] I am no psychologist. Still, I am aware of the potency of these ideas when trying to deal with disputes. I am sure many books have been written about each of these topics by experts, but I will try to summarize what I have come to understand in the context of EDR.

---

[16] Personal communication with Dr. Walter Cieko, August 18-20, 2006, during a workshop on inter-personal relationships and personal dispute resolution in Wilmington, DE.

As I understand it, "**transference**" refers to the unconscious attribution of a personal condition or intention to another person. So, for example, stimulated by the posture, dress, movement, or expression of another person, I unconsciously transfer my personal but hidden-from-myself arrogance and feelings of contempt for certain other people to that person. I am convinced by my own internal, unconscious process that the person is arrogant and contemptuous of others, even through the person may not have those attributes at all. In such an instance, I am transferring my emotions to the other person.

➡️ *The more strongly I deny my conditions or emotions, the more strongly I am convinced that the other person has those characteristics.*

"**Projection**" similarly occurs when I believe someone is manifesting an emotion, such as anger, which I also feel but cannot or will not express consciously. For example, I frequently feel "projected" embarrassment if someone makes a mistake during a presentation in front of a group. The person making the mistake may not be embarrassed at all, but I am "embarrassed for them."

Actually, having been endlessly ridiculed both at home and at school as a child, and now denying such feelings to seem a "grown up" to others, I'm embarrassed **for me, not them**. I am now a polished presenter and recover from my own mistakes without embarrassment, but I experience projected embarrassment when I perceive that others "flub up."

"**Externalization**" refers to our tendency to take issues or problems we possess internally and attribute them to other people or to society as a whole. In unconscious ways, externalization means saying "It's not my problem" or "I'm passing the buck."

So, for example, if I feel that I am being irresponsible by driving a large pickup truck that I do not use for business but for pleasure, I could externalize this internal distress and become a vocal critic of the automobile industry or other people who drive large, fuel-consumptive vehicles.

In environmental circles, it is popular to criticize developing nations for the extent and pattern of their natural resource use and resulting environmental effects without acknowledging that their behavior is based, in part, on the consumption of resources within the U.S. and other developed nations. This is externalization, and in some respects, an expression of a person's unwillingness to accept that they may be a part of the "problem."

Anti-hunting groups may be practicing externalization when they complain about the killing of wild animals, about humans behaving as predators. Such advocates externalize their own repugnance for killing and eating wild creatures onto society as a whole, and they are perhaps unwilling to recognize their own status as omnivorous "predators" in nature and failing to understand that the predator role is part of an important natural balance. White-tailed deer have overrun many communities in the eastern U.S. because of this externalization and role confusion.

➡️ *The more I am in denial of and suppress my emotions or internal conflicts, the more strongly I am convinced that the other person has those emotions or conflicts.*

One statement I've heard is "**that which you resist, you create, enhance, and eventually** ⟵
become." "Resistance" refers to a complex mixture of transference, projection, and shaped experience, resulting in the EDR sense with one disputant adopting the behaviors of another.

For example, over the course of several years I watched environmental groups become legalistic and officiously bureaucratic in their attempt to control public agencies like the Forest Service. As a result of their resistance to public agencies' plans, processes, and actions and their own retreat behind bureaucracy to avoid change, many "e-groups" have become models of entrenched bureaucracy, resistant to change and new ideas.

Often one disputant exhibits "self-righteous" thinking and behavior, placing their values and behaviors above the values and behaviors of their opponent. Self-righteous thinking and behavior is a manifestation of resistance, but one with a "hard left hook." A disputant exhibiting self-righteousness is psychologically positioning herself to be unaccountable for her communication and behavior towards her opponent and possibly EDR practitioners. Such a person is declaring that they are "the law unto themselves" and the appropriate final arbiter of outcomes. Clearly, this behavior would be disruptive to EDR efforts and must be dealt with early in EDR work.

The more I am in resistance to what I am transferring to, projecting onto, or externalizing to ⟵
others, the more strongly I invent, enhance, and eventually become those characteristics.

I frequently mediate or otherwise participate in an EDR with many interests, including development, environmental, and governmental representatives. Each in their own way, particularly early in the EDR effort, will express their perception of the deceit, inappropriate tactics, and untenable ideas and positions of the other.

I have also seen that the parties are practicing transference, projection, externalization, and resistance. They usually unconscious of their practices and unaware that they will become increasingly similar in their positive and negative behaviors over time!

Peter Senge describes this resistance phenomenon, similar to my resistance description earlier in the chapter, and the potential for change in *The Fifth Discipline*.[17]

> *In the mid-1970s, the ideas of [Chris] Argyris and his colleagues were beginning to provide an answer. In "action science," they were developing a body of theory and method for reflection and inquiry on the reasoning that underlies our actions.[18] Moreover, the tools of action science are designed to be effective in organizations, and especially in dealing with organizational problems. We trap ourselves, say Argyris and his colleagues, in "defensive routines" that insulate our mental models from examination*

---

[17] *The Fifth Discipline: The Art and Practice of the Learning Organization*. Senge, Peter M. Doubleday. NY, NY. 1990. pp.182-3.
[18] "C. Argyris and D. Schon, *Organizational Learning: A Theory of Action Perspective* (reading, MA , Addison-Wesley) 1978; C. Argyris, R. Putnam, and D. Smith, *Action Science* (San Francisco: Jossey-Bass), 1985; C. Argyris, *Strategy, Change, and Defensive Routines* (Boston: Pitman), 1985.

and we consequently develop "skilled incompetence" — a marvelous oxymoron that Argyris uses to describe most adult learners who are "highly skillful at protecting themselves from pain and threat posed by learning situations," but consequently fail to learn how to produce the results they really want.

Despite having read much of his writing, I was unprepared for what I learned when I first saw Chris Argyris practice his approach in an informal workshop with a half-dozen members of our research team at MIT. Ostensibly an academic presentation of Argyris's methods, this session quickly evolved into a powerful demonstration of what action science practitioners call "reflection in action." Argyris asked each of us to recount a **conflict with a client, colleague or family member** *(emphasis added). We had to recall not only what was said but what we were thinking and did not say. As Chris began to "work with these cases" it became almost immediately apparent how each of us* **contributed to a conflict** *through our own thinking – how we made* **sweeping generalizations** *about the others that determined what we said and how we behaved. Yet, we never communicated the generalizations. I might think, "Joe believes I'm incompetent," but I would never ask Joe directly about it. I would simply go out of my way to make myself look respectful to Joe. Or, "Bill [my boss] is impatient and believes in quick and dirty solutions," so I would go out of my way to give him simple solutions even though I don't think these strategies will get to the heart of difficult issues.*

Within a matter of minutes, I watched the level of alertness and "presentness" of the entire group rise ten notches — thanks not so much to Argyris' personal charisma but to his skillful practice of drawing out those generalizations. As the afternoon moved on, all of us were led to see (some of us for the first time in our lives) **subtle patterns of reasoning that underlay our behavior, and most importantly, how those patterns continually got us into trouble**. *I had never had such a dramatic demonstration of my own mental models in action, dictating my behavior and perceptions. But even more interestingly, it became clear that, with proper training, I could become much more aware of my mental models and how they operated. This was exciting.*

Later I learned that O'Brien and his management team at Hanover had a similar experience with Argyris' methods ten years earlier. This had led them to realize that, in O'Brian's words, "Despite our philosophy, we had a very long way to go to be able to have the types of open, productive discussions of the critical issues that we all desired. In some cases, Argyris' work revealed painfully obvious gamesplaying we had all come to accept...."

EDR leaders should be vigilant about EDR efforts that establish dispute de-escalation or resolution visions and norms, ostensibly supported by all participants, but which may be unconsciously resisted. In all likelihood, participants have to become conscious of and challenge themselves to change values, beliefs, experiences, and behaviors if the effort is to be successful. Such self-consciousness may also extend to people not in the room, particularly powerful decision-makers and those who could potentially veto a given resolution.

As the EDR effort goes forward, if I can get the opponents to articulate the values, thoughts, and emotions of the other parties, and to do so accurately, we are likely to move ahead towards improved cooperation. Such an exercise builds mutual understanding at the conscious level, and at the unconscious level, it allows participants to accept personal denied values, thoughts, feelings, intentions, and behaviors.

Experiences of the Past Drive Fear-Based Behavior in the Present

Fear is elemental to dispute. The authors of *Contemporary Conflict Resolution*[19] explore the impact of fear succinctly:

> *Azar drew on the work of Sumner (1906), Gurr (1970), Mitchell (1981), and others to trace the process by which mutually exclusionary 'experiences, fears and belief systems' generate 'reciprocal negative images which perpetuate communal antagonisms and solidify protracted social conflict'. Antagonistic group histories, exclusionist myths, demonizing propaganda and dehumanizing ideologies serve to justify discriminatory policies and legitimize atrocities. In these circumstances, in a dynamic familiar to students of international relations as the 'security dilemma', actions are mutually interpreted in the most threatening light, 'the worst motivations tend to be attributed to the other side', the space for compromise and accommodation shrinks, and 'proposals for political solutions become rare, and tend to be perceived on all sides as mechanisms for gaining relative power and control' (Azar, 1990).*

Many disputes are driven by fear, the intuition that, if we do not achieve control and the outcome we desire, we will fail and, perhaps as an extension of our young lives and feelings, we will even die. We respond to **fright** with certain impulses--to **flee, fight, hunker down, submit, appease/placate, or deceive**. We usually act on these impulses.

Sometimes the strength and direction of those actions seem out-of-context or over-reaction to uninvolved observers, because of the intrusion of our reaction to past bad experiences into our present-day behavior. One indicator of what people fear is what they mock. Mockery and related humor exposes what is feared, and sometimes, it exposes the basis for the fear and the past events that drive that fear.

No one can enter EDR work with a fear-free, clean slate because we all reflect and represent our past experiences and carry them into any process. However, what frequently drives tension- and dispute-escalation is that people are afraid that past events and consequences will repeat themselves. So, a part of EDR is to establish sufficient group trust and confidence in EDR processes so that people can let go of fear and fear-based responses and successfully participate.

With this in mind, I usually tell opponents and other EDR participants that "**fear lives in the past**" based our past experience of others and their behaviors under past conditions.

Once we've discussed the past, I tell participants that "**opportunity lives now and in the future.**" I encourage people to recognize the sources of their fear and consciously acknowledge that the events and behaviors that triggered that fear need not be influential going forward. Here is another way of expressing this opportunity-thinking: "**Behind every fear is a want that can be stated as a desired condition or outcome.**"

---

[19] *Contemporary Conflict Resolution: The prevention, management, and transformation of deadly conflicts, Second Edition.* Ramsbotham, Oliver, Woodhouse, Tom, and Miall, Hugh. Polity Press, Malden, MA. 2005. p.88.

As wants and wishes get revealed and understood, I encourage opponents to recognize that the opportunities so presented may allow everyone to get more of what they value. This potential exists in contrast to the likelihood of recycled disputes rooted in fear and perceptions of past performance. The bottom line: everyone has a history as they enter into EDR, and they also can make choices about future conditions.

I have also realized how much every dispute I find myself in is "all about me" rather than the other parties. If I am playing the role of the neutral third party, I must make sure I do not get embroiled in the dispute because of my unconscious thoughts, feelings, and intentions. If I am a party to the dispute, I must make sure I stay focused on the key resource and use issues, not my own unconscious attributions to others.

EDR practitioners sometimes exhibit transference, projection, externalization, resistance, and fear, too. For example, an EDR practitioner may project unconscious emotions or motives on an opponent or another participant and react to them with off-base, inappropriate criticism or attacks. If so, the practitioner is committing the **"bogeyman under the bed"** error in EDR, attempting to solve a problem that does not exist except within the practitioner. This may significantly set back the EDR effort and may give opponents reason to exit.

Chapter 10 addresses aspects of effective and ethical EDR practice and delves more deeply into personal behavior and responsibility concerning different EDR roles.

A Field Example of Overcoming Fear and Building Group Cohesion

"*A pint of sweat saves a gallon of blood*," wrote General George Patton (1885-1945). Leading EDR efforts means getting down to the actual work of dispute resolution as soon as possible, applying the best tradecraft you can, and inevitably taking some risks in anticipation of significant gains.

A few years ago, I stood in a ponderosa pine forest in Oregon, surrounded by a group of people representing the full range of public interests. We were on a Rogue National Forest tour with then-District Ranger Joel King, looking at several potential resource-enhancement projects that the group could choose to fund.

Joel had previously led the group through a half-hour exercise that connected us to the land by our earliest memories and experiences, and at another time, he had asked us to "be silent and listen to what the land has to tell you." This was obviously not your normal government-run field trip. This trip had a "woo, woo" element that intrigued me. I sensed EDR in the air and maybe some small relationship-building miracles unfolding.

We came to a crossroads, quite literally, where Joel and his staff had treated similar timberlands with different levels of cutting and clearing. Where two roads met, creating four quadrants, he had dealt with the land in each quadrant differently and was asking us to note, and to "feel," the differences.

First, we entered a timber stand that Joel and his staff had partially cleared to produce some commercial timber for market and to reduce fuel loadings for fire protection. Then we entered a stand that no one had walked for a long time, growth so dense we could hardly move. Brush was dense and trees close packed — a stand ripe for catastrophic fire and offering little for wildlife. Joel talked about what the land needed, what it was "asking for." People were nodding their heads and talking about what to do in such an over-stocked and vulnerable place.

Joel then pointed out that only fear held us back from taking action — fear of what we had experienced before: betrayal of trust, abuse of resources, unaccountable government employees. He then said with strong emotion in his voice, *"That was the past and now the land demands that we do something else. We need to give up our fear and do what's right for the land."*

My eyes still tear up today as I think about how those people nodded their heads again, even more emphatically than before, infused with a passion for working together to find answers to environmental issues, a passion for environmental peace and justice. At some level, our experience touched and changed us all — the experience Joel created for us that day.

Every day we begin with a fresh slate, and we can choose to eschew our past fear and loathing of our opponents. The past is just an example and not our fate, even if we are dealing with the great environmental issues of our times. EDR that creates a committed community is a means to let go of our fears and embrace environmental peace and justice for people and nature alike. Right, Joel?

Disputes and Blame

At some point, EDR may require a de-escalation of blame. Blame is used in power plays and is usually an appeal to object, process, and behavioral values. For example, many environmental groups will blame agency people for "not following the process," and this becomes the basis for advocacy and litigation. Development groups may blame the environmental groups for production delays and accuse the agency of insincerity and inefficiency in trying to "meet its production targets." An environmental regulator may blame a business leader for not meeting and environmental standard or reporting deadline.

Ah, the "blame game" — what a common part of disputes. I have observed blame in almost every dispute with which I have ever dealt. Blame comes in three forms:

"Situational" or incidental — people are said to have done something unacceptable because of conditions outside their control. When this occurs, I often hear things like, "Well, they had to do that because Congress required them to take that action."

"Characteristic" or intrinsic — people are said to have done unacceptable things as a result of personal values, beliefs, and behaviors they hold that they apply to all situations. In these situations, I often hear statements like, "She's just a jerk. She always speaks first and takes all the credit. It's her nature."

57

➡ **"Personalized" or intentional** — people are said to have done unacceptable things because they hold strong negative feelings towards the other party and intend harm. In these situations, I often hear statements like, "He really hates us, doesn't he? He attacks us because he thinks we're nobodies to be stomped on."

Generally, blame attribution escalates from situational to characteristic to personal. This may parallel dispute progression and escalation from issues, to full-blown conflict, to crisis, and to recovery.

As people gather evidence to support one level of blame, they will often develop evidence that leads them to the next level. It is my experience that blame escalates exponentially. Situational blame is minor compared to characteristic blame. Personalized blame is significantly greater in intensity and effect than characteristic blame.

Once blame attribution becomes personalized, it is much harder to de-escalate, probably because it triggers the human "fright: flee, fight, hunker-down, submit, appease/placate, or deceive" response. People feel attacked when they perceive that blame is personalized towards them. Then, they become frightened, defensive, and perhaps even violent. Sometimes, when hunkering-down occurs, we refer to the person as having a "siege mentality."

Appeasement or placation is a common response to blame in situations where there exist perceived power imbalances among the disputants. Placation may seem to the powerful to be compliance or submission from the less powerful; in fact, the less powerful disputant is likely making a momentary concession with the intention to act in their own interest later. Placation under serves the powerful because they perceive they have agreement and commitment when they do not. In addition, it generally has only short-term value for the less powerful because it leads to ever more forceful behavior from the powerful—behavior designed to force compliance and behavior motivated by mistrust and disrespect.

Appeasement and placation are similar to deception as a response to blame. The difference is that a placater admits some responsibility and offers conciliatory actions and a deceiver uses lies or deflection to divert blame elsewhere.

I believe that blame drives much of the xenophobia, isolation, and cultic behavior I've experienced with environmental and development groups and agency employees. I find this unfortunate because people tend to over-estimate a blamer's intentions.

Frequently, if one opponent views the other as having a characteristic or personalized animus towards them, when I consult the other opponent, they will explain that they actually have no animus at all, or simply a situational dislike for the other person. In the later stages of the process, if one side has escalated the blame to personalized levels, the other side will have as well. "Talking this down" may be the essential first step to effectively resolving the dispute.

Trust

In her book, Laurie Coltri examines trust as a key component to conflict resolution.[20] In her discourse, she describes work by Shapiro, Sheppard, and Cheraskin (1992) that defines trust categorically this way: "calculus-based, knowledge-based, and identification-based." Calculus-based trust rests on understanding the consequences of compliance or non-compliance with rules or agreements. Knowledge-based trust rests on understanding the opponent. Identification-based trust rests on feelings of connection and agreement to the identity, goals, or purposes that one opponent shares with the other. These three definitions conform closely to structural (calculus), compositional (knowledge), and functional or relationship (identification) EDR elements I proposed in Chapter 4.

Effective EDR may require an explicit development of trust and an understanding of trust levels and characteristics for each opponent and some participants, including the powerful people otherwise not present. For example, calculus-based trust may have to be developed before a group will fully commit to a set of norms guiding an EDR effort. Knowledge-based trust may have to be developed for opponents to work together effectively to develop resolution options. Identification-based trust may have to be developed for a collaborative project to move forward.

An excellent book on the subject is The Speed of Trust: One Thing That Changes Everything by Steven Covey[21]. Covey looks at the essential elements that must be in place to promote and sustain trust within organizations and among individuals.

Anger

People involved in EDR often manifest anger. As I understand it, anger is what psychologists call a "masking emotion" — it hides a person's real emotion. The angry person may not readily understand the underlying emotion, either because they are unconscious of it altogether or because they have momentarily hidden it with the anger. Anger is intimidating to other participants, and possibly to EDR practitioners.

Anger can mask almost any emotion, from sorrow or regret to compassion or empathy for others. Anger is also cumulative. Even as people feel anger, they gather "evidence" to support their beliefs and angry behavior. They then re-express their anger with greater energy. This self-reinforcing cycle can lead to out-of-control rage.

When crowds exhibit anger in public settings, anger often recedes as crowds disperse. In rare cases, anger escalates in public settings to the point where mobs form and lawlessness prevails. Usually the difference between anger abatement and lawlessness depends on who leads and how they lead the assembled group. Mob behavior has a special place under the law; usually, people

---

[20]Conflict Diagnosis and Alternative Dispute Resolution. Coltri, Laurie S. Pearson Education, Inc. Upper Saddle River, NJ. 2004. pp. 177-191.
[21] The Speed of Trust: One Thing That Changes Everything. Covey, Steven R. 2006.

caught up in a riot are not criminally prosecuted because they are considered to be mentally disabled for the riot's duration. Such is the great impact of social rage.

In any group activity, and particularly in the early stages of EDR, practitioners may want to speak directly to anger and how the group should try to manage anger through agreed upon norms or rules for personal conduct. EDR practitioners should also recognize the potential for anger escalation, educate participants about anger-escalation potential, and be ready to intervene if anger-escalation appears.

Anger also has a way of being self-defeating. As Benjamin Franklin (1706-1790) said, *"Whatever is begun in anger ends in shame."* For example, people who are asked to speak before large groups, particularly when they are experiencing the strong emotions they have regarding a dispute, will frequently lose control of their emotions and become very angry, expressing themselves and their anger way beyond their planned and normal mode of speaking or feeling. When they sit down, they are embarrassed by their outburst and wonder what prompted it; if they feel shame, the feeling and their resistance to perceived opponents may add to their anger.

Other participants may be threatened by the speaker's vehemence and be so intimidated that they choose not to speak; or, they may be bemused and trivialize the speaker's ideas and values. They may also experience projection and get angrier themselves without understanding this increased emotion when it is their turn to speak. A brew of anger, projection, and fear can drive disruptive and violent mob behavior.

Learning Styles and Resistance as a Factor in EDR

Learning is an important part of developing and maintaining values and beliefs that shape our experiences and behaviors — it is a principal factor in the "believing is seeing" process. Success in EDR may mean understanding learning approaches that help people change their mental models even as they defend and sustain them.

Experts tell me that people learn through four principal senses: **visual, auditory, tactile, and proprioception**. Visual refers to sight, including movement, pattern, and color. Auditory refers to hearing, including sound and intonation. Tactile refers to touch, including pressure, texture, and temperature. Proprioception refers to the position of the body and the limbs. Proprioception is the sense we use to learn to walk, swim, dance, and perform exercise routines. A few people may learn through **smell and taste** and associate thought with these sensations, but the majority of us do not. For most of us, smell and taste more commonly evoke emotions and memories. All sensory experiences can affect behavior.

Children tend to learn through a variety of further means, including mimicry, memorization, repetition, and experience. Adults tend to learn through personal-interest and experiential studies. In this sense, adults show considerable resistance to any learning that conflicts with personal values and life patterns.

EDR practitioners should be looking for **multiple means (for example, tactile, visual, and auditory) to build leaning into EDR efforts**. This means recognizing the many learning styles and the fundamentally different nature of educating adults versus children.

Common Values Related to Environmental Disputes

Understanding how we use the term "values" in working with environmental disputes is essential to success. Simply stated, values are what people think is important or desirable.

For EDR work, understanding values can be difficult. Values are the relatively constant concepts that people hold and express about what is important to individuals, groups, and communities. So, as the numbers of people, groups, and communities involved in EDR grows, the complexity of the related values also grows. To complicate matters further, many of the participants may not understand or be able to articulate the values that they hold.

According to social scientists, there are three general types of values in common usage: personal (individual, psychologically based), social (aggregate, sociologically based), and economic (aggregate, economically based) values. How individuals rank the values they hold reflects the relative importance to them of objects, conditions, processes, or outcomes.

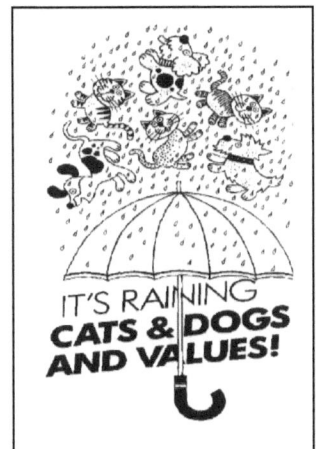

IT'S RAINING CATS & DOGS AND VALUES!

As mentioned previously, all values are personal and unique. However, as we work on environmental disputes with structural, compositional, and function or relationship factors, we see that many personal values are shared with other people, leading to useful aggregations of those shared values. In EDR, we work with all of these concepts depending on the dispute at hand.

In natural resource management, there are several categories of values that are generally recognized, including such traditional commodity values as timber, range, energy minerals, and common minerals. Other categories include non-traditional commodities that are harder to value in terms of economics, such as inter-generational culture or scenic beauty. Values are important to identify and understand because they set the stage for beliefs (which include what we tend to think of as knowledge) and attitudes, which in turn predispose people toward particular intentions and behavior (Rokeach, 1973).[22]

My friend Dr. Pat Reed speaks to one categorization of values people hold towards natural resources.[23] Pat identifies 13 public values as they apply to a national forest:

- Aesthetic value
- Economic value
- Recreation value
- Life Sustaining value
- Learning value

---

[22] *The Nature of Human Values.* Rokeach, M. New York: Free Press, 1973
[23] *Validation of a Forest Values Typology for Use in National Forest Planning.* Brown and Reed. 2000 Forest Science. 46(2): 1-8.

- Biological diversity value
- Spiritual value
- Intrinsic value
- Historic value
- Future value
- Subsistence value
- Therapeutic value
- Cultural value

A person's quality of life is essentially the manifestation and satisfaction of their values. In the case of ecosystem services, quality of life may be expressed in economic terms. But, for many people, it also has emotional and social importance that cannot be expressed in purely economic terms. Economic expression works better for some values than for others. For example, ascribing a higher monetary value to one culture over another does not work well in EDR.

For EDR efforts to be successful, sorting out and communicating values is important. The Brown and Reed list is a starting point for values discussions pertaining to natural resources and ecological services. An equally important list concerns the higher-values discussed briefly in Chapter 2, such values as fairness, timeliness, honesty, good faith, etc. This higher-value list is important because it speaks directly to people's expectations for the behavior of others in the EDR and for the nature of the EDR processes to be followed.

The worth of an EDR outcome for some participants may be more directly related to satisfaction of meta-values than the actual control, use, protection, or ownership of resources. I have heard many public-process participants say, "I actually don't much care what you folks decide to do, and I'm here to make sure everyone gets listened to and treated fairly."

Although values tend to become "fixed" as people mature into adulthood, the same people sometimes change their values based on experience. A new tofu dish at dinner might prove tasty and satisfying to someone who had made rude noises about tofu before. After the experience of that dish, the person may change an "object-related" value; he now likes tofu served that way and may be open to more experimentation. Object-related values involving such experiences as taste, color, texture, and appearance change relatively easily.

Another person undergoes a personal crisis caused by a cancer diagnosis. He recovers and changes a long-held "process-related" value: he no longer avoids annual checkups to avoid hearing "bad news." Process-related values involving what is to happen and how it is to happen are more difficult to change than object-related values.

After two years of therapy, a woman realizes that she has been treating her spouse unfairly and

changes a "rights-related" value. She has gone to a weekly card party "for fun" for years but had objected on religious and financial grounds to his occasional loss of money at poker. She stops protesting when he plays poker "for money" with his friends. She accepts that he has the right to choose how to spend his money and time. Rights-related values are relatively hard to change in part because they may reflect the owner's high-order fears and control needs, and in part, because they reflect broader, economic and other social values common to society, cultures, or religious groups.

EDR practitioners should recognize that opponents can voluntarily change their values and should sometimes structure EDR work to enable, but not require, those changes. Practitioners should also understand that "higher-order" values often override "lower-order" values. For example, as a family selects a restaurant for dinner, the choice to "go out for a steak" (object-related) may be over-ridden by a vegetarian family member's protest about unfair treatment (rights-related) if she is to be forced to pick from a menu developed for a meat-eating customer base.

Short of crisis and recovery, perhaps the only way EDR practitioners can achieve consent, consensus, or collaboration in their work is by assisting people to change their values or, more likely, by helping to invoke and work through higher-order values that override and resolve an object- or process-related values dispute.

In public dispute discussions, opponents and other participants often express fears about the behaviors of other disputants. These fears are values-based and reflect past experience, real or perceived. The fears conceal desires for changed relationships and different outcomes. EDR practitioners may find it quite advantageous to explore these fears-to-desires transformation opportunities early in an EDR effort as they explore and map the values that opponents hold.

A Simple Model to Describe Values and Their Influences

Over time, I developed a simple model to illustrate individual behavior in complex dispute situations. Here's how it looks:

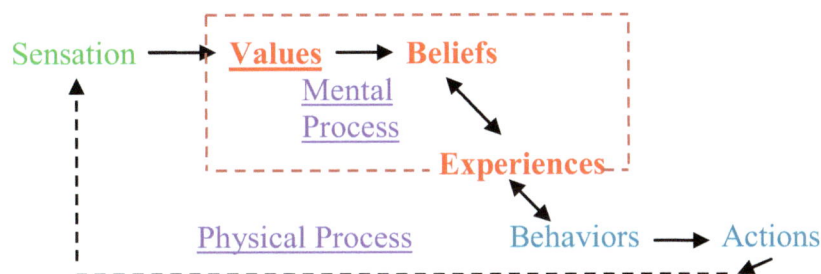

Sensation ⟶ **Values** ⟶ **Beliefs**
Mental
Process
Experiences
Physical Process   Behaviors ⟶ Actions

In humans, sensations occur then quickly stimulate emotion and thought in the brain. As sensory information flows into us, our values, beliefs, and past experiences activate and create a set of behaviors and actions in response to the sensation.

An old axiom is that "seeing is believing," but more often than not, the way the human mind works is actually the other way around: **believing is seeing**." People process complex life experiences through a relatively simple model. As they do this, they manage their experiences, and their perceptions of the effects of any actions they take, to reinforce their values and beliefs.

For example, I enter a bank. I see a teller stuffing money into what I perceive to be her lunch bag. Based on this sensation and my values about how the teller should be treating money in the bank, I develop the belief that she is embezzling. Processing this through my past experiences, I approach the manager and she tells me essentially to "mind my own business." I am miffed.

My first action is to leave the bank. And, once I've calmed down, now deeply mistrustful, I continue to watch closely every time I come into the bank to gather further evidence of embezzlement--evidence that I can eventually share with higher authority than the bank manager.

We experience life subjectively, and evidentially, we create our own reality at a personal level. The whole bank-embezzlement business began with my viewing the teller putting money into a bag I thought she used for her lunch, but the bag she used was a customer's <u>deposits</u> bag not her lunch bag. And, based on that viewing and my interpretation of it through my values, beliefs, and experiences, I created a highly flawed, subjective reality and a pattern of actions for the long-term that reinforced my mistrust and potential disputes between me and my bank.

In dispute situations, **such subjective "evidence gathering" and reality building can become critical** because they may either reinforce and intensify the dispute or act to move people towards resolution. If people are gathering evidence to support their perception that their opponents are deliberately inhumane, brutish, devious, and dishonest, they are unlikely to seek resolution. If they are managing their perceptions so that their opponents are viewed as human, thoughtful, caring, and honest, they are far more likely to support resolution efforts and find cooperation.

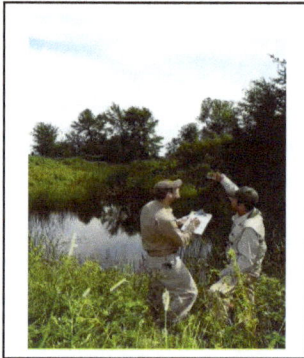

In research and development, elaborate protocols and applications of the "scientific method" have been developed to prevent or off-set such subjectivity. These methods can be beneficial for creating an informative and educational context for dispute-resolution work as well but may not play much of a causative role in helping opponents change values and adopt new behaviors.

Disputes and the Influence of Concepts about "Quality"

I believe that occasionally environmental disputes are disagreements about quality; or perhaps put more clearly, they are presented or summarized in "quality" terms.

To hear folks talk, Americans pursue quality endlessly: "the best car on the block," "highest quality clothes," "best vacation money can buy," "water quality," "air quality," "environmental quality." All these terms can be rolled up into the idea of quality of life mentioned earlier.

The case can be made that almost all environmental conflicts are related to human concepts and perceptions about quality, manifested as debates over the present protection or use of resources or desired future protection or uses of resources. In short, for there to be an environmental dispute, people have to have differing views about quality, present or desired in the future.

As I have told many audiences, I never had a mountain hemlock tree or a chipmunk, a coho salmon, a phytoplankton, or a spotted owl come into my office to complain about my management, my failure to meet production targets, or the encroachment of fire or other species upon habitats. Instead, humans showed up at my office to argue for the plants and animals and conditions of the forest, inadvertently reinforcing my belief that there are no environmental issues, only human ones. Because these issues concern natural resources, those issues always

include questions of quality, whether the advocate is speaking about environmental protections or resource production.

Modern philosopher Robert M. Persig speaks to quality in his books, *Zen and the Art of Motorcycle Maintenance,*[24] *Lila,*[25] and *Lila's Child.*[26] Persig experientially and anecdotally explores the idea that "quality" is composed of two elements: that part which is "true" and that part which is "good." The "true" part is objectively real, actual, "touchable," correct, and factual. The "good" part is what is subjectively most beautiful, best, or most desirable. He compares and contrasts perceptions and experiences of static with dynamic quality.

To the purchaser, a car must have utility (be real), with wheels and an engine, and many other elements to allow it to function safely, efficiently, dependably, and quietly. It also needs to be the right size and shape for the intended uses. These are objective measures. The owner may also want a car that is sleek, well-designed, powerful, fast, ergonomically supportive, fuel efficient, and a pleasing color — all subjective measures.

Today's incredible diversity of car choices, compared to what was available just after World War II when I was a child, make the purchaser's pursuit of a quality car more complex on the one hand and more likely of success on the other. As it is in nature and as regards decisions about the environment, diversity is a wonderful phenomenon in car buying, but having a wide range of choices does not facilitate simple and easy decisions.

Balanced with considerations of cost and finance, the real, good car is what the purchaser seeks and obtains. To the owner, the car can represent a reliable, life-enabling, static asset or a dynamic, life-changing experience.

Environmental disputes are filled with quality elements, assertions about what is "real" or "true," factual and consistent with science, and about what choices are "good" or desirable and consistent with personal esthetic or community social values. For some people, nature should be static and remain unmodified by humans. For other people, nature should be treated as dynamic with intense human modification and use.

Persig's philosophical observations on quality and my own thoughts about the Reed and Brown values list convince me that each person's concept of environmental quality is unique. I think this is easily understandable when you consider that each person has a unique physical, emotional, educational, and social experience.

Even if we have full agreement among participants about the reality of the dispute, what participants consider to be the desired "good" is purely individual. This opinion may be shared generally by a group of **like-minded people, often called an "interest" group** because of these shared values. In practice, however, the individual nature of values regarding what is "good" means that people considered to be in the same interest group often disagree with one another,

---

[24] *Zen and the Art of Motorcycle Maintenance.* Persig, Robert M. William Morrow Co., NY, NY. 1974.
[25] *Lila: An Inquiry into Morals.* 1991
[26] *Lila's Child: An Inquiry into Quality.* Glover, Dan with Persig, Robert (A chronicle of internet dialogues) 2003

too, sometimes in quite fundamental ways. Although they may wish to act collaboratively to achieve a common goal for a time, they may have strongly differing views about what is "good" that separates them apart later.

They may also have strongly differing values regarding what standard of "true" to apply to a given conflict. Some people are satisfied that the minimum scientific and procedural standards are being met, but other people may ask for higher standards or greater scientific investigation before their values can be met.

Some people want science to be directed towards subjects that will best meet their values. For example, environmental groups may wish to emphasize science that discovers rare species or ultimately sets higher standards to protect the environment. Development interests may emphasize science that can lead to new products reaching the marketplace. Both approaches address the "real" of how nature works; both also point to the "good" of what may be made of the knowledge.

Quality dialogues also expose differences in those "higher-values," which concern such things as "fairness," "process quality," "timeliness," "rights," "freedoms," and other cultural or societal values. These more esoteric values are also composed of both "true" and "good" elements. These are the values over which members of interest groups often disagree with one another.

"True" ideas that arise around these higher-values may center on the accuracy of perceptions of Constitutional, legal, regulatory, or procedural rights held by individuals or groups. "Good" ideas are likely to focus on subjective fairness, the appropriateness of impacts on people's time or resources to participate, or the proportionality of impacts from a given condition or action.

One way of viewing the sum total of people's values is that it allows individuals to participate in a dispute with an inherent "values-preference scale." Although how they choose to apply their values-preference scale may be modified in many ways (for example, by acquiring new information, being exposed to changing ranges of choice, engaging with other people's values and understanding them better), their values will largely remain intact throughout the dispute, particularly the meta-values.

For example, what a person believes is "fair" practice is very likely to be the same after the dispute resolves as it was before. That person's perception of whether a specific EDR was fairly handled may be changed by their experience of the resolution and the skill of the mediator, but they will still hold the same overall "fairness" value.

People's differences over what is "true" or "real" may sometimes are resolved by finding the best current information about the conditions or outcome in contention. If a science panel or peer-reviewed journal can be found to address people's concerns, disputes can be diminished and sometimes set aside. The more directly applicable the information is, the more substantial the effect in diminishing the dispute. Generally, the more the information is applicable by inference or interpretation only, the less effective it is in diminishing the dispute.

People's differences over values or value preference scales have little potential for a preemptive use of information in EDR efforts, however. Usually, the core of the conflict lies in the values each opponent holds, and real, accurate information is but one of the justifications they have for holding those values.

Why Then Disputes?

The authors of *Contemporary Conflict Resolution* refer to the work of John Galtung,[27] which models dispute as a triangle with contradiction, attitude, and behavior at its vertices.

"Contradiction" refers to values-preference disagreements. In a symmetric power dispute (where each party holds the same power), the contradiction refers to the opponents, their values, and the values conflict. In an asymmetric power dispute (where power is not balanced), the contradiction refers to the opponents, their values, and the values conflict that stems from their asymmetric-power relationship.

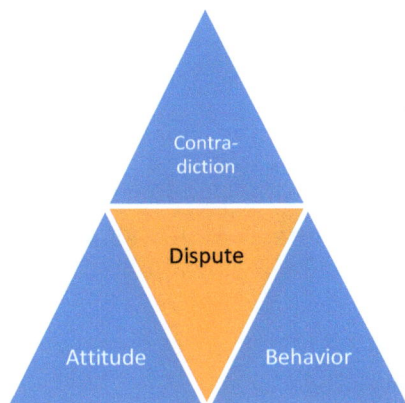

"Attitude" refers to the perceptions or misperceptions opponents have of one another, and it includes feelings, beliefs, and intention (conative) or will considerations. Attitudes get more and more negative towards opponents as disputes intensify. "Behavior" is similar to and reflective of attitude — it can be cooperative and nurturing or coercive and destructive.

Galtung believes all three components must be present for a dispute to exist; otherwise, a disagreement among parties is simply a latent dispute or values conflict. Once disputes materialize, opponents organize around the three components, complexity develops, and the source of the original dispute may be hard to understand or define. To address confrontational behavior and the propensity for violence, Galtung suggests that we ask for behavioral change and a change in attitudes. To address structural injustice or imbalance, he suggests we change structural elements to remove contradictions and injustice.

In the systems sense, disputes can occur when systems break down. In *Collaborative Approaches to Resolving Conflict,*[28] the authors note three categories of breakdown. The first is "transactional redundancy," which occurs when people repeat unchanging relationship patterns. The second is when "a sub-system becomes ineffective" — a condition that results when people no longer provide the same functional or relationship support that they once did but that they are still expected to provide. The third is when "members exceed their roles." In this case, disputes emerge when someone exceeds expectations as regards their role or their power.

Not to diminish or dilute the importance of any work, and if we compare Galtung's triangle and the *Collaborative...* authors' three elements, we get some matches to my three, broader, ecologically based categories for EDR in Chapter 4:

---

[27] *Contemporary Conflict Resolution: The prevention, management, and transformation of deadly conflicts, Second Edition.* Ramsbotham, Oliver, Woodhouse, Tom, and Miall, Hugh. Polity Press, Malden, MA. 2005. pp.9-11
[28] *Collaborative Approaches to Resolve Conflict.* Isenhart, Myra and Spangle, Michael. Sage Publications, Thousand Oaks, CA. 2000. pp.8-9.

*"...EDR definitions to match the ecological categories of "structure, composition, and function." **EDR structure** should be considered the physical, biological, spatial, legal, and regulatory elements involved in an environmental dispute, including legal aspects of resource ownership.. **EDR composition** should include the physical and biological components present, adding to them cultural (moral, ethical, and traditional) values, the human-built environment, and the means people use for communications. **EDR functions** should be considered to include human-to-human and human-to-nature **relationships** and the content of communications as symbolic of and conducive to human relationships and desired outcomes..."*

Galtung's "contradiction" element shares much with my notion of EDR composition. His "attitude" and "behavior" elements similarly compare well with my EDR functions and relationships descriptions. The authors of *Collaborative...* focus on key elements that might fit well in my EDR functions and relationships category.

"Right versus Wrong" and "Right versus Right" Disputes

Zane and Elaine Cornett of the Eugene, OR-based training company "Integrations," often speak about the distinction between what they term "right-versus-right" conflicts and "right-versus-wrong" ones. Galtung's contradictions category fits well with their ideas as do part of the *Collaborative...*author's concepts, such as "when members exceed their roles."

A **"right-versus-right" conflict** is one in which one appropriate social value (e.g., freedoms, processes, or objects) held by one person conflicts with a similar appropriate value held by another person. For example, this conflict could be over human abortion in which the accepted values of a woman's right to privacy and control over her womb conflicts with another person's values about the sanctity of and desire to protect human embryonic life.

An **example of "right-versus-wrong"** might be someone simply walking up to a stranger and punching the stranger in the nose. The puncher's action does not reflect an appropriate social value—that the puncher can hit anyone without provocation—and ignores the punched person's right to go unharmed.

Right-versus-wrong disputes tend to be resolved relatively easily; for example, judicial means will likely be used in the case of the puncher. Right-versus-right disputes, on the other hand, tend to be very difficult to resolve, particularly when they involve higher-values such as rights or freedoms (rights of the woman versus the rights of the embryo).

In environmental disputes at national scale, such as debates over human influences on global warming, we see endless right-versus-right conflicts. Some of these concern Persig's "real" element for quality. Do humans actually contribute anything meaningful to global climate change and warming or are we just a minor player, along for nature's ride? Scientists offer significant bodies of evidence for both "real" positions and advocates attempt to make their opponents look "wrong" by citing the evidence that supports their position.

Equally, Persig's "good" element also comes into play in the right-versus-right disputes. People say it "would be good" if the U.S. polluted less and was less dependent on foreign petroleum imports. Other people say it "would be good" if we just let capitalism sort things out—once the price of it gets so high people can no longer afford to travel, pollution will be reduced and the planet will recover and so on.

For EDR practitioners, the recognition that right-versus-right disputes exist and that they often form the basis for very difficult EDR interactions and efforts is an important insight. This insight also has to be offered to EDR participants and discussed at length. Dispute-resolution momentum is not likely to develop if participants cannot understand or acknowledge the validity of values held by other participants and let go of their passion to be "right." The Practices book describes some means for helping participants validate the values held by other participants.

A Simple, Hypotheticated Case of Believing Is Seeing

One day an Oregon woman's skin senses warmth and her eyes see sunshine.

She holds personal values that her skin should remain youthful-looking and cancer-free as long as possible. She believes that SPF 45 sunscreen, if not avoiding the sun altogether, will prevent skin damage. Consequently, she has adopted behaviors in the past to avoid the sun, or when being in the sun is necessary, applying sunscreen. She feels that her experience of behaving this way has been effective in keeping her skin youthful and disease-free. She applies sunscreen when she goes out to read a book in her sunny garden, but she avoids hats because they affect another of her values: her hair must always look "just so."

She also communicates her values to her husband, saying "I'm a mushroom person." She also acts to impose her values, beliefs, and behaviors on her husband by urging him to apply sunscreen, mentioning her concerns for him and what she has learned from her past experience.

He holds different values and beliefs, so he sees the situation differently than she does. His beliefs have also shaped his experience. He does not apply sunscreen while in the garden, but he persists in wearing a ball cap that covers his balding head and shields his eyes. His behaviors and experience are different because his values and beliefs are different.

Thus a low-level dispute and power-struggle develops and remains ongoing for 20 years, marked by power plays and dispute-driven communications. The husband considers himself an easy-going, flexible man; he's unconscious of his innate stubbornness. He transfers his unconscious stubbornness to his wife and mutters under his breath about her being "pig-headed." He is also unconscious of his desire to always be right; so when his wife demands, hands-on-hips and tight-jawed, that he protect himself, he projects his feelings of self-righteousness onto her and vehemently calls her a "nag."

The wife considers herself a compassionate, caring spouse; she's unconscious of her desire to control people who disagree with her. She transfers her desire to control to her husband, muttering under her breath, "That guy just has to be in charge of everything, even if it kills him." She also believes her desire to protect him should be apparent and transcendent; she is unconscious of her "righteous" anger when he does not agree. So when he calls her a nag, she says, "I don't know why he gets so angry when I'm just trying to take care of him."

They both resist one another. He gathers fringe scientific evidence from the World-Wide Web about how sunscreen doesn't work. He repeats the information frequently to refute her "less-authoritative" assertions, which he says come from sunscreen advertisements.

She gathers evidence and makes dire predictions about his future health, referencing published health studies and statistics about skin disease, particularly cancer. She counts the number of times he goes out without protection, and she occasionally applies sunscreen to him while he is sleeping in the sunshine without asking him first. He is indignant when he finds out.

Once she wrote "FOOL" backwards on his chest with sunscreen while he was sleeping in the sun so he could read the white letters, against a red, sunburned background, in the mirror the next day.

It becomes a crisis one day when the wife develops mild Stage I melanoma on her arms, and her husband says, "See that sunscreen stuff and all your fussing never did you any good." A month later, the crisis deepens when the wife's dermatologist looks casually at the husband's ears, asks to examine him, and diagnoses him with Stage IV melanoma. His wife says, "If you had only worn sunscreen like I told you to."

Blame ripples through their relationship, then escalates and becomes personalized.

The dermatologist tells the wife, "Sunscreen only lasts for about two hours. Did you replenish it often enough?" The wife thinks she may have forgotten to do so fairly frequently. After all, she had to watch her husband so she could remind him to protect himself, and she was distracted and concerned by his anger. It's really his fault because of the kind of guy he is, and he's in trouble now because he resisted her advice just to be spiteful towards her.

The doctor tells the husband, "Not wearing a hat that shields your ears caused cell damage and led to your cancer." The husband admits that he only wore a ball cap, mostly out of stubbornness and to model the evidence that he was right and his wife was wrong. The husband asserts that it's his wife's fault because, even though she nagged him about sunscreen, she never mentioned a hat to cover his ears.

As both spouses consider treatment for their melanomas, they find that they hold a shared value that transcends the values, behavior, and blame that characterized their dispute and power struggle. They find that having disease-free skin and sustaining their long-term relationship are worth far more to them than the question of whether their behaviors were appropriate. They're both treated successfully.

The polarity bleeds gradually out of their power struggle, and together, they abandon the dispute. They go home and both wear broad-brimmed hats, use sunscreen, replenish it every two hours, and sit in the shade whenever possible from then on.

Thinking about Social Behavior and Disputes

Laurie Coltri is the author of a book titled *Conflict Diagnosis and Alternative Dispute Resolution.* Although her book focuses on interpersonal disputes, she presents another interesting cognitive model for understanding disputes.[29] She presents social behavior as having seven steps: **stimulus from opponent, stimulus reception, opponent behavior interpretation, response option generation, option weighing, choice, and action**. Her model compares closely to the diagram and model I presented on page 63 in this chapter.

Her portrayal suggests a linear progression from stimulus to response-action. I agree with her steps but experience them in myself as less linear, as more iterative and free-floating. Regardless, her descriptions and definitions are valuable because they move us away from the general model I presented to one more specifically focused on dispute.

Ms. Coltri also presents ten conflict themes that appear variously in some disputes:

1. An individual will behave in ways that make sense to him or her.
2. Each individual's interpretation of reality is subjective.
3. Conflict participants use the conflict itself to make judgments about the motives of the other conflict participants.
4. The influence of mental processes on the perception of reality in interpersonal conflicts is largely unconscious and automatic.
5. Expect interpersonal conflict to be characterized by widespread subjective perception and misperception on the part of the conflict participants, which, in turn, contributes to the persistence of conflict.
6. Each individual is motivated to improve basic well-being, happiness, comfort, and pleasure, and to minimize discomfort, pain, and damage to the self.
7. Individuals' expectations about the results that their behavior will produce are subjective.
8. Individual choices in a conflict will be the result of reconciling numerous, diverse, frequently unconscious, and often contradictory motivations.
9. Individuals in a conflict frequently don't attain their intended goals.
10. **Interpersonal conflict tends to be a self-fulfilling prophesy**.

These provide valuable insights into people's social behavior as it relates to EDR. I will expand on a number of these themes in later chapters.

Defining "Communities" in Useful Ways for EDR

If Coltri gives us some useful ideas about individuals' behavior when involved in disputes, we will also be well served to consider those individuals in the context of the human communities to which they belong. Communications and public-involvement practice shows that individuals, groups, and communities can be categorized, at least to some degree, by their values, interests, context, and conditions. These categories are useful in the process of integrating communications into EDR outcomes, objectives, and techniques because they constitute basic

---

[29] *Conflict Diagnosis and Alternative Dispute Resolution.* Coltri, Laurie S. Pearson Education, Inc. Upper Saddle River, NJ. 2004. pp.77-87.

audience categories, segments of the overall audience with perhaps many common, and sometimes unique, values and histories.

We speak of "**communities of interest**" when we refer to individuals or groups that focus mainly on topics or subjects like "old growth" or "threatened or endangered species." Sometimes these communities declare themselves, and sometimes EDR practitioners have to conduct polls or focus group activities to help discover who has which interest-based values.

We refer to "**communities of place**[30]" when we think of individuals or groups that focus mainly on conditions within a certain geographic area. It is not uncommon for people considered part of a community of place to hold membership in communities of interest as well.

We speak of "**communities of tradition**" when we refer to individuals or groups that focus on traditional relationships or uses, such as Indian Tribes, Spanish land grants, and people practicing logging, mining, or ranching lifestyles dating back many generations. Many times, people in these communities are focused on arguments about whose opinions, practices, or occupancy should have primacy. Therefore, they are also often part of communities of place and interest.

We speak of "**communities of fate**" when we refer to individuals or groups likely to be adversely affected by a dispute or condition which, unless they engage with the EDR effort, they are powerless to control. These could be people living below a failing dam, ranchers with livestock and buildings in front of a grass fire, or poultry farmers concerned about the latest spread of avian influenza. Because of the perceived or actual conditions affecting communities of fate, they often display the greatest urgency and have the highest possible need for accurate communications.

For EDR purposes, we also speak to **dispute communities** when we are defining what people, businesses, and other entities are involved in a particular dispute. In addition, EDR practitioners and leaders may want to form a **dispute-resolution community** made up of those individuals and entities that have to be involved for a particular EDR effort to be successful. Dispute-resolution communities are most likely wanted for some full-blown conflicts, crises, and recoveries rather than for issues abatement.

Sometimes people refer to being "**called to community**" or "**fully immersed in community,**" which speaks to the human tendency to bond with other people who share similar values. This tendency can become troublesome if it becomes extreme because it results in "**tribalism,**" cultic self-righteous rejection of opponents or other participants.

Perceived communities of **victims** and **oppressors** can exist within any of these broader communities. Sometimes communities that perceive themselves as victims attempt to practice acting-out behaviors, referred to as the "**tyranny of the victim,**" acting out role-reversal against the perceived oppressor. EDR success may depend, at least to some degree, on finding the means to reconcile these historic compositional and relationship issues.

---

[30] *The Experience of Place: A completely new way of looking at and dealing with our radically changing cities and countryside.* Hiss, Tony. Alfred A. Knopf, Inc. NY, NY. 1990.

The stakeholders who belong to each of these categories have specific information and communications interests, which represent specific needs on the part of the EDR practitioners to understand the values of the groups and how they fit into the structure, composition, and functions or relationships of the dispute. Later we will look at how to build effective conflict management communications even for very large scale, multi-issue, full-blown conflicts. One of the most important aspects of communications in this regard will be an accurate description of the looming crisis as the "least preferred alternative" to resolving the conflict.

There are two additional communities, which are a definition of the community overall. Which community a stakeholder belongs to depends on how they choose to involve themselves in the dispute. So therefore, we can speak in terms of a **"dispute community"** and a **"dispute-resolution community." The dispute community consists of all those individuals and groups that choose to involve themselves in a dispute, directly or indirectly. A dispute-resolution community consists of the individuals and groups that choose to involve themselves or who must be engaged in EDR efforts for the efforts to be successful.** Participants in these communities come from communities of interest, place, tradition, and fate.

The "Dumbbell Curve" — Comments on "Polarity" within Communities

Social statistics frequently show what is known as a "bell curve." When polls are taken or demographic information assembled, the display often looks like a cross-section of a fried egg, thin on the edges and thick in the middle. The data tend to cluster around the middle, thus creating the thicker bulge — this clustering is called "central tendency." Out on the edges of the curve are the most disparate data, and the differences between the data clustered at the center and at the edges are considered important.

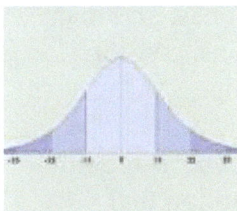

In environmental disputes, the people who are presumed to be represented by the data at the edges are often the people most strongly advocating a given resource protection or use. These folks find it very hard to move towards the center because they believe that to do so would mean the surrender of values important to them, and sometimes core values of the highest importance. Sometimes their unwillingness to move seems to be fear-based and includes a solid rationale premised upon past experiences and behaviors by opponents to support the fear.

After contending with these highly disparate advocates for many years, Forest Service Chief Emeritus Dale Robertson referred to these folks as occupying the opposite ends of a "dumbbell curve." He often spoke of the need to work with the "silent majority" of people in the center who respected government services and supported the agency. I certainly understood his frustration with highly positional and uncompromising interests.

Americans' Overall

Disputant X   Disputant Y

The results of many polls demonstrate that Chief Robertson's words were right: a majority of Americans like, respect, and trust public agencies to protect and develop public resources.

Chief Emeritus Jack Ward Thomas, with much the same frustration, referred to the polar-opposite advocates as **"the professional gladiators"** who **"enter the arena" to win or lose, "live or die" while pursuing their goals and values**. Dr. Thomas respected the energy that these individuals displayed but deplored their tactics and the effects of those tactics.

As much as I experience the same frustrations and respect the concept and its potency, I also find the notion of polarized interests, icily glaring at each other across the field of battle, along with other "warlike" thinking, of little use in EDR. I also believe that this absorption with polarity directly undermines the potential for reconciliation of the values in dispute. If we spend our time and energy taking measure of, or lamenting, the distance between the poles that opponents are presumed to represent, we'll have a hard time describing let alone finding the middle ground (or whole new ground, as the circumstances might require).

This "polarity" thinking also contributes to the potential for the dispute to be **"triangulated."** Triangulation occurs when the opponents are able to use a third party to serve as the medium for communicating, perpetuating, and perhaps escalating, their dispute. Unless they are conscious of the potential for triangulation, public agencies and institutions or non-governmental mediation groups often get placed, or place themselves, "in the middle," between opponents.

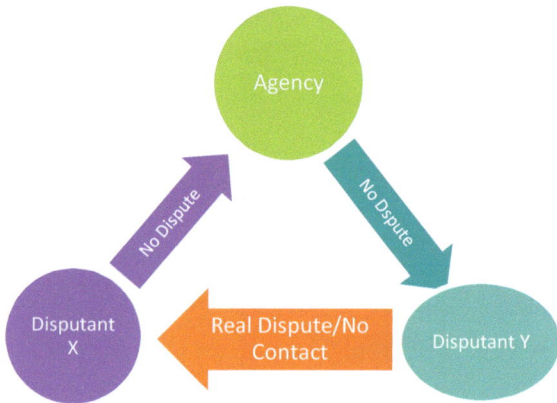

One institution, the judicial system, is specifically designed to serve triangulation. Other quasi-judicial institutions, and people with related skills, such as mediators and arbitrators, can also fulfill the role to some degree. The executive and legislative branches, and many non-governmental organizations, are not particularly effective in the role.

What I have found useful in EDR as regards avoiding triangulation is the notion that individuals and interests are more like "planets in a values universe," moving dynamically around and with one another depending on the energy they feel around one subject or another. On one subject, such as the restoration of forest functions through harvest of second-growth timber, environmental and development advocates may be nearly similar in their support of certain actions, but their meta-values and goals probably still differ. On another subject such the clearcut harvest of old-growth timber (and even on the definitions of these terms), they may disagree significantly about actions and outcomes.

I structure communications and interactions to expose these many values — values opponents agree on and those they do not. I also structure communications in ways that enable opponents to communicate with one another in a neutral and supportive environment so that the potential for triangulation is minimized. In part, this environment is created when I speak to the rights and privileges everyone in the room enjoys as citizens and participants in a free society.

It is crucial to understand the dynamics of values in EDR work because, in part, if EDR advocates and practitioners believe the positions adopted by opponents represent their actual and immutable values, they misunderstand the potential for dispute resolution.

"Life Strategies" as Considerations in EDR

Triangulation may be a part of certain "life strategies." In Body-Centered Psychotherapy--The Hakomi Method: The Integrated Use of Mindfulness, Nonviolence, and the Body,[31] Ron Kurtz explores people's various strategies for experiencing life:

- ✓ **Sensitive/withdrawn** (withdraws; seeks safety)
- ✓ **Dependent-endearing/self-reliant-independent** (trusts, then when rejected, separates; seeks acceptance and support)
- ✓ **Tough-generous/charming manipulative/expressive-clinging** (deceives; seeks authenticity and freedom from persecution)
- ✓ **Burdened-enduring** (waits "it" out; seeks independence)
- ✓ **Industrious/over-focused** (takes refuge in action; seeks appreciation and freedom to play or relax)

EDR leaders and practitioners should be knowledgeable about these strategies. They must recognize that the different participants will experience and react to the EDR effort differently. Each one's sense of success will be conditioned by their strategy. Positive results for the whole dispute-resolution community may rest on EDR leaders and practitioners understanding the differences among these strategies and skillfully adapting processes and techniques to accommodate them.

For example, many top executives and some public officials use "tough-generous" methods to get what they want. These include forceful, autocratic behavior and the imposition of their ideas and actions on others. EDR leaders and practitioners can deal effectively with this strategy by recognizing that the "tough-generous" participants are practicing deception, consciously or unconsciously. Those participants would actually prefer an authentic process and experience that protects them personal attacks and attempts at manipulation.

Looking Forward in the Discussion

Understanding individual dispute psychology and social contexts for EDR are essential to effective EDR. Equally important are understanding the nature and uses of power in our social-political system and how processes have to be developed to nurture and use rational human behavior to create successful EDR. These topics are covered in the next two chapters.

---

[31] Body-Centered Psychotherapy--The Hakomi Method: The Integrated Use of Mindfulness, Nonviolence, and the Body. Kurtz, Ron. LifeRhythm. Mendocino, CA. 1999.

Chapter 6: Exerting Power and Control

Real or effective power is the ability to determine the outcome of a course of events, including an environmental dispute

People holding power are often influenced by power brokers, power plays, and the resistance of others

Fear from past experience shapes our reactions to current triggers and we may choose to: flee, fight, hunker down, submit/appease, or deceive others to deal with the conflict

In Chapter 5, I presented a broad set of understandings about dispute psychology and sociology, including how values drive actions in peoples' lives. This chapter delves more deeply into how people attempt to exert control over environmental conditions and the decisions that affect them.

Power and Control as Essential Elements in Disputes

In environmental disputes, 'power' concerns people's ability to control the use or protection of resources, particularly scarce resources, or to control the outcomes of a series of events affecting the environment. The attainment of power can also be seen as an outcome or reward, a result of successful competition or cooperation, or even of successfully handling a crisis or a recovery in the aftermath of crisis.

When there are decisions to be made about environmental management and natural resources in America, most people have the power to participate and give advice, often called the **"power to advise" or "the power to influence." Other people, far fewer in numbers, have "the power to prevail."** This second, usually smaller group possesses **effective power** — they make decisions and exercise control over resources and outcomes. This chapter discusses power and control, and how those concepts apply to disputes.

We are all familiar with power. We exercise a considerable amount of power over our possessions and, if we are work supervisors, over our employees. We have extensive choices about how we live our lives. We guide and control our experience of life, sometimes consciously and sometimes unconsciously, according to our values.

We are also limited by many things. For example, everyone has a boss who has expectations and requirements for our performance. Some actions may not be feasible because of physical, biological, ecological, social, technological, or financial limitations. Nature places significant limits on our actions: few of us will ever travel to the moon because of physical laws such as the law of gravity and the natural effects of distance and vacuum. Many small nations with few resources lack the social will and financial resources to care for their environment, which may nearly equal the inability to defy gravity if the country in question is sufficiently poor or politically and socially chaotic.

Some people are designated by law to control resources and decisions about the use or protection of resources. If we do not have that power, we look for ways to influence the decisions and control the resources we care about. We exercise our advice-giving opportunities and attempt to influence the choices of people with controlling power.

Within our government, we have **a system of "checks and balances" that ensures power sharing among the executive, legislative, and judicial branches**. The Framers of the Constitution established these checks and balances so that Americans would not be oppressed by their government in general or by any one branch more specifically. In addition, social, cultural, and business institutions also exist that use government functions and social persuasion to impose checks and balances on government and within society. These include churches, electronic and print media, and many advocacy groups, including those for environmental protection and resource development.

The four dispute pathways I describe in this book are in part reflections of the checks and balances embodied in the Constitution. For example, scandal is the attempt by one opponent to enforce the rule of law or social convention on another, often using the judicial authorities of government or media. Anarchy is the attempt by one opponent to assert their right to propose and perhaps impose change over another, often using their freedoms under the Bill of Rights. All reflect assertions and uses of power.

Kinds of Power

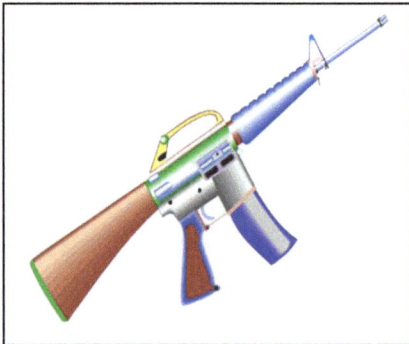

Power can be described as **"real" or "manifest,"** meaning there is unquestioned direct cause-and-effect control of resources or outcomes. Chairman Mao said, *"Power grows out of the barrel of a gun."* He was speaking to **manifest power**: pull the trigger, a bullet leaves the barrel, and someone may be injured or die. Start the chainsaw, apply it to the base of a tree, the tree falls, sections are hauled to the mill, someone buys lumber and builds a house.

Power can also be further described as **"appointed,"** meaning that a person or group can exercise control based on their election or appointment to office. This is sometimes called **"position power,"** or **"the power of the chair (referring to the person in charge)."** Appointed power is limited to what law, regulation, and legal interpretations will allow and depends on the position occupied.

In our system of government, Congress, state legislatures, or other legislative bodies develop laws or otherwise provide direction for action in the public interest, and our Constitution delegates the execution of the laws to agencies and individuals in the Executive Branch. In this way, through our elected officials and our system of government, Americans regularly give appointed power to natural resource managers and political figures concerned with environmental management.

As we do with other complex situations requiring cooperation, we accept that "someone has to be in charge" of delivering public environmental protections and services in order for society to work properly. People with appointed power are often formal leaders within the community.

Power can also be described as "**tacit power,**" meaning that other people will attribute power to a person because of charisma or because they have the notion that appointed or real power is greater than it actually is. Tacit power is also granted to some people because of personal characteristics, including community leadership, specialized knowledge, religious piety or affiliation, reputation, wealth, past performance or experience, education, and appearance. People holding tacit powers often have great persuasion skills and credibility with their followers, and many are informal leaders within their communities.

Tacit leaders can wield great influence over elected officials because of their real or perceived ability to influence voters and others whose opinion will be listened to by the voters. As former House Speaker Tip O'Neal often said, "*All politics is local.*" This statement acknowledges that people's relationships to resources and issues and our one-person-one-vote electoral system concentrate real political clout in local interests and individuals when they sufficiently motivated and mobilized.

Manifest, appointed, and tacit powers are all "**effective powers.**" When someone exerts these powers, they exercise effective control over environmental resources and events.

For example, a Bureau of Land Management Area Manager can exercise her appointed power to accomplish a timber sale. The timber contractor who buys the sale can use the real power of his chainsaw to cut the trees designated for sale. A local environmentalist can use her tacit power to gather a group together and protest the timber sale, and perhaps gain some concessions from the agency and the logger that will protect certain resources.

In the future, the BLM Area Manager can choose to use her appointed-power discretion to drop or modify a timber sale because it will not be financially viable or will be too controversial. The timber contractor can use his powers of persuasion and economic strength to influence elections so that politicians favorable to timber development are in office. The environmentalist can rally other environmental groups and work through the courts to stop or delay timber harvests in the future.

Perceptions of Power

People often perceive someone's use of power as either "**punishing**" or "**nurturing.**" Sometimes this perception is shaped by actual observation of how power is used, a cause-and-effect perception; sometimes it is shaped by the perception of whether power is being constrained adequately by accountability measures like review boards or the courts.

In EDR efforts, the higher degree to which power is seen as punishing, the less likely complete dispute resolution is to occur. Punishing uses of power can abate issues or even resolve conflict for a time in some cases, but, as you will read in later chapters, this use of power can contribute little to resolving values differences among opponents. Thus, the punishing use of power tends to create a series of win-lose outcomes and push the recycling of disputes.

The more power is seen as nurturing, the greater the likelihood of complete dispute resolution. These perceptions are related to the personal sovereignty and "peace and justice" expectations citizens hold as put forth in the Constitution. Nurturing power can also be ineffective if it is not focused on timely outcomes using clear methods and strategies. Nurturing power that is seen as lagging behind more efficient and effective dispute remedies can do little but affirm or ratify resolutions and may not be able to play a role in shaping them.

People perceived to have power, and who have cause to wield it, are often frustrated when, during an environmental dispute, that power is "checked" by another government entity or by a private citizen or group. For example, many elected officials with whom I have worked were frustrated by delays in timber harvest imposed by the courts. They point to the loss of jobs, reduced economic benefits, and degradation of infrastructure. I certainly agree that such checks are frustrating, and yet, "power held in check" is part of our government's "check and balance" systems as crafted by the Founders. I find it appropriate but unfortunate that our current system frequently grants the **power to stop, delay, or veto** without providing the reciprocal **power to enable, achieve, or act**.

Doing Nothing is Also Power of a Sort

Winston Churchill was once present at a fine dinner of British naval leaders — admirals and Lords of the Admiralty. After a time, the distinguished body began to drink toasts and tell stories about great British naval traditions and victories. At some point, Mr. Churchill rose to his feet and said, *"Don't talk to me about naval tradition. It's nothing but rum, sodomy and the lash"!* Needless to say, his mordant and contrarian views caused some upset among those dedicated to the honorable history of the British navy.

If the British Naval Lion had a "dark underbelly," so also exists a **dark and difficult aspect to American bureaucracies**. In bureaucracies and governments, people who hold the power to prevail and to act in the public interest sometimes allow its "evil twin" to hold sway, the **power to do nothing**. Many citizens are frustrated by government officials and other interests who refuse to act or seem overly committed to the status quo.

Sometimes, those who refuse to act are motivated by a desire to avoid risk. By delaying decisions or actions, they hope to have the matter defined and decided by others, reducing risk to their own personal interests, including career path. In some cases of risk aversion, a decision maker will make a flawed environmental decision to force the decision into another venue such as the courts or delay action until an exasperated party takes the matter to court.

W.B. Preston said, *"In any contest between power and patience, bet on patience."* Often true, but "patience," or "waiting your opponent out," may also be deliberate foot-dragging and passive-resistance or -aggression. Sometimes this represents cowardice. Sometimes it represents the unwillingness to let go of the familiar and still-useful status quo. Sometimes it's simply all about who is to wield control and power.

There are many reasons for this reluctance to use power, including the tendency for passive-aggressive people to work in government agencies, the perception of the potential for litigation or other risks, lack of sufficient information to proceed, risks and uncertainties about

what to do at large spatial and time scales, the normal checks and balances of our democratic government, and the inherent inertia of existing societal agreements and relationships.

As Machiavelli pointed out 400 years ago, **the status quo has many supporters because many people are benefiting; however, altered conditions may have few supporters**, whose enthusiasm for change mostly tends to be lukewarm at best, because the benefits and beneficiaries of a new order are ill-defined whereas those of the old order are clear.

Power Struggles, Power Plays, and Power Brokers.

Whether disputes are stated in quality terms, or more expansively described in terms of values or higher-values, dispute participants are engaged in what is often termed "a **power struggle**." The term sums up the disputed values — the opposing personal, social, and economic values — of the participants. This tension is expressed as oppositional desired outcomes and forms the basis for environmental strife.

All disputes exhibit power struggles. In EDR work, I sometimes find it useful to diagram the power struggles in terms of "who, what, when, and to achieve what outcomes" components. In such cases, I emulate some of Peter Senge's *Fifth Discipline*[32] systems diagrams, particularly those illustrating "enabling" or "reinforcing" forces that stand in opposition to "balancing" or "countering" forces.

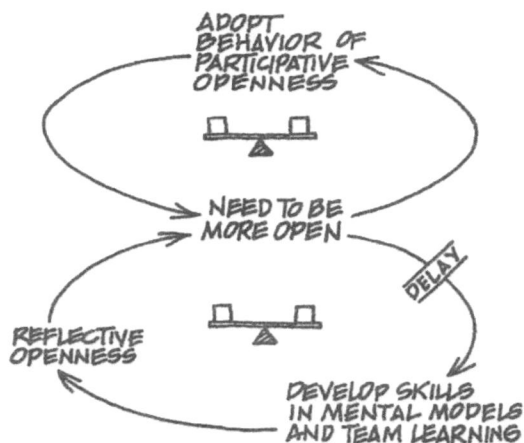

This work can help reveal otherwise unstated values, beliefs, behaviors and expectations that, once known, can allow progress on dispute resolution to occur. Trust increases as "agendas" are revealed in an objective and supportive manner.

Sometimes, if issues are not managed and escalate into full-blown conflict, power struggles can become embedded and institutionalized. At this point, fanaticism can appear. Philosopher and historian George Santayana's (1863-1952) maxim applies well to these situations: "*Fanaticism consists of redoubling your efforts when you have lost sight of your aim.*"

Unless the structural, compositional, and functional/relational elements that lead to a dispute are dealt with, a crisis can sweep away power struggles only to have them reappear during recovery.

Power struggles are also characterized by "**power plays**." As issues in dispute escalate to full-blown conflicts, opponents will develop strategies about how to deal with the dispute. As each opponent acts, the tactics employed are often power plays. For example, an environmental group might file an appeal to influence an agency choice, and if that fails, they intend to litigate or support legislation. The appeal is a power play supportive of their desired outcome, and of their strategy to litigate or pursue legislation if their desired outcome is not achieved. Another consideration may be whether a particular disputant has **escalation power** (the ability to intensify a dispute) or **de-escalation power** (to reduce or resolve it).

---

[32] *The Fifth Discipline.* Senge, Peter. p.278

Another power play is the attempt to **dominate the dispute dialog**, particularly in communicating with the public at large or highly influential groups. In this context, the power play involves getting certain messages or narratives before them target audiences and trying to oppose or censor the messages and narratives of opponents. Also, certain advocates, interested onlookers, and agency people can find themselves having their doubts, dissent, concerns, or criticisms being controlled by more powerful people in their organizations or communities.

Censorship of this kind can lead to dispute escalation, particularly in the accretion of issues leading to full-blown conflict and later crisis. For example, the act of censoring dissent within agencies can become a national-scale ethical issue, and when added to a local issue about resource protection or use, can contribute significantly to the dispute duration and intensity.

Power plays accompanied by desensitizing toward and the dehumanizing or objectifying of opponents can lead to defamatory communication practices. In the broader public context, tactics include gossip and "smear" campaigns. In meetings or more structured public settings, tactics often include open ridicule, a form of blaming called "**scapegoating**," "**diminishment**" (wherein one opponent minimizes the value or quality of another's thought or deed), "**reduction to absurdity**" (taking an idea to an extreme never intended by the opponent), or "**marginalization**" in which one opponent distorts the communication of another or does something to diminish the opponent like mispronouncing their name.

Like censorship, defamatory communication practices can lead to dispute escalation and may precipitate a crisis from a full-blown conflict. EDR practitioners should be vigilant about these verbal power plays and correct them whenever possible.

In the psychological sense, if one opponent directs defamatory comments towards another, EDR practitioners should expect the victim to experience emotional pain and then act defensively; later they may move to a "**fright: flee, fight, hunker down, submit, appease/placate, or deceive**" response. Sometimes, an opponent may employ this approach to "put the other guy on the defensive," but the tactic often backfires because invoking a fright response often means that the dispute escalates and opposing positions become even more firmly entrenched.

Before beginning an EDR effort, practitioners should inform opponents about the effects of defamatory and other power-play tactics. In fact, practitioners may find it imperative to gain agreement on group rules and expectations so that power plays will not be used — this may be a critical dispute-resolution success factor.

People with appropriated or tacit power often find themselves surrounded by a "**sycophant circle.**" Sycophants seek to share in power by loyally and personally serving the powerful person's needs and interests. They constantly filter communications and reinforce the powerful person's values; they are the quintessential "yes" people, the people who tell the "emperor" that he is "beautifully clothed" when, in fact, he is "naked."

Once sycophants attain power, they often attempt to broker their tacit power, controlling the access of people and ideas to the powerful person. Because of this phenomenon, powerful people can be placed in a position of rarely hearing the truth in an objective sense. Over time, people attempting to "**speak truth to power**" can find themselves at great risk because they may speak contrary to the **isolated, possibly narcissistic condition of the powerful person.**

82

Some powerful people understand this phenomenon and create "**barrier busting**" means to stay in touch with reality, such as "open door" and "Ombudsman" opportunities. But the number of powerful people this applies to is small at best. Thus, EDR practitioners should understand the sycophant circle. They can either use key contacts within the circle or find other means such as peer-to-peer contacts at the level of the powerful person to assure clear, timely communications and decisions.

As EDR efforts go forward, the pattern of power plays, and the communications surrounding them, can often reveal much about the overall strategy an opponent intends to pursue. When strategies become clear, EDR practitioners can then fashion means and methods to deal with the strategies while selectively responding to the tactics.

Power struggles often involve "**power brokers**." These are people who may or may not be actual parties to the dispute but who offer the apparent ability for one opponent to prevail over another. Power brokers often occupy positions with appropriated powers, such as Congressmen and Senators. Sometimes, employees of power brokers may wield almost as much power as the power brokers themselves because of the trust their employers put in them.

In other cases, power brokers are people with extensive tacit powers, such as legislative-branch lobbyists with cash and connections or local informal leaders who can introduce "the right people." In EDR work, power brokers can be a great asset for dispute resolution, and they can also be leaders of the counter-force or balancing effort. Consequently, successful EDR work may depend on understanding the power brokers and their influences. Some power brokers serve as principal advisors to environmental decision makers — public relations professionals sometimes refer to this role as serving as a "**maven**."

To be effective in advising the decision makers, EDR practitioners should attempt to communicate through the power brokers, or mavens, as well as directly to the decision maker. Similarly, EDR practitioners should contact principal staff working on or monitoring the dispute for the power brokers in order to communicate plans and actions.

EDR practitioners will want to make sure people holding the real or appropriated power concerning an issue or conflict are hearing this message: that EDR professionals are working on a solution with appropriate parties. If they do not hear that message, and sometimes even if they do, they may intervene and thereby escalate the dispute. Thus, routine communications with staff, power brokers, and decision makers is critical to successful EDR.

The Effects of Perceived or Real Bias

As it is with nurturing and punishing uses of power, **the more people wielding power are seen as biased, the more its uses will be questioned**. However, in an odd twist of influence, the effect of a perceived bias is to cause people not holding the power to cater to the power-holder in patterns that are most likely to gain them influence over outcomes.

This is much the same effect as occurs when punishing power is used. Punishing power may cause people to engage in "malicious compliance," which appears as conformity on the surface but actually represents resistance. "Work to rule" tactics are an example of this, wherein people slow work processes down by conforming exactly to contract standards — work that could take 10 minutes is drawn out to twice that perhaps if that is what work agreements state. Biased power can generate a similar skew in behavior with people conforming to accomplish their short-term intentions yet resisting that bias over the longer-term.

I have witnessed public interest parties who wanted to influence a natural resource decision I was making be affable and kindly, but then make veiled threats to sue me or harm me physically, be assertive about process or scientific findings, and argue the law and case law — whatever they thought would influence my control of outcomes. If they had discovered a bias in my approach, they would have oriented their advocacy towards the most effective influence on that bias. Because I had a bias towards fair process and swift action, but not necessarily one alternative course of action over another, these public interest parties did not have much with which to work.

Resistance to Power

Public natural resource managers commonly encounter resistance to their appointed powers. Many times, this takes the form of "**counter-dependent**" behavior, a common manifestation of resistance. People exhibiting this behavior are often aggressive, defiant, and dismissive of legal authority. They position themselves counter to the agencies and individuals serving them and "act out" their feelings in uncivil ways.

The root of the behavior is the belief that the laws and regulations developed by legislative bodies are not consistent with what the resistors want. In short, the rules lack legitimacy through public support, and agencies trying to implement the laws and regulations are seen as oppressive under these circumstances.

Counter-dependent thinking and behavior may contribute to anarchic communications and behavior. Still, counter-dependent behavior is only one part of the anarchic impulse. The matching part of the impulse is belief in a plausible replacement for the status quo, a new order, which settles issues in dispute.

During EDR work, I have always found it important to clarify and interpret the intent and impact of laws and regulations for local people, to explain the background and importance of what Congress or the state legislatures are trying to achieve. Local misperceptions often clear up and the counter-dependent behavior diminishes and sometimes disappears.

For example, people often voice concern for how their tax dollars are being spent and demand a refocus of those dollars on an expenditure that they find more desirable. They may say, "I pay your salary and you have to do what I say. I want you to sell more timber (or create more wilderness)."

To reframe the discussion, I usually did a simple, slightly off-topic presentation for them:

"On the Umpqua National Forest, we spend about $20 million per year. That's a lot of money and we respect that people are contributing that through their taxes and fees for service such as

campgrounds. There are about 140 million taxpayers supporting families in America. I know they don't all pay the same amount of taxes, but let's pretend for a moment that they do. This means that each taxpayer pays about 15 cents a piece for the management of the Umpqua. For a family of five with one breadwinner, that's about 3 cents each. If we asked the 25,000 households in Douglas County, Oregon to pay for everything it would be $800 a household, not twelve cents. I think the current arrangement is the best bargain in Douglas County given the millions of dollars of economic activity management creates and the low cost to the people living here. Now, just because you pay very little for our management of your resources doesn't mean we don't care about how you want us to manage. We do care and we invite you to participate in and advise us about every decision we make, whether that's about offering more timber for sale or wilderness proposals for Congress to consider."

Generally, after I make these comments and handle some questions, people are able to refocus on the natural resources issues they care about and move away from counter-dependent and nonproductive confrontation, to move away from what Fisher and Ury refer to as rights- or past-position-based arguments.

Addiction and Power

Sometimes we call people "**power hungry**", "**power junkies**", or "**control freaks.**" These terms refer to people with an extreme desire for power and control. In Chapter 5, I presented some background on psychological and social motivations for control and how differences in values can be the core reason for disputes.

I also believe that some people become addicted to the accumulation and use of power and to control over others. For some, I would speculate that exerting effective control works like a drug, giving them a "high"—an ecstatic experience above and beyond other sensory gratifications like sex and touch. Such people may drive environmental disputes for the simple purpose of gaining power and control, or at least the public attention or notoriety that could lead to power accumulation through an elected office or membership on a corporate board.

The most extreme examples of this phenomenon might psychopathic criminals like Jim Jones and Charles Manson who took total control-unto-death over their followers. More common and less extreme examples would be political and business leaders[33] who "know the words but not the song", a phrase used to describe psychopaths.

I speculate that if psychopathic behavior is not a birth trait, then it may be the result of addictive cycles over a "power junkie's" lifetime. For such people, the gratification for their control need leads to a high, followed inevitably by a "low" which then requires more gratification to reacquire the "high." The motivations for the "high" could be many—increased personal security, social acceptance, ambition, elimination of rivals, avarice, lust, sloth, to name a few.

---

[33] *Snakes in Suits: When Psychopaths Go to Work.* Babaik, Paul and Hare, Robert. Harper Business 2006)

Like drug addicts, **power junkies may find that other people become inevitably less valuable, except and unless they can contribute to getting the junkie high. Other people become objects to be used rather than real people with real personal values, lives, and thoughts**.

A less extreme set of related behaviors is termed "narcissism" based on the Greek myth of Narcissus in which a young man grew so enamored of his image that he fell into a pond and drowned. Narcissistic people shape their functions and relationships with other people so that their values are given higher priority than those held by others.

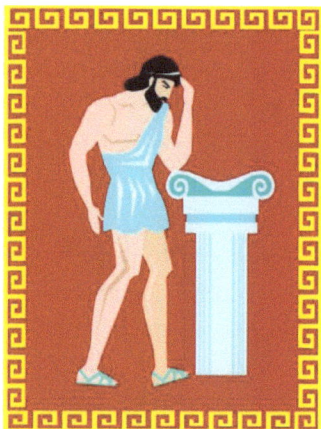

Narcissistic people act with the apparent belief that they are superior to others and should be treated so. They often operate with a "**double standard**" in which they permit themselves to act with little constraint and require others have to meet much higher standards. Unlike psychopaths, narcissists are conscious of the humanity of other people, at least at some level. They simply believe that other people should be in service to them. They create strong boundaries to capture and hold supporters while pushing away or isolating skeptics and detractors.

Understanding that power junkies and narcissists are present in a dispute community allows EDR practitioners and leaders to incorporate their values and behaviors into EDR methods and means. If power junkies and narcissists join a developing dispute-resolution community, for example, their behaviors can make EDR very difficult because of negative effects on other participants' attitudes and behavior.

In a more positive vein, power junkies and narcissists frequently avoid dispute-resolution community, preferring to remain outside as neutrals or detractors. Power junkies may see that their addiction will not be fed there and narcissists may realize that they will not get the group to be in service to them.   I have had them show up and, becoming aware that the group displayed an unsupportive culture, depart for greener pastures.

Because power junkies and narcissists can achieve power positions, later in this chapter I discuss "Gaining the Commitment of the Powerful to EDR".

The Importance of Understanding Limits on Power and EDR Possibilities

People proposing to conduct or participate in EDR should make a good faith effort to understand the power that they and the other participants wield. A previous example illustrates how explaining the mechanism for paying the bills on public lands can refocus people's attention on issues we could address. Sometimes I took stakeholders through a discussion of the 400+ laws the Forest Service had to obey while providing public service. I explained our government system with the legislative, judicial, and executive branches, and its checks and balances. I explained that my hands are not necessarily tied by the law but that all my decisions and actions had to be consistent with law (EDR Structure).

Just like understanding the characteristics of natural systems, understanding the nature and complexity of the powers represented by the participants in the dispute can be difficult. But because people's perceptions and expectations are shaped by their understanding, the study, discussion, clarification, and expression of those powers is very valuable.

I have been in many situations where the public expected to be able to vote on a natural resource matter – and implementing majority rule was a power that no one in the room held. I had no authority to permit a vote on resource-management choices, called a "referendum" or "initiative" in many places. Policy experts suggest that this strategy would be a bad approach for many reasons, including the idea that the complexity of resource-management choices does not easily lend itself to the simplifying effects of referenda and political campaigns that are, by their nature, driven by simple rhetoric and elected-time-in-office considerations.

In similar circumstances, some participants have obviously believed that they could control the outcome by shouting louder and bringing more people to testify — a form of "mob rule" that is contrary to laws governing use and protection of the environment.

Many times in public settings, people have expressed ideas that made it clear that they thought my appointed powers were far greater than they were. Sometimes, they thought I could do more and was holding out on them or that I did not understand my own appropriated power.

I would tell them the story of King Canute, an ancient British king. As the story goes, his courtiers claimed that King Canute wielded sufficient manifest power to control everything in his kingdom, a divine power of hereditary kings. King Canute took them all to the sea and ordered the waves and tides to stop rolling in; as the tide rose and waves continued to wash the shore in defiance of his orders, King Canute demonstrated the difference between real powers and appointed or tacit power. I leave it to your imagination as to whether he made his courtiers stand in the way of the waves and rising tide to drive his point home.

Like King Canute's courtiers, participants in an environmental conflict might have to "get wet" a few times before they realize how limited various participants' effective power may be. In our system of laws, unconstrained manifest or appointed power over environmental matters, at least on public lands and waters, is constrained to very limited circumstances, focused mainly on declared emergencies such as wildfires or floods. Other times, most powers brought to a dispute are highly constrained appointed powers and broader tacit powers of persuasion and influence.

Appointed power tends to endure, but tacit power is more fragile. Appointed power is supported and buttressed by law and societal norms. Tacit power can vanish if those wielding it are ineffective or grow detached from their constituencies.

Crisis can be triggered if people do not understand the limits on their powers and attempt to control resources or outcomes beyond the limits of their authority or influence. Another way of saying this is, if people over-promise what their powers can deliver, support for taking action can disappear quickly. People will leave a coalition or collaborative effort if they feel that their partners are incapable of meeting their commitments. If a crisis ensues, depending on its nature, power may be redirected to another entity or the powers of the ineffectual entity broadened so that they can be more effective in the future. For example, after Katrina, the Senate proposed to do away with FEMA and to give more money and authority to the Corps of Engineers.

Americans resist autocrats and other forms of bully. We try to minimize the punishing or coercive power of one entity over another in order to balance the protection and prosperity of all against the desire for personal freedom. We accept autocracy when unilateral efforts or uniform controls must occur (e.g., national defense or crime control). Thus, people who act in autocratic ways at inappropriate times are often acting outside their effective power and will be subject to correction in some form.

Public agency decision makers can fall into a pattern of autocratic behavior if they do not understand the limits on their appointed powers, and often those limits are quite significant. Consequently, EDR efforts that begin with a frank discussion of limits on power are likely to be more successful in the long term.

I have led many successful efforts in which, after a brief review of who has what authority, the agencies and interests set aside power-dispute discussions and simply agreed that, as a coalition of interests, they had the power to make effective natural resource and environmental decisions. This is the real basis for collaboration, at least for agencies, and can establish a cooperative pattern compelling to other participants.

I usually try to guide the **authority conversations in the direction of "shared power means effective outcomes" as early in an EDR process as possible**. In my experience, if wrangling over who has which powers continues throughout the EDR process, EDR is likely to fail in the later stages. This happens because, if the opponents remain in fundamental conflict throughout, they will be uncommitted to resolution or recovery.

A classic state-federal power dispute in the West is over "who owns the water." Water is an incredibly important part of any discussion of development in the arid West, both currently and historically. In fact, early in the opening of the West to development, people died in conflicts over the control of water.

When state and federal resource managers sit down to deal with environmental issues concerning water, unless the courts have effectively adjudicated water ownership and management, the agency people may fall into disputing who owns or manages the water for the public. In the case of the Diamond Lake Restoration effort that I led with others from 2002 to 2006, the issue came up in the first meeting of the state-federal-local agencies working group. Lake-bed and water ownership had not been adjudicated, so the positions and authorities of the different agencies were unresolved.

After articulating our agency positions on the matter of ownership, we elected to set our differing opinions aside and do what was right for the lake and the people of Oregon, secure in the knowledge that one member or another of the coalition held the power to do whatever was required. Because it was not disputed, the lake-bed-and-water-ownership issue was soon seen as irrelevant and immaterial to "fixing" the dangerous ecological conditions in Diamond Lake.

If I had elected to pursue the lake-bed-and-water-ownership dispute and acted autocratically towards the other coalition members, the coalition would have likely failed to coalesce and later disintegrated. And therefore, the public would not have been served. I understood the limits on my power, which, given the lack of adjudication that left federal authority unclear, could have gotten in the way of swift and effective action.

Gaining the Commitment of the Powerful to EDR

Einstein (1879-1955) pointed out that, *"The significant problems we face cannot be solved at the same level of thinking we were at when we created them."* In other words, problems at one scale often require thinking and action at different scales, greater or lesser.

Extending this idea to environmental disputes, two disputants acting alone often cannot resolve a dispute, however well-intentioned or well-supported they may be. Although they may be able to abate an issue that exists between the two of them, they may lack the resources to settle their own larger, values-based dispute for the long term. In many cases, they simply lack resolution power because someone else holds it at greater or lesser scale.

For example, an environmentalist and a logger may be able to sit down and resolve an issue about protecting a grove of trees. But if they agree to spare the grove, the disputants will likely have to get their resolution confirmed by a reluctant land owner. Their attempts at reaching agreement may also be frustrated by environmental or industry interest groups who advocate politically and legally over broad geographic areas. Stopped by the unhappy land owner and caught up in political wrangling over logging effects and rights, they may never resolve their fundamental disagreement over land condition.

Governments and certain NGOs and experts are often called upon to use their powers and skills to resolve disputes for others. In some cases, EDR is the explicit reason the organizations or agencies exist. In other cases, EDR is implied by their missions because, if EDR is not used, their mission will go unfulfilled or be compromised.

At times, EDR practitioners will be faced with the dilemma. They have an excellent understanding of what structural, compositional, or functional and relationship changes have to occur to completely resolve a dispute. However, **they do not have the people or entities with dispute-resolution powers in the room or committed to the EDR effort**.

So, as you will read later, EDR practitioners must develop the understanding of which powers are important early in an EDR effort and engage the powerful as early as possible — engage powerful people who may never have the time or interest to personally take part in the EDR effort at any level.

Some of the powerful may also be power junkies or narcissists and altogether unsupportive of the EDR process. Still, they must somehow be engaged. And, even with these limitations, the practitioners must make sure that the powerful develop a commitment from the powerful to a successful outcome, and that **their commitment remains sufficient throughout the process**.

The authors of *Contemporary Conflict Resolution*[34] note that powerful people wedded to the dispute, particularly people wielding appropriated or tacit power, may find they have a stake in

---

[34] *Contemporary Conflict Resolution: The prevention, management, and transformation of deadly conflicts, Second Edition.* Ramsbotham, Oliver, Woodhouse, Tom, and Miall, Hugh. Polity Press, Malden, MA. 2005. p.161.

continuing the conflict and exhibit significant intransigence when faced with the prospect of resolution. For them, **resolution that achieves peace and justice may mean a significant loss of prestige and status and an unacceptable role change**.

Thus, the authors also discuss the idea of "**peace-building from below**," working from the grass roots to secure peace and justice.[35] This is certainly a solid approach at smaller ecological scales. And, in most cases, it will be necessary but not always sufficient to gain the support of the powerful. So, beyond grass-roots accords and momentum building, EDR practitioners and leaders must find people with power from within contemporary society to play a key role in designing and implementing any EDR agreements that display substantive structural and compositional changes.

Explicit commitments from power holders need to be negotiated and confirmed and then re-enforced and re-affirmed throughout the EDR effort. Caring on-lookers, charismatic interveners favoring EDR, power-holders from other jurisdictions, and mavens may all play a significant role in this effort. EDR leaders may have to develop these agreements as the resolution goes forward, the potential for success improves, and the imminent success becomes clear to power holders and other citizens.

EDR practitioners and leaders should anticipate that disputants will be tempted to betray and exit the EDR effort and then use powerful people to achieve a "win." However, everyone involved should understand that this will result in a recycling of the dispute-at-hand in another form and at another time because the inherent values dispute has gone unaddressed. Early in the EDR process, practitioners and leaders should communicate with those powerful people who are key to successful dispute resolution about the importance of supporting the process and not allowing disputants to co-opt them.

Power and Ecological Scale

Environmental disputes always contain some elements reflecting ecological phenomena and values (see Chapter 4). Powers held by different people and institutions at different geographic scales matter when considering the basis for dispute or the potential for EDR.

Although they do not specifically address environmental disputes, authors Cumming, Cumming, and Redman, writing in *Ecology and Society*[36], point out that "*Scale mismatches occur when the scale of environmental variation and the scale of social organization in which the responsibility for management resides are aligned in such a way that one or more functions of the social-ecological system are disrupted, inefficiencies and/or important components of the system are lost.*" Such mismatches can represent key structural and compositional factors leading to a dispute.

The authors go on to say, "*An important difference between societies and ecosystems is that some individual humans, especially those in organizational roles, are able to influence ecosystem patterns and processes at scales well beyond what might be expected, and far exceeding those at which the influence of any individual organism of another species might be*

---

[35] IBID, p.217.
[36] *Scale Mismatches in Social-Ecological Systems: Causes, Consequences, and Solutions.* Cumming, G.S., Cumming, D.H.M., and Redman, C.L. 2006.

felt. Human influence can be a direct result of the number of people represented or led, or can occur via informal rules, transitory regulations, or more permanent laws. The connection between representation and power contributes to a sociological concept of scale in which different levels of an organizational hierarchy respond and act at particular spatial and temporal scales that may range from small to very large. Recognition of the importance of social scale has been an underlying motive for the development of political ecology, which focuses first on local land users and their social relations and then traces those relations to higher scales of decision-making power (Blaikie 1985, Schmink and Wood 1992, Peterson 2000)....

EDR practitioners should be aware of the **several ways geographic-scale mismatches can contribute to disputes**. These include the potential for people at one scale feeling that the powers held over "their" resources by someone at a different scale are illegitimate and to be resisted (an EDR composition factor). Another source of dispute is the assertion that people managing at local scales are not complying with requirements imposed across larger scales (an EDR structural factor). In addition, a person with large-scale power may elect to do nothing when people at more local scales have a strong sense of urgency (an EDR relationship factor).

Practitioners may want to find ways to create power symmetries to address these factors, including bringing people powerful at large scales into local EDR efforts, either in person or by proxy.

Every party to a dispute who can scale their preferences or values is rational, whether other people share their values and preferences or not

Dispute-resolution models may be rational, rationalizing, or both; models may call on relationships or social contacts and functions or upon personal or organizational transformation to resolve disputes

Mathematical models or formulae rarely work to resolve disputes although they may form an important element in informing disputing parties

---

As discussed in Chapter 5, each person has unique values regarding what constitutes "good," "bad," "beautiful," or "desirable." We tend to agree on some values, at least in general terms, such as life being a better choice than death most of the time. However, we almost never fully agree on a how a range of objects, outcomes, processes or choices should be ranked on a scale of "good," "better," "best." The more parties to a dispute there are, the greater the variety of values. Put simply, each of us scales our value preferences differently than anyone else.

The basis for all environmental disputes and related power struggles discussed in Chapter 6 rests here, in the disparate values brought to the situation and the emotions stemming from the denial of, or perceived threat to, our values. This disparity is compounded if some of the participants are not fully conscious of the values they hold, or if they are highly motivated to exert control over other people. Dispute management and resolution requires that we effectively find out what values people hold and how those values apply to the situation, how they can be a factor in settling the dispute. This chapter presents a discussion of rationality and some rational disputes-resolution models that might apply to environmental disputes.

The Relativity of "Truth"

In *Compass and Gyroscope* (1993), Kai Lee speaks to science as a means for society to set direction and forecast futures while providing stability for culture and industry. No other methodology or institution provides such a pragmatic foundation.

For dispute resolution, interpretations of fact or of truth (what is "real") are often found by finding the interpretation that most clearly explains key parts of the dispute's structure and

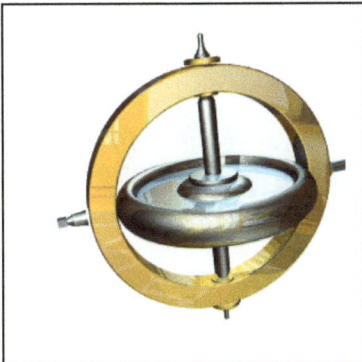

composition. For example, if the dispute is about protection of native tall-grass prairies, then EDR leaders seek out the best science available concerning the structure and composition of the tall-grass prairie before them.

Yet, even as they stabilize and undergird the context for dispute resolution, they should know that science and scientific interpretations can change. In biological sciences, theory revision is almost continuous, and dispute leaders have to stay up to date with changing scientific information and its applicability to current disputes.

When the concepts of what is "good" and what is "real" are combined, they coalesce into a person's quality definitions, and the resulting value judgments or value preference scales are completely unique and may have no likelihood of preemptive ordination or modification by science. Attempts to drive dispute resolution with scientific interpretations may be only partially effective because people's hold other important non-scientific values. Their values may also be composed of and colored by beliefs about "good" and "right" and influenced by sources more trusted than scientific sources such as gossip, conventional wisdom, or the Bible.

Rationality and Disputes

Regardless of our differences over what we value and prefer, most of us believe that other people are "rational" when they agree with us — when they share our values or behave and act as we do. Conversely, we find it easy to describe someone with different values and stated preferences as "irrational." So, we tend to believe rational people are those who share our quality concepts.

Such subjective definitions of rationality are usually sufficient because each of us has a unique view of the world, and when someone else shares that view, we can call that shared value "rational" without harm to our convivial relationship. However, when we are attempting to manage a dispute, which is always essentially a dispute over values and preferences, applying labels like "rational" and "irrational" can lead to self-righteous resistance and be counterproductive.

So, let me describe what I learned in graduate school to be "rationality" within the context of dispute management. **A "rational person" is one who has an internally consistent values system and lives by it.** That values system is not always clear. A person may not be able to fully explain their values when asked because they may not be fully conscious of them until they are asked to state a preference. Then, they have to draw upon their values to describe the preference, and they can do so even for an object they have never seen before or an experience previously unheard.

So, a rational person is someone with a logically consistent set of values who, while their values change gradually over time, can state those values in a scalar manner. This means that they can explain their values in terms of what they least prefer to what they most prefer.

An irrational person is someone who cannot scale their preferences or who holds values that so significantly different from their other values that they "gridlock" in the face of options and are effectively unable to choose. Such people are few in number, often mentally ill, and subject to manipulation. Please see Appendix B for an example and discussion of these ideas about "rational" and "irrational".

To summarize succinctly, *I submit that every party to a dispute who can scale their preferences is rational,* regardless of whether other people share their values and preference scales or not.

94

Rationalizing

If determination of preference scales and rankings lacks rigor or clarity (sometimes because values are held unconsciously), decision-making occurs by hunch or intuition. Choices get made without logical or rigorous understanding. **Individuals and groups often "huddle together and muddle through,"** allowing the course of events to shape their perceptions and decisions without a conscious rationale for their actions or any understanding of likely effects.

When asked why a certain decision was made, you will often hear a rationalize give a "just because" answer. This implies that the person has not been consciously rigorous. Or you may hear a hastily formed rationale complete with decision-making process and supportive thinking. This invention of support for intuitive decision-making is another instance of rationalization and rationalizing behavior. Although the term is less important than the reality, I refer to this as **"inductive self-justification."**

Rationalizing is common and is perfectly acceptable; it's just not very easy to share values presented this way with other people or to replicate the same thinking later or with larger groups. Rationalizing can also offend people who rely on explicitly rational methods.

Because people "wander" into choices when they exhibit this rationalizing behavior, when pressed to explain their rationale, they can get defensive and exhibit "fright: flee, fight, hunker-down, submit, appease/placate, or deceive" behavior. Because they have not clearly and consciously articulated their values or have not rigorously evaluated their choices, other people, including their opponents, who press for exact details can be frustrated by the vague answers they get.

To get good performance in EDR work, we have to understand that people will use inductive self-justification from time to time, particularly until they are exposed to the need for, and the methods of, increased rigor. And even when these go-from-the gut people understand the need for deductive rigor, they may not be able to present their thoughts that way. Practitioners have to make sure rationalizing participants are respected in the process and by other participants and their ideas incorporated as readily as those presented in a clear, linear form.

In addition to inductive self-justification, rationalizing can involve a person inventing a rigorous approach after choices are made. This **"post-justification" can also be frustrating for other parties to a dispute because they sense that they are listening to a "made up" rationale,** which, although it has the appearance of rigor, is not truly rigorous. People who use this post-justification approach may also benefit by exposure to the need for and the means to achieve increased decision-making rigor.

In beginning work with disputing parties, I have found it important to explain both inductive self-justification and post-justification. I emphasize that these approaches are normal, and that they are acceptable in most settings. But for dispute management, we will develop more explicit and better means and methods for dispute resolution.

Rational and Rationalizing Dispute-Resolution Models

EDR models tend to fall into three potentially complementary but somewhat-discontinuous categories. The first of these include "**rational models**" — often means and methods that reflect Western thought about science and management. These models are mostly "linear" (steps or actions follow an order reflecting the model's purpose), and they are often reductionist (breaking things down into small enough pieces to be understood and acted upon). They are based on cause-and-effect linked, step-wise accomplishment of tasks, such as data-gathering, analysis, objective-setting, option formulation and selection, and implementation — complete with monitoring for results and further understanding.

Sometimes, steps are repeated to incorporate changes from knowledge gained at later steps. This recycling is referred to as "iteration" and is intended to bring several steps into harmony. When applied in field settings as natural resource management, this is sometimes called "adaptive management."

Federal and many State agencies use rational National Environmental Policy Act processes, or something similar, to arrive at environmental decisions. So, in many circumstances, EDR practitioners can construct rational models that advance through linear, reductionist steps to search for resolution. These methods will appeal to people who organize the experiences of life in a linear fashion (often called "left-brain" people, after the operationally dominate brain hemisphere).

This figure comes from the Forest Service Manual (1900-1) governing National Environmental Policy Act processes. Note that EDR is not displayed in the diagram except perhaps by inference in the "public involvement" center.

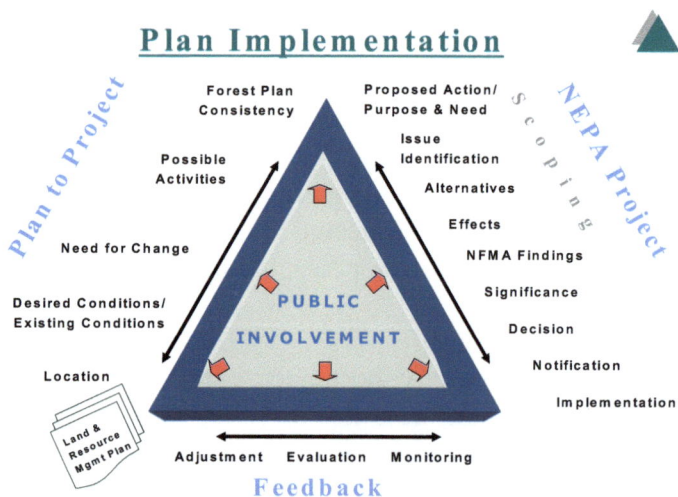

Plan Implementation

The second category is "**rationalizing models**," which include many aspects of public involvement in conjunction with rational models. So, as we search for consent, collaboration, or even consensus with citizens during a rational process, we are evoking (and inviting) rationalization on their part. We are asking them to accept actions or conditions contrary to at least some of their values, often unconscious values, actions or conditions that they might otherwise oppose. We want them to rationalize choice and acceptance by exposing them to a rational process.

We might also ask them to rationalize actions or conditions by evoking creative or "traditional" models. These can include dispute-resolution models from history or pre-history, aboriginal cultures, faith organizations, "Eastern" or "non-Christian" beliefs, early-Christian, or traditional societies. For example, although they may not act on the idea, people still express the belief that two opponents representing larger interests or groups can settle disputes through personal combat — that gladiators or duelists might be the most direct and immediate way to settle a values conflict. These models and ideas may appeal to people who organize their experiences of life in a non-linear, sometimes creative fashion ("right-brained" people).

We also see the third model as well which attempts to rationalize actions **using symbols or archetypes**[37]. This would be the **"evocative model."** In using threat and war symbols to characterize disputes, politicians and pundits try to evoke traditional "warrior archetype" responses. They wish to stimulate emotional rather than rational response and gain control of outcomes without rationale, even outcomes that lead to actual war. For example, when Saddam Hussein was characterized as a madman with weapons of mass destruction intent upon attacking America in concert with Osama Bin Laden, those communicating the information were attempting to evoke a "Let's go to war," or warrior, response.

In another example, when the Korean conflict was initially characterized as a United Nations "police action," the potential for expanded war was greatly understated and Americans and their allies had "law and order" expectations. Consequently, because American troops were sent to "police" things, they were mobilized with less-than-desirable and -capable equipment and support. When the dispute escalated to include the Chinese Communists and war, Americans back home were unprepared. Rationalizing archetypes had to be shifted; the Korean conflict became the "Korean War."

Environmental interests often attempt to evoke traditional archetypes around "motherhood" or nurturance, reverence for "God in nature," or Druidic faith and ritual. Under some circumstances, EDR methods here might include ceremonies, rituals, or appeals to the wisdom of Druidic or American Indian elders.

Development interests often attempt to evoke other traditional archetypes around "support for the working man," "titans of industry," "free enterprise," "jobs," and "taming" nature to reach "new frontiers." EDR methods here might include discussing or gaming what it might mean to "leave it up to the marketplace" or having a fistfight or gunfight.

Inevitably, rational and rationalizing thinking patterns, and evocative symbols and archetypes all come into play as we work on EDR. As disputes escalate, these models and their effects often get clearer, even though they have been present in subtle ways all along. Consequently, as they work, EDR practitioners are well served to develop and update their understanding of the models and how they apply.

Rational Dispute Resolution Models—NEPA and Adaptive-Management

I have already displayed and discussed one of the most common rational models being used today for environmental management — the National Environmental Policy Act processes used by federal agencies and entities using federal funds. Many states and local governments have similar processes.

---

[37] Joseph Campbell and the Power of Myth. Campbell, Joseph and Moyers, Bill. Mystic Fire Video (1988)

These processes are "terminal" in nature, meaning that achieving the goals of the process ends the process. For example, an agency uses the NEPA process to make a decision to build a bridge. Once the construction is done and measures to protect nature from construction effects are in place, the NEPA process is terminated.

I also mentioned "adaptive management" as a science-management model increasingly common in environmental-management efforts. This is a terminal process focused on gaining and applying knowledge in conjunction with construction or active environmental management. The process is cyclical and repetitive. In order to accommodate uncertainty at any given time, it allows for continuous scientific monitoring, analysis, evaluation, and adaptive change in actions taken over the long-term.

For example, in the face of considerable unknowns, land managers might adopt an adaptive-management approach to use statistical field sampling and science monitoring of annual plant presence and vigor to evaluate the effects of prescribed fire across a landscape, over many years. The knowledge gained would then permit resource managers to change the frequency and intensity of future fires and the planting of native species to suppress invasive plant species and re-create viable, productive prairie-plant communities.

Both models can work separately or together, depending on community needs. Yet, neither the NEPPA Process nor adaptive management inherently incorporates EDR. In fact, most agencies' NEPA drives conflicts of all kinds. And, unless EDR is consciously built into adaptive-management processes and practices, it can drive disputes as vigorously as NEPA. So, at times both processes may require the incorporation of EDR to be successful.

Other Rational, Behavioral Models

Other rational models exist. In his book, *The Conflict Resolution Toolbox: Models and Maps for Analyzing, Diagnosing, and Resolving Conflict* (2005)[38], Gary T. Furlong gives us rational models that seek to change values, behaviors, and ultimately human relationships in pursuit of conflict resolution. They may have some applicability to EDR, although, so far, their applicability seems to mainly be on the home or workplace.

Furlong describes eight models he discovered while he was pursuing his doctorate:

> #1 – The Circle of Conflict Model
> #2 – The Triangle of Satisfaction Model
> #3 – The Boundary Model
> #4 – The Interests/Rights/Power Model
> #5 – The Dynamics of Trust Model
> #6 – The Dimensions Model
> #7 – The Social Style Model
> #8 – The Moving Beyond Conflict Model

---

[38] *The Conflict Resolution Toolbox: Models and Maps for Analyzing, Diagnosing, and Resolving Conflict.* Furlong, Gary T., John Wiley & Sons Canada Ltd., Mississaugua, Ontario. 2005

Discussion of each model includes diagnosis, strategy or prescription, application specifics, and worksheets to help the reader. Each is also supported by hypothetical case information.

To help my readers understand some of the "building blocks" of dispute analysis and resolution models, and to allow some contrast with my EDR typology, diagnoses, and processes, I will share Furlong's summary of each model. I have the expectation that readers will consult Furlong's book if they want more specifics:

The **Circle of Conflict** is a model that diagnoses and categorizes the underlying causes or "drivers" of the given conflict. It categorizes these causes and drivers into one of five categories: Values, Relationships, Moods/Externals, Data, and Structure. Further, the model offers concrete suggestions for working with each of these drivers, and directs the practitioner towards Data, Structure, and a sixth category, Interests, as the focus for resolution.

The **Triangle of Satisfaction** is an extension of the Circle of Conflict, though it easily operates as an independent framework for the practitioner. This model deepens the area of Interests, suggesting that there are three types of interests: result or substantive interests, process or procedural interests, and psychological or emotional interests. The model offers specific strategies for working with the three different interests in conflict situations.

The **Boundary Model**, similar to the Circle, assesses the root cause of conflict from a structural and behavioral point of view, but suggests that conflict occurs because of how people relate and interact with boundaries. Our lives are filled with boundaries of many kinds, and may include: laws, contracts, cultural expectations, norms, and limits of any sort. It suggests that conflict occurs when parties disagree on boundaries, expand or break boundaries, or refuse to accept the authority and jurisdiction inherent in a boundary. It also offers specific approaches to work with conflict caused by boundary issues.

The **Interests/Rights/Power Model** does not assess the root causes of conflict, but rather focuses on the different processes people use to deal with conflict, categorizing all approaches to conflict as being one of three types: Interest-based, Rights-based, or Power-based. The I/R/P model diagnoses the characteristics of each of the three types. Finally, the model offers broad direction on working with each of the three different processes, along with a guide for choosing effective types of processes for resolving conflict.

The **Dynamics of Trust Model**…looks at the dynamics of trust and how we attribute blame. Attribution Theory, one of the most important areas of psychological research, is boiled down to help practitioners understand how trust is broken, and how blame and lack of trust can make resolution difficult if not impossible. The model also gives practitioners specific strategies for rebuilding enough trust to facilitate the resolution process, through activities such as Confidence Building Measures (CBM), procedural trust, and attributional retraining.

The **Dimensions Model** takes the broadest look at diagnosing conflict by proposing that conflict takes place along three different "dimensions." These three dimensions are the Cognitive dimension (how we perceive and think about the conflict), the Emotional dimension (how we feel about the conflict), and the Behavioral dimension (how we act or what we do about the conflict). The model identifies how separating a conflict into these dimensions can help the practitioner intervene, and offers specific strategies for working with each of the dimensions.

The **Social Style Model**…is significantly different than all the rest of the models because it focuses on understanding personality conflict, and conflict related to communication styles. Based on research similar to the Myer-Briggs Personality Type Indicator but offering a much simpler framework for assessing personal styles, the Social Style model suggest four basic personality and communication styles, or types, [analytical, driving, amiable, expressive] and offers clear skills and strategies for working with these personality characteristics in conflict situations.

Moving Beyond Conflict… One of the main barriers to resolution comes when people can't let the conflict go and move on with their lives. A dispute can become such an important part of an individual's life that he or she will not allow it to end. It feels as if something important is being lost. This is very similar to the process of grieving, and the Moving Beyond model helps identify the stages or steps parties must often go through in order to let go and move beyond it.

These models have many components in common with the EDR model discussed in the companion "Practices" book. They also represent opportunities to explore the basic building-blocks of rational and rationalizing dispute-resolution models and methods.

What the eight models lack is the understanding of environmental dispute stages and pathways. They also miss the importance of geographic scales, and at least some elements of EDR structure, composition, and functions/relationships. The more complex EDR typology and categories I present reflect more of the complexity, scale, and duration of environmental disputes, which sometimes reflect multi-issue, multi-resource, international and inter-generational participant factors.

Conflict Transformation and Reconciliation as Procedural Intent for EDR

EDR practitioners and participants may want to view dispute resolution as a social-psychological transformative process. The authors of *Contemporary Conflict Resolution*[39] describe five "generic transformers of protracted conflict":

1. **Context transformation** – changing the social, political, economic, or ecological context for the dispute.
2. **Structural transformation** – examining the actors and their incompatible values. If symmetrical power relationships exist, this transformation may mean changes in the

---

[39] *Contemporary Conflict Resolution: The prevention, management, and transformation of deadly conflicts, Second Edition.* Ramsbotham, Oliver, Woodhouse, Tom, and Miall, Hugh. Polity Press, Malden, MA. 2005. pp.163-165.

method of sharing power. In asymmetrical situations, it may mean ways to give more power to a weaker opponent.

3. **Actor transformation** – changing players, values, behaviors, affiliation/ membership/constituencies, and the adoption of new values, beliefs, priorities, and actions.

4. **Issue transformation** – changing interests, positions, and issues, including reframing and re-imaging.

5. **Personal and group transformation** – people reshaping their values and lives based on experience and education.

According to the authors, such transformations require "real changes in parties' interests, goals, or self-definition," and many times this can only be considered during a "hurting stalemate," an "imminent mutual catastrophe," a reconsideration of behavior in light of experience, or an "enticing opportunity."[40]

This transformative model assumes that experience and participant commitment will change values to then modify attitudes, beliefs, behaviors, and actions. So, practitioners might fashion an EDR process as follows:

- Gain commitment to EDR process and outcomes
- Create positive imaging for self, opponents, and mutual functions and relationships
- Release anger and blame safely
- Drop fears and frustrations
- State and pursue wants, desires, and interests
- Create collaboration
- Refuse to recycle disputes and act to build community

EDR participants may also want to view dispute resolution in terms of creating the potential for reconciliation among people within dispute-resolution communities. The authors describe "four dimensions of reconciliation":[41]

Aspects of reconciliation	Stages of conflict de-escalation
1. Accepting the status quo	Ending dehumanizing speech
2. Correlating stories and histories	Overcoming polarization
3. Bridging opposites	Managing contradicting values
4. Reconstituting relations	Celebrating difference

These match up well with contemporary thinking about acceptance, requiring people to pass through stages of denial, bargaining, rage, depression, and acceptance to get to element 1. They also match well with ideas about transitions being from one condition (1) through a "neutral zone" (2 and 3) to the new status quo (4).

---

[40] IBID, pp.166-167.
[41] IBID. p.232, adapted from Table 10.1.

Values and the Lack of Mathematical Ways to Represent Them in Dispute Work

Mathematical models for resolving environmental disputes do not exist. Attempts to build them will invariably exacerbate the underlying environmental conflicts. Here's why.

Over the past 25 years, many mathematical means have been proposed for expressing and ranking environmental values. For example, one model is "comparative valuation." Comparative valuation usually follows the pattern of a numeric scale and is often based on individuals stating cash-value-representing resource-value or willingness-to-pay-for-resource-use. Participants are then asked to rank order their use or value preferences for natural resources and assign a comparative monetary value. So, one day's fishing might be ranked at $45 per day and the sight of a grizzly bear at $30 per sighting. A numeric preference scale can then be built, with cardinal numbers rather than ordinal as we use in forced ranking.

This approach is fine for ranking individual value preferences, although the limitation to monetary or numeric values can hide actual values because money is simply a surrogate, or symbol for, many values in play. So, money scales are shorthand for a person's broader values and inadequately reflect the person's rich fabric of interests and desires. As Albert Einstein (1879-1955) said, *"Not everything that can be counted counts, and not everything that counts can be counted."*

For groups of three or more people, there exists no mathematical way to scale and to aggregate human values and then use the aggregations to make choices for the group without doing harm to the values of the participants. In *Social Choice and Individual Values,* Nobel Laureate Kenneth Arrow detailed the reason why mathematical approaches will not work for choices made by groups. Our unique preference scales make this impossible, and Arrow's "General Possibility Theorem" spells out this reality.

So, in situations where an aggregation of preference scales might seem the best way to end an environmental dispute, it is actually the worst way. People will have heightened concern about, and sensitivity towards, any practice or process that offends their values in such a situation.

IT'S A MAD MAD MAD MAD WORLD" of Dispute Resolution

the biggest entertainment ever to rock the screen with laughter!

STANLEY KRAMER

"IT'S A MAD, MAD, MAD, MAD WORLD"

From Wikipedia

The film *It's a Mad Mad Mad Mad World* is based upon several dispute-resolution failures. The film begins with the automobile injury of a man who had stolen and hidden $350,000 many years before. The thief's last words reveal the location of the money to 5 men. The 5 men return to their 4 vehicles and 3 companions. All 8 people gather and attempt to negotiate a "fair" way to split up the loot. Everyone wants the money and mistrusts the others. When they can't agree, the cutthroat, hilarious, madcap chase to the money is on.

The participants and vehicles have the following pertinent characteristics:

Vehicles	Death Witnesses	Other Participants
#1 - Volkswagen	2 men	none
#2 - Moving Van	1 man	none
#3 - Chrysler-Imperial	1 man	2 women
#4 - Plymouth Station Wagon	1 man	1 woman
TOTALS 4 vehicles	5 men	3 women

The eight people discuss four schemes for dividing the money:

1.   One share for each <u>vehicle</u> (4 even shares);

2.   One share for each witness to the death of the thief (5 even shares);

3.   One share for each <u>person</u> discussing the conflict (8 even shares);

4.   One share added up by vehicle, death witness, and total people — each person's reward contingent upon each person's qualifying in one or more categories above (4 + 5 + 8 = 17 even shares).

During the discussions, one driver frantically and accurately calculates what each vehicle, witness, and person would receive using each scheme.

His calculations and everyone's objections are as follows:

1. An even share for each four vehicles:

Volkswagen	$87,500
Van	$87,500
Imperial	$87,500
Station Wagon	$87,500

The three women and the two men in the Volkswagen veto the scheme because the shares per person are not in their favor.

2. An even share for each of five death witnesses yields:

Volkswagen	$140,000
Van	$70,000
Imperial	$ 70,000
Station Wagon	$ 70,000

Everyone except the Volkswagen men veto the scheme because the Volkswageneers get too much.

3. An even share for each of 8 total people:

Volkswagen	$87,500
Van	$43,750
Imperial	$131,250
Station Wagon	$87,500

The van driver vetoes the decision because he gets too small a share; and

4. Seventeen shares distributed by 1, 2, and 3:

Volkswagen	$102.940
Van	$61,765
Imperial	$102,940
Station Wagon	$82,355

The van driver and the man and woman in the station wagon veto the scheme because they are receiving the least.

As each participant evaluates his share and casts a veto, the following preference scales emerge:

Volkswagen	2 4 1 or 3
Van	1 2 4 3
Imperial	3 4 1 2
Station Wagon	1 or 3 4 2

Every participant has a different option-preference scale and sees no benefit in compromise. Coalition building is impossible because all participants hold veto power over cooperative actions, and no one coalition can result in greater winning power than any other. The race is on!

The movie also offers some insights into the fragility of effective power. Unbeknownst to the eight people, a ninth participant in the hunt, a police captain, who observes their tumultuous progress and expects to scoop up the money after the 8 find it.

Near the end of the movie, the policeman exercises his appropriated and tacit powers over the other participants to take possession of all the money. However, the policeman then shows that he intends to keep the booty for himself when he directs his car away from the police station. Seeing this, the other participants realize the policeman's appropriated power has disappeared with this violation of the public trust. The participants rescind the grants of tacit power they normally accord to any policemen. And the chase is on again.

The fitting conclusion of the movie is a crisis. The $350,000 is literally tossed to the winds, distributed randomly to thousands of spectators. The participants, including the policeman, are all jailed, losing everything — a fitting crisis and conclusion.

Question: can you think of any division scheme or coalition structure that would have eliminated the chase? Remember: anything goes in the "mad mad mad mad world" of dispute resolution.

EDR Using "Asymmetrical" Math

Even though a precise mathematical process cannot be used for group decision-making and EDR, there are other cases where a mathematical process can be used to rationalize agreement and acceptance. This process can work even as it violates, perhaps because it violates, mathematic precision.

A FULL-BLOWN CONFLICT FABLE: "THE OLD MAN'S HORSES"

Back in biblical times, a certain wealthy old man had three sons. The oldest son was due to inherit all of the old man's possessions, including livestock amounting to 360 sheep, 270 goats, 90 camels, and 17 horses. With the oldest son's permission, the old man decided to provide an inheritance for the second and third sons so that they could be happy and, with hard work, perhaps could prosper.

The old man's testament read:

1. The first son was to receive virtually all the old man's property except some tents, household goods, and one-half (1/2) of the livestock;

2. The second son was to receive a tent, household equipment, and one-third (1/3) of the livestock;

3. The third son was to receive a tent, household equipment, and one-ninth (1/9) of the livestock;

4. All remaining animals were to be given to the Temple in Jerusalem; and

5. All sons had to be satisfied with their shares and the remaining livestock conveyed to a representative of the Temple in Jerusalem before any one son could begin to enjoy his inheritance. This provision would mean they would remain close and the extended family wouldn't fight.

A few months after making these provisions, the old man died.

True to the agreement, the sons took possession of all the property except the livestock. Then, the sons met and began dividing the animals. All went well as they separated the following animals:

	Share	Sheep	Goats	Camels
First Son	1/2	180	135	45
Second Son	1/3	120	90	30
Third Son	1/9	40	30	5
Temple	Remainder	20	15	10

This split of sheep, goats, and camels went well—the math worked. Unfortunately, when the sons came to divide up the horses, they began to have problems. No matter how hard they tried to divide the 17 horses according to their fractional rights, the math did not work.

After several days of wrangling, each son began to see his inheritance slipping away. Grazing and water were limited where they camped and animals were suffering. The sons needed to split up their father's estate and move on. Animals began to stray and get sick. The sons began to accuse each other of greed and stupidity for not compromising, but none would concede horses to the others.

Over the next few days, the conflict intensified until the families began to live in fear of hostility intended to "redefine" the shares. Theft and even murder seemed real possibilities and everyone tightened security and stopped communicating. Each waited for the others to act.

When the second son's wife could no longer stand the tension, she sent a servant to the Temple in Jerusalem asking for help. She told him to find a wise man and explain to him the history, numbers of animals, and the bleak impasse which existed. The servant quickly reached a rabbi known for his wisdom. After some careful thought, the rabbi saddled his horse and rode to the three sons' camp.

When he arrived, the rabbi called the sons out to the horse corral. Their desperation and anger barely controlled, the sons watched as the rabbi dismounted and turned his horse in among the seventeen. Then, the rabbi quickly divided the horses according to the following scheme:

	Share	Horses
First Son	1/2	9
Second Son	1/3	6
Third Son	1/9	2
Temple	The rabbi's own horse	1
		18

Shamefaced, the sons led their horses back to their tents. The rabbi mounted his horse and rode off to a nearby town to hire herdsmen for the Temple's new sheep, goats, and camels.

Moral: ***Many conflicts end when someone takes a different view of the facts, and is willing to fudge the math to end a conflict.***

If the rabbi had been available to help out the Mad, Mad, Mad World characters, he could have called all nine of them to a meeting , had their vehicles towed away while they were inside, and when they emerged from the meeting, handed them $38,888 each and told them to walk home.

Moral: ***Change a significant composition element in a full-blown conflict and you may resolve the dispute short of a crisis.***

Chapter 8: Disputes and Consequences — War, Games, and Real World Examples

---

Dispute resolution often is thought of in war-like, or near-pure-conflict, terms

Effective environmental dispute resolution often means moving disputants away from thinking and acting in near-pure-conflict ways and towards near-pure-cooperation behaviors and actions

---

If all disputants are rational and rational models exist for dealing with the dispute, then why do such disputes often get beyond the issues stage to become full-blown conflicts and even crises? One reason may be our cultural tendency to couch these disputes in war-like terms. Another may be our tendency to make all such disputes "win-lose" outcomes rather than "positive" outcomes.

One way we can show dispute participants who are prone to win-lose approaches how "positive outcome" approaches might work is for EDR practitioners to engage them in cooperative games.

Expressions of War

War can be described as a series of intense, full-blown, armed conflicts (i.e., battles) resulting in the supremacy of one disputant over the resources, events, territory, and ideas held by another disputant. So, in terms used in this book, war is an extreme example of full-blown conflict intended to precipitate a crisis.

Because war is so destructive and common, much conflict-management literature and methodology is dominated by warfare studies, rules, strategies, tactics, and techniques. And as a result, power and dispute discussions often express conflict in war-like symbols and language.

From Wikipedia, British Challenger Tank

It should be intuitively clear but is worth stating that the means used for managing warfare can be quite different from those used for settling an administrative appeal over a small timber sale or a minor boundary conflict between two neighbors. And, only some of these war-management approaches are useful at lower dispute-intensity levels in civil society.

Rarely do we encounter pure war-like conflict, or pure utopian cooperation for that matter, in environmental dispute work. But we also have good reason to try to move many disputes from greater intensity to less, from higher levels of strife to lower, from high conflict to low. This means we should be trying to build dispute-intensity-lowering structures, components, and functions/relationships into our EDR work. Many times, that will mean **discarding war language and symbols in favor of those conveying environmental peace and justice**.

Even Wars Have Rules and Agreements

Sometimes people think that war is a death-dealing free for all with no rules. Sometimes war is simply about killing the enemy by any means available, say at the height of a battle; most times it is not.

The international agreement known as the "Geneva Conventions" is a formal code maintained today by the United Nations (http://www.unhchr.ch/html/menu3/b/92.htm). They describe some of the ways in which wars are to be conducted and people and combatants are to be treated during war. The first Convention was approved in 1864 and many others have been formulated since.

Together, the Conventions are considered the international war law. They are the basis for war crimes trials for individuals who fail to keep to the code. So, because of the Conventions and other international law such as arms treaties limiting the use of certain weapons, wars have their own set of formal codes. They are death-dealing but not a free-for-all. They also have tacit agreements that develop through diplomacy and battlefield conduct, such as an informal armistice on the war front during Christmas, that reflect ideas of peace and justice.

War conduct codes have teeth. Violations can bring about consequences for the violators in the form of war-criminal prosecutions. In addition, violations of tacit agreements can bring problems because once they break down, trust is lost; disputes tend intensify quickly and continue intensifying, perhaps leading to a turn in battle or strategic position.

Are War Examples Useful to EDR?

The simple answer is "Yes, but…."

Initial EDR rule sets and conduct agreements can be treated like war codes and treaties. Parties can agree and then revisit elements at some later date. But, to avoid triggering war archetypes and behaviors, EDR practitioners and leaders should not use the language of "war codes" or "treaties" to describe the agreements, using terms like "enforceable agreements" instead.

Thinking of the Geneva Conventions, some concepts about how truces are to be managed might be transferable to environmental disputes, but the humane treatment of prisoners-of-war would not likely be applicable to a native-species and grassland-restoration controversy. In addition, broadly used war concepts like "search and destroy" might apply well to identifying EDR issues and the intention to abate them, but better words might be found to describe the process and methods.

In addition, like "search and destroy" in warfare, broadly applicable techniques, such as environmental mediation can extend across a wide range of disputes and levels of intensity, even if they cannot work as well with all kinds of disputes or at all intensity levels. And, just as troopers engaged in search and destroy maneuvers depend on artillery or radio communications, broadly useful EDR techniques have limits and must often be supplemented with other techniques.

So, you might engage in **a mediated settlement followed by a signed settlement agreement**. But if a series of facilitated meetings are not put in place for months or years after the agreement is signed, it may become dysfunctional and implementation may fail.

In way similar to consequences for war-code violators, there are consequences for code- and tacit-agreement violations along the four EDR pathways: distress, scandal, anarchy, and catastrophe. The consequences can be in the form of more stress imposed on already stressed disputants—stress that can trigger crises cascades and a breakdown in EDR progress. Because code and tacit-agreement violations add unpredictably to the intensity of disputes, a crisis may be triggered much more quickly than anticipated.

There may also be "rapid accumulation" similar to the effects of insurgents or commandos attacking normal combatants in clandestine and unpredictable ways. For example, after years of war in Vietnam, crises that might be plotted along all four EDR pathways became almost daily occurrences.

As Vietnamese died and families hid and grieved, personal and community **distress** peaked again and again. **Scandals** over atrocities and misused money and resources kept cycling. **Anarchies** in the form of desertions and insurrections grew. Exploding munitions and Agent Orange denuded landscapes, created soil erosion, and injected pollutants into the environment, adding up to ecological destruction at the scale of a **natural catastrophe**. **Crises cascaded** and overwhelmed civil and military order.

In the last years and months of the war, the North Vietnamese pushed hard to create a rapid collapse of the South Vietnamese government and allied war effort. International communications and propaganda were part of their push. Their efforts worked.

As bad as it was "in-country," the effects were reported daily back in the U.S. And the "rapid accumulation" and crisis cascades in the war zone were paralleled by political and social unrest in the U.S and among its allies. So, breakdowns in civil order eventually became profound in the U.S. and among its allies, paralleling those in Vietnam. In EDR, sometimes peripheral participants and onlookers such as the media increase participants stress or even trigger a crisis by reporting pejorative information or engaging in an unforeseen power play. Their actions may be intentional or unknowing, but the effect is the same. EDR practitioners and leaders should anticipate these effects and be ready to respond.

Core Concepts in Games

I introduced win-lose or "zero-sum" thinking briefly in Chapter 2. Because of the influence of war in traditional dispute definitions, and because much of government is based on zero-sum concepts, game theorists have spent most of their energy on defining zero-sum strategies and tactics. These include "**mini-max**" and "**maxi-min**" strategies in which opponents try to maximize their gains or advantages while minimizing their losses. These strategies are often seen in contract or other negotiations, too.

Another strategy, "**tit-for-tat**" (http://www.abc.net.au/science/slab/tittat/story.htm), is the most successful theoretical zero-sum game. A tit-for-tat approach means that, each time your opponent makes a move, beneficial or adversarial, you respond with a move that yields the same, or a similar, effect. Zero-sum modeling shows that tit-for-tat combined with other tactics, such as finding the best location for combat or using weapons most efficiently, is most likely to lead to success.

This strategy has a corollary strategy called "GRIT," or "**Graduated Reciprocation in Tension Reduction**" (http://www.beyondintractability.org/essay/disarming_behavior/). GRIT happens when one opponent tells the other that they intend to reduce dispute intensity in stages through specific actions at specific times, and if the opponent makes any adversarial counter-move at each stage, they may get a tit-for-tat (or "**tit-for-double-tat**") response. "Tit-for-double-tat" means that the responses will be at an intensity twice as great as the opponent's adversarial action. The GRIT initiator reserves the right to decide whether to reciprocate or not with a plan for clear communications essential to GRIT success.

Then, the initiator carries out each GRIT detail. By delivering the tat (or double-tat) after an adversarial move, the GRIT initiator intends to impress the opponent with the importance of accepting the GRIT outcome. The action-response-reaction cycles of the GRIT process not only inform the opponent but are part of an attempt to impose tacit rules and gain tacit buy-in to continue and complete dispute de-escalation. This method may be used when communications are minimal or non-existent under conditions of insurrection, anarchy, or widespread criminal behavior, such as prolonged riots.

All these strategies assume zero-sum conditions and some power parity between the opponents in their ability to inflict harm on the other while winning or controlling the outcome to favor their values. In EDR work, this parity may not, and often does not, exist. In power-theory terms, zero-sum games assume nearly "**symmetrical**" power relationships when, in fact, relationships we commonly encounter in EDR work are

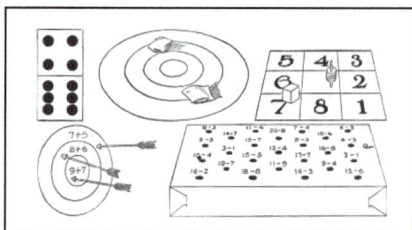

actually "**asymmetrical**" — and sometimes significantly so. In asymmetrical power situations, one opponent holds considerably more power than another, at least initially.

In addition to simple power-symmetry considerations, opponents may be using different methods, one favoring political influence and the other litigation. So, environmental-dispute-winning strategies focused on zero-sum methods and outcomes do not often work, even though they seem expedient at the time they are implemented. When these strategies fail, they often lead to escalation.

In addition, EDR practitioners may find that deceptions like **bombast, blustering, bluffing, and confusion** around power differences and asymmetries obscure the true nature of the dispute and the actual powers each opponent holds. So, the deception can make meaningful resolution discussions difficult or even initially impossible. Taking time to create clarity and communicate realities may be essential to successful EDR.

Consequences of Win-Lose Gaming

In *Contemporary Conflict Resolution,*[42] the authors speak to the consequences of win-lose and win-win strategies and games:

> *Traditionally, the task of conflict resolution has been seen as helping parties who perceive their situation as zero-sum (Self's gain is Other's loss) to reperceive it as a non-zero-sum-conflict (in which both may gain or both may lose), and then to assist parties to move in the positive sum direction. Figure 1.5 shows various possible outcomes of the conflict between Cain and Abel. Any point towards the right is better for Abel, any point towards the top is better for Cain. In the Bible the prize is the Lord's favour. Cain sees the situation as a zero-sum conflict: at point 1 (his best outcome) he gets the Lord's favour, at 2 (his worst) the Lord favours Abel. All the other possibilities lie on the line from 1 to 2 in which the Lord divides his favour, more or less equally, between the two brothers. Point 3 represents a possible compromise position. But it is the other diagonal, representing the non-zero-sum outcomes, that is the most interesting from a conflict resolution perspective: the mutual loss that actually occurred, at 0, when Abel was slain and Cain lost the Lord's favour, and the mutual gain they missed, at 4, if each had been his brother's keeper.*

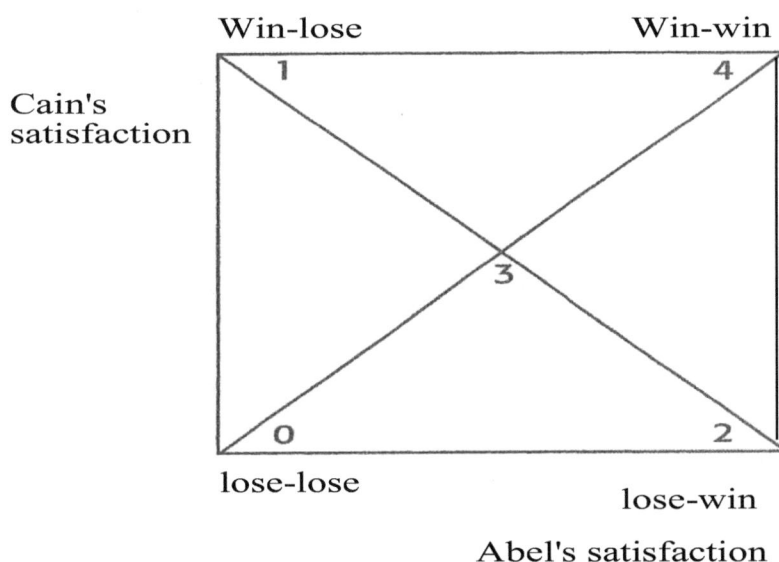

---

[42] *Contemporary Conflict Resolution.* Ramsbotham, et al. Polity Press. Malden, MA. 2005.

In environmental disputes, **often the truth is the first casualty of conflict**. As shown in this example, the **last casualty is often the real opportunity to have the outcomes the disputants originally sought**. EDR participants should be reminded of this truth throughout the effort.

Pure Cooperation or Collaborative Games

In comparison to zero-sum or war models, positive-sum, or "pure-cooperation," games are rare. Some positive-sum models include "**satisfying**" games. These models emphasize values and interests clarification and cooperative strategy development to achieve those values and interests.

A variation on these models for achieving desired conditions and values are the **"loss minimization"** or **"regret minimization"** models. As discussed more thoroughly in Chapter 5, these models present thinking based on fear; however, behind the fears lays a desire (a premise) that can usually be stated in terms of positive-sum satisfaction.

Like zero-sum games, positive-sum games proceed through a series of "frames" subject to rules and performance scoring that rewards cooperation with higher scores. Opponents might score two or three times more if they cooperate with one another than if they betray their opponent, as would normally occur in a zero-sum game.

In a win-win or pure-cooperation game, the cumulative scores of the opponents define success, and there is often a multiplier for equal scores between the opponents or for reaching a certain score threshold. For example, if two opponents engaged in a pure-cooperation game achieve 100 points each (equal scores summing to 200), they might both receive 200 points. If one gets 20 points and the other 80 (unequal scores that when summed are 100), they only get to keep their respective 20 and 80 points.

In using these game models, EDR practitioners may ask opponents a series of questions meant to help them understand the disputed values they hold. This effort sometimes begins after a "nominal group" or some other public involvement effort reveals an issue or conflict. Nominal-group exercises help reveal public preferences about environmental matters by creating and ranking lists of what topics are most important to participants.

If disputed values emerge from questioning disputants, EDR practitioners may then ask disputants to engage in a dialog about how the disputed values might be satisfied. Sometimes, beneficial dialog begins with "upper-level" values, such as what constitutes "fair" process and behavior and how to attain it. They then move the discussion "step-wise" through dialog about process, object, and social and economic values, seeking means and actions that "satisfy" their values and resolve the dispute.

As a corollary to a step-wise dialog, EDR practitioners may decide to use a more highly structured approach to exploring values satisfaction, including asking opponents to "force rank" their listed values. "**Force ranking**" refers to the process of putting a list of outcomes in order of their importance (first, second, third, etc.) with no ties between outcomes. Once each opponent force-ranks their values list, EDR practitioners compare the lists and convene a dialog about how to attain the disputed outcomes and resolve the dispute.

Sometimes this conversation begins with a thorough discussion of the values not in dispute to make sure of their meaning to all parties, to create a context for discussing the disputed values, and to begin the process of developing group cohesion.

Even more structured approaches exist. Similar to *Getting to Yes* interest-based bargaining, EDR practitioners may try to have opponents agree on a set of criteria reflective of their values list. They may also ask them to rank the relative importance of one criterion to another and assign weights to each to express their importance. If agreement on the criteria and weighting occurs, EDR practitioners can guide the opponents through a structured evaluation of alternatives meant to address the criteria and the values they represent. Jim Suhr, a now-retired Forest Service engineer, developed a method called *Choosing by Advantages*[43] that works very well and represents this approach.

Time limits aid games that use "satisfying" approaches whether the limits are voluntary or, better yet, imposed by contract, law, or other authority. **For many "pure cooperation" efforts, if dialog can continue indefinitely, it will**. EDR professionals — including mediators, negotiators, and arbitrators — often try to create agreements about time limits before scheduling meetings or dialogs. They then use the agreements to focus dialog, move it along, and find initial dispute-settlement parameters. With initial settlement parameters in place, the professionals allow more time later to iron out the details with the opponents.

Pure cooperation games also include questions about who leads the dispute-resolution efforts, in particular who represents the opponents. If the representatives are bent on war or used to pursuing zero-sum strategies, they will make little progress towards peaceful resolution.

If EDR practitioners find themselves faced with opponent representatives who have no interest in EDR, it is perfectly reasonable for the EDR practitioners to ask the opposing boards of directors or leadership groups to appoint new representatives. Failing different representation, it is also perfectly reasonable for the EDR practitioners to ask for a clarification of rationale and changed behavior. Sometimes this means sidebar conversations with the players about behavioral expectations, and sometimes it means working to establish group norms, agendas, and timelines conducive to EDR success.

---

[43] *The Choosing by Advantages Decision Making System*. Suhr, Jim. Greenwood Publishing Group. Digital. 1999.

Playing Super Games

A "**supergame**" can also be called a "**meta-game,**" which is a "game about the game." For example, two players are asked to play poker while game controllers with video cameras record their behavior and card play.

In poker, ordinarily only one player, the one who gets "called," has to show her cards at the end of a play. If she wins, the other player does not reveal his cards. If he has better cards, then he shows those cards to beat the first player and win.

By videotaping each player, their bets, and the cards played, game controllers are capturing information not usually available. If, after each hand, the controllers allow the players to review the videotapes and then replay the exact same cards, the controllers have introduced a supergame, one that provides quite different information about the opponents and their behavior than what is revealed in the game alone.

An "EDR supergame" might be the use of expert observers to review and analyze the behavior of participants and provide a weekly report to participants, revealing behaviors and agendas even the participants themselves may not be aware of. Or the reports might be given to the EDR practitioners to help them modify the means and methods in use for working with the disputants or powerful people not in the group.

"Gaming" Congress, State Legislatures, and the Courts

Some government institutions do not serve as a good context for EDR "gaming" because they reflect "war-like" or battle-replacing thinking. The Congress and state legislatures have traditions of partisan politics, which guide competing interests and disputes to resolution with strong rules-based and seniority-based processes. However, unless the law or a contract requires them, similar rules and seniority conditions do not apply to EDR.

Unless a dispute reaches the courts, **judicial-style rules and culture generally do not apply to EDR either**. The federal and state judicial branches are intensely adversarial, built to replace medieval justice-by-combat or later dueling models. The judge takes on nearly regal powers in the courtroom. Thus, we rise when the judge enters and wait to speak until asked to by the judge. We may be imprisoned for not following the court's rules, for being impertinent or argumentative, or just for wearing a hat in the judge's presence.

Both legislative- and judicial-branch behaviors rest on "zero-sum" concepts around which "win-lose" and "winner-takes-all" cultures exist. Both branches also allow for and depend on positive-sum cooperation and compromise, too, but zero-sum thinking and relationships dominate shared cultural values,

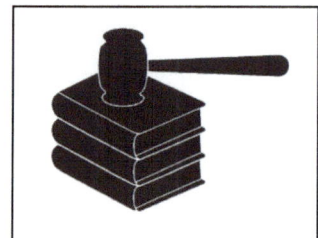

114

behaviors, and actions within the legislatures and the courts.

In legislative actions, if compromise and cooperation are lost, dispute resolution simply means dominance by vote of zero-summing majorities. In the courts, compromise and cooperation come down to a ruling by a judge.

Along the way to votes and rulings, legislators and judges try to resolve issues among disputing interests through pressure to compromise and cooperate. If efforts prove ineffective, disputants move into a zero-sum setting where control rests in the hands of legislators or judges. Once there, disputants may advocate for a "win" on their terms, but at the end of the day, they often find that their desires are unmet, or are only partially met, and regret giving up control of potential outcomes.

Besides dispute settlements, opponents may have other reasons for seeking legislation or a court ruling, such as setting new policy or creating legal precedents. These goals are also subject to the entities' zero-sum cultures.

Legislative and court schedules often impose time pressures or limits on dispute-resolution efforts. If EDR practitioners try to impose time limits in non-zero-sum situations, they may find that imposing time pressure actually escalates the dispute and increases the severity and intensity of tactics. Under positive-sum concepts, EDR practitioners may impose time constraints, but they set soft limits subject to quick revision if EDR progress is made.

One of the reasons environmental disputes become intractable and recycle the same issues repeatedly is that there is often no means to set time limits or to eventually "win" or "lose" in the zero-sum sense — no opponent holds sufficient power to fully subdue the other opponent. So, each participant repeats dispute patterns, exercising whatever power options they feel will most likely achieve their desired outcomes. The "game" becomes a "tit-for-tat" exercise. EDR practitioners have the opportunity to describe that for participants as a means to motivate them to adopt positive-sum approaches.

Finally, within the context of Constitutional intent, outside strong rules-based institutions such as courts or legislatures, zero-sum methods are counter to the core concepts of environmental peace and justice and individual sovereignty and responsibility that undergird successful EDR.

Games to Help Understand Disputes--The Five "Dilemmas"

In a zero-sum game, the winner takes all and the loser gets nothing. In a positive-sum game, many can "win," or at least gain from cooperation.

The authors of *Contemporary Conflict Resolution*[44] make the point that positive-sum work means "**making the cake bigger**": setting the issue into a wider context or redefining the parties' interests in such a way that they can be made compatible, sharing sovereignty or access to the contested resource, offering compensation for concessions or trading concessions in other areas, and managing the contested resources on a functional rather than a sovereign basis. Interest-based work is positive sum. In contrast, **bargaining is zero-sum, splitting a "fixed cake."**

Games can be non-cooperative with no shared communications or actions. They can also be cooperative with players acting together in teams or as one group.

Games can also be strategic with players in charge of change, or they can be passive with players having to work with whatever conditions they are given as in card games.

Games can be static with strategies fixed by players before play begins, or they can be dynamic with strategies flexible and changing during the game. Games can be deterministic and played with the facts fixed at the start of the game, or they can be probabilistic with facts changing or being added during play.

If EDR practitioners want to illustrate some of the advantages and disadvantages of zero-sum behavior in common dispute situations, they should focus on zero-sum, non-cooperative, passive, static, and deterministic games. If they want to illustrate some of the advantages and disadvantages of positive-sum behavior, practitioners should focus on games that emphasize positive-sum, cooperative, strategic, dynamic, and probabilistic performance.

One of the zero-sum games most studied is the **"Prisoners' Dilemma,"** which has many variations. This game assumes two people commit a robbery, hide their loot, get picked up by suspicious police, and are imprisoned. They are quickly isolated and the police interrogate them, and pressure them as individuals to confess or to implicate the other. Because there are no witnesses and no evidence in hand, the police have to get one of the prisoners to "break," and then the prisoner who implicates the other will go free; otherwise, both will go free.

The Prisoners' Dilemma is played several different ways. Sometimes, it is assumed that the criminals have a prior agreement to remain silent. Sometimes, this is not a condition. Sometimes, the police are allowed to deceive or coerce the prisoners, and sometimes they are not. Sometimes, the incentives for betrayal change during play, and sometimes not. For example, sometimes the payoff from the loot varies or the number of years of imprisonment.

---

[44] *Contemporary Conflict Resolution: The prevention, management, and transformation of deadly conflicts, Second Edition.* Ramsbotham, Oliver, Woodhouse, Tom, and Miall, Hugh. Polity Press, Malden, MA. 2005. p.175.

Play proceeds through a series of "frames," or rounds, usually involving different communications from the "police" to the "prisoners" until betrayal occurs or the prisoners are both freed. Sometimes, in the interest of time, play is limited to a certain number of frames.

Regardless, participants in a Prisoners' Dilemma game are exposed to issues of communication, cooperation, competition, threat, risk, exposure, and betrayal. Typically, play results in betrayal even though pure cooperation would mean both benefit by gaining their freedom and possessing half of the value of their theft.

I add several other "dilemmas" to any zero-sum or positive-sum gaming discussion. The first game is the **"Gambler's Dilemma."**

A gambler sits at a poker table with five cards in her hand. After the first cards are dealt, she has three-of-a-kind, a good hand and a possible winner. She requires only one card to have a hand that has a higher probability of winning, either four-of-a-kind or a full house. The probability of her receiving the card she wants is very low.

Her first dilemma is what to bet before she asks for the card. Good gamblers always try to "build the pot" by getting other players to bet heavily in counterpoint to what the good gambler bets or bluffs. With a big pot, the gambler's winning hand will then mean much more money for her.

The gambler has to decide what the right bet should be, balancing the play of others and their behavior regarding past hands (called "reading the *tells*," which includes other players bluffing, or faking and their reaction to her past bluffs) with the strength of her current hand and the probability of drawing cards that will improve her likelihood of winning. She also has to be concerned that too large a bet may scare off the other players or that they are accurately reading her *tells*.

Her second dilemma occurs when she receives her next cards. If she has a winning hand, she knows how to proceed. If the strength of her hand does not improve, she then has to decide whether to bluff, to again pretend that her hand is better than it is. As a strategy, bluffing results in good poker players making more money than straight play.

Even though the Gambler's Dilemma is a win-lose game, the players are communicating and cooperating at some level. Using only two frames (first hand, second hand), the Gambler's Dilemma offers a different set of issues about communication, cooperation, competition, threat, risk, exposure, and betrayal than the Prisoner's Dilemma.

Another game is the **"Paratroopers' Dilemma."** Two paratroopers are dropped behind enemy lines on a moonless night to secure a bridge prior to an attack by allies at noon the next day. Both of them have to be present to secure the bridge, one at each end.

To reduce the threat of detection, they perform a High-Altitude, Low-Opening (HALO) jump, leaving the plane at 40,000 feet and dropping to 800 feet before they open their parachutes. Because extreme cold and lack of oxygen at 40,000 feet could kill them, they have to wear insulated clothing, oxygen bottles and face masks, and other bulky equipment.

Therefore, they have to omit a lot of other equipment that paratroopers normally carry. Each one is limited to maps and a Geographic Positioning System (GPS) unit, knives, guns, and a little ammunition, one landmine and some explosives, a small medical kit, a small reflective "space blanket," two days' food, and radios with only a one kilometer range.

They jump and, because of unpredictable wind conditions, come down ten kilometers away from the bridge and ten kilometers away from each other. Radios do not work at this range, other than to create static when they are "keyed."

One paratrooper has a GPS unit that works but has lost his map when a pocket on his pack opened during the jump. The other paratrooper has held on to her map, but her GPS unit is broken after a hard landing. They are bruised, confused, and anxious but they have the advantages of being well-trained and experienced, being familiar with their equipment and having landed undetected.

They have twelve hours to reach the bridge to fulfill their mission. If they fail in their mission, tactical advantage and many allied lives will be lost, and the entire battle may be jeopardized

Play proceeds in increments that represent one "on the ground" hour and is therefore limited to twelve frames. The game can be "static," meaning that strategies and variables do not change throughout play, or it can be dynamic with strategies allowed to change each hour or multiple hours or with variables changing to introduce detection by the enemy or injury to a paratrooper. Players find this game creates very different experiences around communication, cooperation, competition, threat, risk, exposure, and betrayal than the Prisoners' or Gambler's Dilemmas.

Another game is the **"Forester's Dilemma."** After a major fire, a forester is asked to tell a landowner what it will cost to plant trees to restore a landscape and how likely it is that attaining those desired future forest conditions will be successful. The landowner wants to reforest because he expects to pass the commercial forest on to his children and grandchildren as "wealth." In turn, they want to realize some cash value but also prize the landscape for hunting, fishing, bird-watching, camping, and berry-picking.

The forester has no problem estimating how much it will cost to clear the fire-killed trees and plant the first year's seedlings because that information is readily available. He can also calculate how the sale of fire-killed trees can offset some of the reforestation costs.

However, the landowner also wants to know how successful the restoration will be over many years. The landowner wants to know how much normal environmental losses due to seedling drying, or cattle and wildlife grazing on seedlings, will cost and how much other actions promoting tree growth will cost over that time, too. Now, the forester has to project likely long-term survival for seedlings and effectiveness of other actions, considering variables such as rainfall, heat, fire, and competing vegetation and predators.

The forester knows that, if the seedlings survive 15 years, they will grow into a commercial forest about 50 years later. He also knows that the landowner's relatives have some ideas about present and future conditions that may mean keeping some areas free of trees or planting trees more widely spaced than in a commercial forest. He has to project conditions, forecast tree survival, design forest openings, and calculate per year costs for reforestation and management actions such as clearing and applying herbicides.

The Forester's Dilemma is an "expert" game in which the forester has to estimate threats, risks, and costs. Scenarios have to be built and tested against values held by the landowner and the heirs. Several independent "foresters" play the game for fifteen frames, consulting a "landowner and family" panel who usually have an initial set of values that may remain static or can change with, say, the death of the landowner at frame ten. Environmental conditions can also remain fixed throughout, or the game controller can randomly change weather, fire, disease, mitigation cost, or other variables. The competing foresters can be kept isolated and uncommunicative, or they may be allowed to communicate in limited or completely open ways. At each frame, each forester is asked to describe restoration plans, future reforestation and other costs, and the likelihood of success.

The winner of the Forester's Dilemma is the player who best satisfies the "family" panel's expectations. Like a boxing match, each frame is scored by each panel member against a scoring system given them by the game controller. "Forester" players find this game creates very different experiences around communication, cooperation, competition, threat, risk, exposure, and betrayal than the other Dilemmas.

A last game with zero-sum and positive-sum qualities to consider is the **"Elders' Dilemma."** I developed this game idea from the Alaska Youth Practicum I participated in and supported as Deputy Regional Forester for Natural Resources in the 1990s.

In this game, players are separated into teams of four to five individuals whose assignment is to develop land use and management plans that reflect the values important to a native community. The teams are asked to look at a series of maps and spreadsheets that are available to everyone and describe several parcels of native land, the resources

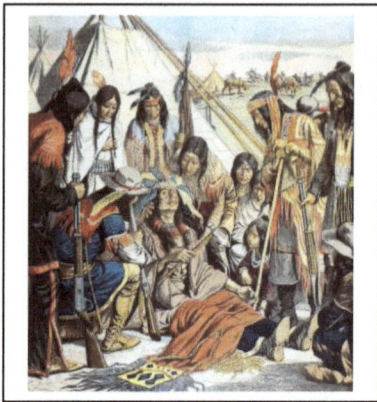

present on those lands, existing transportation systems, and nearby towns and natural resources.

Once participants have had a chance to study the materials, they are introduced to a panel of "Elders," people who know the resources and their traditional uses and who are advocates for community and ethnic support and continuity. Throughout play, the Elders will be available to the teams to answer questions, and occasionally, they will make presentations to the teams about shared values and priorities and the importance of traditional spiritual uses and connections to resources.

Participants are then introduced to a panel of "Developers," who will provide information and insight regarding the means to develop resources for economic benefit. They also meet a panel of "Environmentalists," who will provide information about environmental conditions, laws, and beneficial practices. As advocates, the Developers and Environmentalists are expected to exaggerate some ideas or overstate some issues, but they may not lie to or coerce team members.

Play begins with the teams assessing and presenting their understanding of the resource values they have on the "native lands." Play progresses through explorations of desired outcomes, to alternative development, to descriptions of effects, to a final management plan complete with financial projections and plans.

The Elders introduce different considerations connected to the land and to the native community, and some of this group's members live locally and some far away. The community also needs health and financial services, transportation, education, and housing. The Developers and Environmentalists introduce ideas about investment options, environmental impacts, and legal status.

The Elders Dilemma is played through 12 or more frames, which can last 2-3 hours each over a two-day period. The teams develop and present their ideas at the end of each frame and make a final presentation to the Elders, Developers, and Environmentalists at the end of play. Each frame is scored, with the final frame weighted more heavily than the preceding ones. The winning team has the highest score.

Learning Cooperative Approaches from Real Life

Perhaps the best examples of EDR success begin with spontaneously self-forming, self-satisfying EDR groups, which are **sometimes called "collaborative" groups**. The Quincy Library Group and the Malpais Borderlands Project are two award-winning examples of environmental opponents coming together without EDR professionals or public agency people involved.

Practitioners of EDR should closely examine the factors that led to the emergence and success of collaborative efforts. They may even ask representatives from collaborative groups to attend training sessions and discussion meetings to inform opponents about opportunities firsthand.

By using a case-study approach, EDR practitioners can inform and engage opponents in the concepts, conditions, and behaviors that contribute to creating cooperative groups and actions. There are many factors to consider.

Most self-initiated (pure) cooperation happened because **the opponents were tired of fighting and appalled at the effects of intractable environmental disputes on themselves, their families, their communities, or natural resources they care about.** They went looking for a better way and found it in collaborative dialog and action, bringing agency and EDR helpers in only after they had decided to change from a zero-sum approach.

Their commitment to high-order values of community and prosperity allowed them to step back from long-term process-value, resource condition-value, economic-value, and object-value disputes. EDR practitioners and caring onlookers can encourage and nurture such courageous acts through dialog and application of techniques that reveal higher-order values. However, pure cooperation behaviors cannot be required in most cases, but must arise of their own accord.

In fact, public agency personnel and EDR practitioners can inadvertently sabotage collaborative groups by trying to control timing, processes, or outcomes, or by sending the wrong messages about performance or expectations to an emergent self-motivating collaborative group. These groups are often fragile in the beginning, the advantages of coalition building are unclear to the members, and suspicions of one another are still running high. These groups also lack supportive structural elements, such as laws or regulations that enable funding for projects.

EDR collaborative groups form to satisfy high-order values, often local economic, community-perpetuation, or community-prosperity social values. Thus such a collaborative group is a coalition that intends to use collective powers to meet higher-order values.

However, other coalitions form to meet mid- or lower-order values, such as to complete a timber sale without protestors or develop a new wetlands-exchange protocol for their state. It is important to note that EDR practitioners must strive hard to understand the motives for coalition formation before trying to apply EDR strategies and techniques. If the motives are obscure, the EDR effort will often be off-target and ineffective. This is because the coalitions exist because of shared value-preference scales that the EDR folks must understand if they are to be successful.

The coalitions also exist to determine the outcome of a series of events and to share in the results according to the power and resources they contributed to determine the outcomes.

This means that some coalitions will be short-lived in order to achieve lower-order values and others will be long-term in order to achieve higher-order values. EDR practitioners must understand: what coalition members feel is at stake for them as far as risks and rewards are concerned, what the coalition schedule looks like, and how they plan to divide the results of their collaborative efforts.

Because each coalition or collaborative group member has a unique set of values, some individual and some shared, when it comes to dividing the results, they may all get most, if not everything, they want from their mutual efforts. Understanding this values-optimization potential, EDR practitioners can help coalitions and collaborative groups by applying values-clarifying techniques and ranges of options to help optimize them.

Based on the cases examined, EDR practitioners can facilitate discussion among opponents regarding what structural and compositional conditions and functions/relationships would have to exist before a collaborative effort can address ongoing disputes. This "gaming" has a very practical side because it could lead, in short order, to skills development, attitude change, and movement towards dispute-resolution in both the short and longer terms.

Other Examples of Environmental Cooperation and Collaboration

One challenge for EDR practitioners is to understand how people can develop structural incentives for pure cooperation in a world seemingly dominated by win-lose thinking. A partial answer may lie in understanding legislative incentives that encourage cooperation behavior and how these examples might be used to inform and motivate opponents.

Congress and some state legislatures have developed laws to encourage collaboration with the use of public funds to achieve environmental and public use improvements. These include the *Secure Rural Schools and Community Self-Determination Act* (2000, rev. 2008), which structures Resource Advisory Committees (RACs) that guide the investment of tens of millions of dollars annually in Forest Service and Bureau of Land Management lands. Each RAC is composed of 15 members, representing a broad cross-section of public interests: environmental, development, local and tribal governments, and elected officials. These committee members review proposals from the agencies and public interests and recommend investments within and near the public lands.

Some state and local laws also allow developers who use advisory groups or make provisions for green space or the conservation of habitats to add more sale units, whether commercial or residential. When tied to advisory groups with a broad spectrum of representatives, these structural components create incentives for cooperation among opponents and often mean increased profit for the developer. There are other laws that require a quid pro quo of environmental mitigation; for example, if wetlands are filled and developed in one place, wetlands may have to be created or enhanced elsewhere.

Currently, **the mechanism of a multiplier-reward for pure cooperation is not common in these structural approaches**. To the extent such a reward is utilized, the

multiplier effect occurs through the shared experience of the opponents and resulting compositional effects, such as "log-rolling" and "horse-trading" and improved relationships and communications. Log-rolling among cooperators refers to creating mutual action from which both may benefit as in two men rolling a log at the same rate in the same direction so neither loses control and both reach the log's resting place. Horse-trading refers to cooperators or opponents making demands and offering compromises or concessions to settle a dispute in a quid pro quo manner.

Practitioners can also look to compositional factors, such as opponents' values around economic support for local communities, as a place to develop shared social values and cooperation. Similarly, practitioners can help opponents develop mutual relationship values through effective techniques, so that trust builds and collaboration can take place.

Computer and On-Line Games

Wow! What an amazing number of computer games are on the market today, and electronic gaming systems are rapidly expanding in capacity and complexity. Many of these games are combat-style games, and most games are competitive zero-sum games with scoring and record-keeping. All are simulations of effective-power and outcome-control situations.

Almost every computer game promotes "mini-max" or "maxi-min" game strategies, meaning that a player attempts to score the most while minimizing an opponent's score (if there is an opposing player). Some contain "tit-for-tat" components wherein the move of one player can be opposed equally by another player; electronic tic-tac-toe and chess are examples of such games.

I've never seen a game that emphasized issue management. I know of one that promotes understanding of crisis recovery, however. The "Sim" series simulates cities and infrastructure being impacted by natural events such as earthquakes. Recovery has to be attempted to "win" the game and scores are recorded.

For EDR efforts to be modeled and supported by games, game makers will want to develop more positive-sum games, building rules and incentives into the games that train players to understand and later emulate cooperative methods and conclusions. This is hardly an insurmountable task but it flies in the face of popular taste that emphasizes zero-sum games and dominance by one opponent over another. Positive-sum games can also be part of a super-game educational curriculum.

At the end of the day, positive-sum games and super games may only be developed at the request of EDR practitioners or supportive foundations like the U.S. Institute for Environmental Conflict Resolution. This direction is one well worth pursuing for game-mined people who care about developing broad-based public awareness, understanding, and skills in EDR.

Chapter 9: People Involved In EDR

Effective EDR depends on the participants; they must want it to work

The U.S. Institute for Environmental Conflict Resolution has established eight principles for EDR work: informed commitment; balanced, voluntary representation; group autonomy; informed process; accountability; openness, timeliness; and implementation

Besides the actual disputants, some of the people involved in EDR may be agency representatives, third-party interveners, supporters, cooperators, courts, and caring-but-untrained on-lookers; roles differ among these participants

Participants must be prepared to act according to principle and the ethics associated with their role

---

Social and Behavioral Norms for Effective EDR

"The true measure of a man is how he treats someone who can do him absolutely no good" (Samuel Johnson, 1709-1784). EDR will not work unless people want it to work. EDR as part of the journey to environmental peace and justice — both short- and long-term — has to guide all practitioners and participants.

In this context, I propose a basic Code of Conduct for EDR Practitioners and Leaders:

*"In all my advice and actions, I will **Do No Harm.** To this end, I will:*

- *Accept work intended to resolve environmental disputes and reject work that increases strife or polarity*
- *Make recommendations and act in ways that move people and communities towards environmental peace and justice*
- *Commit one hundred percent to EDR outcomes and processes agreed to with EDR community members*
- *Meet EDR community member expectations for agreed-to services and products, delivering on time, to standard, and within budget*
- *Treat participants with dignity and respect at all times*
- *Communicate honestly, candidly, and diplomatically with all participants*
- *Reveal any personal conflicts of interest or biases that might affect the EDR effort or outcomes*
- *Protect confidential business, government, and individual information as permitted by law"*

USIECR Principles for Federal Agency EDR

Operating under their own EDR Code of Conduct, some practitioners may find the sound Environmental Conflict Resolution Principles established by the interagency steering committee of the U.S. Institute for Environmental Conflict Resolution of use as additional background for building an EDR program. The USIECR website www.ecr.gov displays a variety of case examples that purport to uphold these "Basic Principles for Agency Engagement in Environmental Conflict Resolution and Collaborative Problem Solving:[1]

- **Informed Commitment** – Confirm willingness and availability of appropriate agency leadership and staff at all levels to commit to principles of engagement; ensure commitment to participate in good faith with an open mindset to new perspectives
- **Balanced, Voluntary Representation** – Ensure balanced inclusion of affected/concerned interests; all parties should be willing and able to participate and select their own representatives
- **Group Autonomy** – Engage with all participants in developing and governing the process, including the choice of consensus-based decision rules; seek assistance from impartial facilitator/mediator selected by and accountable to all parties
- **Informed Process** – Seek agreements on how to share, test, and apply relevant information (scientific, cultural, technical, etc.) among participants; ensure relevant information is accessible to, and understandable by, all participants
- **Accountability** – Participate in the process directly, fully, and in good faith; be accountable to all participants, as well as to agency representatives and the public
- **Openness** – Ensure all participants and the public are fully informed in a timely manner of the purpose and objectives of the process; communicate agency authorities, requirements, and constraints; uphold confidentiality rules and agreements as required for particular proceedings
- **Timeliness** – Ensure timely decisions and outcomes
- **Implementation** – Ensure decisions are can be implemented consistent with federal law and policy; parties should commit to identify roles and responsibilities necessary to implement agreement; parties should agree in advance on the consequences of a party being unable to provide necessary resources or to implement the agreement; ensure parties will take steps to implement and obtain resources necessary to implement the agreement

These principles provide ideas that EDR practitioners may find useful for goal and objectives setting, and they provide broad guidelines for conducting EDR activities. These principles are similar to the public involvement direction for the Forest Service and other federal agencies and current literature on "collaboration" in the emphasis on using facilitators/mediators and collaborative methods.

EDR Practitioners

EDR practitioners probably fall into one of three categories: agency people and trained third-party "neutral" interveners.

Agency people generally have laws and regulations to guide their work — rules that define their roles pretty well. Agency people also often have appointed powers, "the right to prevail," as they serve as decision-makers and problem-solvers on environmental issues.

They also have responsibilities for public involvement, and those activities can serve as a valuable means to bring opponents together — known as a convening and facilitating function. Agency people can also create a collaborative working environment by conducting their work "in a fishbowl" — with no secrets and public oversight of their work. They also have the means and skills to communicate intensively with opponents and other participants, and they can support the communications needs of other practitioners.

Some agency people may also be professionally trained mediators, counselors, planners, or others trained in EDR or Alternative Dispute Resolution. Their agencies may make them available for EDR work either as a part of their duties or upon request.

To be effective in their roles, agency people generally have to nurture a continuously open work environment — no matter how controversial a dispute becomes. To do otherwise is to nurture a "siege" environment and to join the dispute. In one sense, by remaining open during disputes, agency people keep their agency and actions as neutral as possible, almost as neutral as third parties can be.

Third-party neutral interveners are usually trained professional mediators, negotiators, or arbitrators. In these categories, many are attorneys who may have specialized in these skills during law school and have extensive practice after graduation. They generally manage EDR processes, including communications among opponents and other participants and the media.

Other trained third-party neutrals include social workers, counselors, social scientists, biological scientists, and economists. Other participants may bring these individuals into a dispute to provide expert topical information, or to provide participants with services, such as counseling to relieve personal distress.

Some non-governmental organizations employ professional third-party neutrals and make them available to perform EDR. Other professionals are self-employed or a part of legal, environmental planning, construction, or engineering firms.

Third-party neutrals usually have codes of professional ethics that guide their roles in EDR. They are sometimes licensed under state or local laws, and thus they may have regulations that guide their practice similar to agency people.

One of their most important responsibilities is to remain "neutral," just as their category suggests. No matter how intense a dispute becomes, the third-party neutrals are supposed to remain detached from the dispute itself and guide processes or provide information or other services so that the dispute can be resolved.

Caring-but-Untrained Participants

Caring but untrained participants often assist agency people and trained third-party neutrals in EDR. Many times, these people are members of an affected community of interest, place, tradition, or fate. They become involved in the EDR effort because they have values vulnerable to violation if the EDR effort is not successful. Although it is common to see doctors, pastors, or other professionals adopt these roles, people from all occupations can serve. Sometimes, Members of Congress or state legislators adopt this role, too.

Untrained participants often have life experiences or come from disciplines that help them with disputes at issue-abatement levels. However, **as full-blown conflict and crisis emerge, they may not have the skill or the experience** to continue the EDR effort without further training and assistance, such as professional coaching or direct assistance from agency people or trained third-party neutrals.

Agency people and trained third-party neutrals have a great deal to gain if the untrained folks get the support they need to be successful. At a minimum, having this kind of intervention and leadership will likely improve the chances for EDR success and the likelihood that the resolution will work long-term.

Caring but untrained participants usually have **no code of professional ethics or legal basis for their activities.** Although this flexibility is an asset in some ways, it may work against them if the untrained folks begin behaving in ways considered prejudicial to the interests of a specific opponent or to the public at large. These folks generally should not try to serve as the party "having the answer," but rather, as the force for "bringing people together to find an answer."

They may also serve as "shuttle diplomats," carrying messages and ideas back and forth between disputants and making sure the communications are respectful and build towards dispute resolution.

When legislators serve as untrained neutral third parties, because of the partisan nature of legislative bodies, opponents carefully watch the legislator's neutrality. A legislator's credibility and utility generally suffers if the legislator's behavior seems excessively partisan and biased towards one opponent over another. If legislation is likely to help resolve some structural aspects of the dispute, a generally neutral, bi-partisan approach will increase the likelihood of EDR success and the passage of the legislation.

For more discussion of ethics and relationships, see "The Ethics of Intervention" in *Contemporary Conflict Resolution*.[45]

EDR Cooperators and Key Supporters

Many other organizations and individuals can help EDR practitioners as **cooperators**. These include the courts, non-governmental organizations and businesses not a part of the dispute or EDR, churches, media, and educational institutions including schools, colleges, and universities.

In some cases, the cooperators may only lend their processes, names, or credibility to serve as a mechanism for bringing opponents together. In other cases, the cooperators may serve as part of an EDR team that broadens and deepens the EDR effort and improves its likelihood of success. This enhancement may be due to the nature of the EDR, the specific skills of the cooperators, or the fact that they can provide many more options for solutions or monitoring.

For example, the courts can provide a legally enforceable decision once mediation is over and a settlement agreement reached. Having legal enforceability may be just the reassurance that one opponent requires to accept the settlement. The courts may also place itself in the role of neutral implementation monitor through the offices of a special master or umpire — a role that may guarantee compliance and prevent dispute recycling.

Disputants and Other Participants

Early in the work, EDR practitioners will likely ask disputants and other interests to help develop a set of rules or norms for conducting the EDR effort. Although setting these in place is tough going at first, the rules or norms are essential to success in most cases. After adopting them, participants must be accountable for adhering to the rules and norms, and for asking for changes if needed, particularly the disputants who might be prone to exit citing the group norms as an excuse.

Where professional advocates, paid to prevail in disputes rather than participate in EDR, represent disputants in EDR, resolution possibilities lessen. Where disputants employ advocates trained in or simply accepting of EDR, the chances of success are greatly increased.

Some other participants get involved in a dispute to improve their chances of gaining electoral office, to create or enhance business opportunities, or to develop new interest or advocacy groups. EDR practitioners should keep them well informed about the importance of successful EDR and guide them into effective participation.

---

[45] *Contemporary Conflict Resolution: The prevention, management, and transformation of deadly conflicts, Second Edition.* Ramsbotham, Oliver, Woodhouse, Tom, and Miall, Hugh. Polity Press, Malden, MA. 2005. pp.275-287.

"Unmasking"

In any mediation and certain negotiations, practitioners may experience the moment when a **disputant "unmasks" and reveals their apparent true agenda, "bottom lines," or "best and final offer."** Although the timing varies considerably, in my experience, I find this unmasking, if it happens, occurs somewhere around the fourth or fifth offer "sets," "frames," or "rounds."

A similar phenomenon occurs with distress disputes in which, as people try to articulate the issues they have with their opponents, **they may have to be asked three or four times to get to the point of stating "what's really bothering them."** Practitioners sometimes use verbal "hooks" to help opponents "drill down" to key issues, asking, "So, is that what's really bothering you, or is there something else?" Alternatively, they may use effective listening and ask, "So, (blank) seems to really concern you, and it's obviously important to you, but is that what really bugs you or is there something more?"

Experienced negotiators and mediators actually "push" unmasking other ways:

1) Setting real deadlines and reinforcing them with opponents while stressing the implications of failing to meet them

2) Offering appropriate settlement or improvement suggestions.

In financial or contract negotiations or mediations, these settlement suggestions may have a "mid-point" quality, the point at which third-party neutrals suggest an average of the high and low figure on the table.

In all of these cases, disputants may not know what is really bothering them or what their bottom line is unless practitioners push to discover the points with precision. Practitioners should be assisting and watching for this unmasking, and they should be prepared to act on the insights when and if they appear, validating them, and grounding them by stating their relevance to the dispute and its options for resolution.

However these events unfold, **practitioners have some ethical issues to ponder**. When does their "push" become too influential, exerting control over the outcome? When does withholding information or emphasizing certain information create too much emphasis on one choice over another, or perhaps send a message about practitioner bias to one disputant or another? When one disputant obviously reacts to information or a push differently than the other, what is the responsibility of the practitioner to reveal or use these differences? When one disputant unmasks, should the practitioner notify the other disputants? Should practitioners shift to different rules or processes if disputants unmask?

EDR practitioners have significant challenges and obligations. In the end, as Winston Churchill (1874-1965) said, *"Sometimes it is not enough to do our best; we must do what is required."* In every dispute situation, an honest search for environmental peace and justice is what is required.

A Commitment to Transformative Processes

Opponents and other participants are involved in both the dispute and the EDR effort to maximize the attainment of their values or desired outcomes. However, if EDR is to work completely, they have to accept its basic purposes and results and accept the roles played and actions taken by EDR practitioners.

Sometimes, perhaps most times, EDR reaches only partial success because the fundamental values conflicts are not resolved or because opponents are not trained (or refused training) in how to manage issues for the long term. I have always accepted partial success, but I have never been satisfied with it because the long-term costs of recycled environmental value conflicts is too high to be tolerated within my value system.

Still, I once spoke to an eye surgeon of great skill. We were talking about how patients come to accept cataract surgery. He said, "Well, you just wait until the cataracts are ripe." With visions of shriveled fruit in my mind, I asked, "How do you know when they're ripe?" He answered with a smile, "It's not really the cataracts; it's the patient. The cataracts are ripe when the patient can't stand bad vision anymore." Okay. I got the point.

Some dispute-resolution work only happens when **the disputants are "ripe" for it, when they are ready to have their "vision" transformed for the better**. Practitioners may have to treat "symptoms" for a long time before they get a chance to work on the true basis for the dispute and assist others through transformation in a dispute-resolution community.

Everyone participating in EDR has a role and accompanying responsibilities. In addition, people's values regarding EDR play a major role in determining EDR success. Thus, getting practitioners and participants to understand their roles and responsibilities, as well as getting them to articulate their values towards EDR (versus the dispute itself), is likely to prove critical to success.

Back in Chapter 7, I mentioned that the authors of *Contemporary Conflict Resolution*[46] describe five "generic transformers of protracted conflict":

1. **Context transformation** – changing the social, political, economic, or ecological context for the dispute.
2. **Structural transformation** – examining the actors and their incompatible values. If symmetrical power relationships exist, this transformation may mean changes in the method of sharing power. In

---

[46] *Contemporary Conflict Resolution: The prevention, management, and transformation of deadly conflicts, Second Edition.* Ramsbotham, Oliver, Woodhouse, Tom, and Miall, Hugh. Polity Press, Malden, MA. 2005. pp.163-165.

3. **Actor transformation** – changing players, values, behaviors, affiliation/ membership/constituencies, and the adoption of new values, beliefs, priorities, and actions.
4. **Issue transformation** – changing interests, positions, and issues, including reframing and re-imaging.
5. **Personal and group transformation** – people reshaping their values and lives based on experience and education.

One of the values to be nurtured is participants' commitment to transformation in appropriate ways. Until a sufficient number of transformations occur, environmental disputes may recycle or escalate and progress. The nature and extent of transformations necessary to prevent recycling will vary according to the dispute's scale, structure, composition, and functions or relationships. As a matter of principle, both EDR practitioners and participants share responsibility for working towards appropriate transformations.

As Mark Twain (1835-1910) said, *"Always do right — this will gratify some and astonish the rest."* A positive intention and clear communications can be a powerful force in driving transformation.

Some People Have Concerns about EDR Efforts

Some people criticize EDR efforts because they feel they are infeasible or offensive to American mainstream cultural or minority cultural values (e.g., personal sovereignty expressed as "rugged individualism").

Other critics of conflict-resolution efforts[47] question whether "**a conflict- resolution, - consensus-promoting strategy, based on impartial mediation and negotiation…is appropriate in cases where war is fuelled by 'greed' rather than 'grievance'**." Taken out of the international context of warlord-ism and criminal factions leading nations, this is a debate about the legitimacy of opponents; if opponents are simply are looking for economic or power gain, rather than environmental peace and justice after EDR, disputes will prolong or recycle and may intensify. So, people question whether practitioners should undertake EDR under these circumstances. I submit that the Code of Conduct I propose will help EDR practitioners decide if they should engage.

Another criticism is that **contemporary conflict resolution efforts are incompatible with certain cultures and religions**. As one example, the authors of *Contemporary Conflict Resolution* compare contemporary views of conflict with Buddhism's four noble truths and find that EDR is consistent with these beliefs[48]:

---

[47] *Contemporary Conflict Resolution: The prevention, management, and transformation of deadly conflicts, Second Edition.* Ramsbotham, Oliver, Woodhouse, Tom, and Miall, Hugh. Polity Press, Malden, MA. 2005. pp. 6-7.
[48] IBID, p. 314.

1. Conflict (suffering) is part of the human condition.
2. Understanding the deep roots of conflict is the first step to transforming it.
3. By engaging with and transforming the roots of conflict, peace can emerge from conflict.
4. Peace is a way of life, a process, not something that lies in the future, but something to be engaged in now.

Jesus taught essentially the same beliefs, particularly if you equate Buddha's thoughts on suffering and conflict with Jesus' teachings on sin and un-forgiveness. In America, some traditionally conservative churches are thought to be against environmental quality in favor of resource development for human uses. Sometimes, this is called "prosperity theology"—those God blesses should expect worldly riches. Other churches support environmental causes, including environmental justice.

Whether a particular Christian tradition embraces prosperity theology or another view nurturing the environment, many churches value and support the American Green Cross initiative (http://www.americangreencross.org). The American Green Cross mission is:

Wherever and whenever there is a threat to America the beautiful, we want the American Green Cross to be there.

Our beautiful country has never been more threatened with environmental disasters than now. We seem to have lost our way as American stewards of the great natural blessing that God has bestowed upon us.

America is scarred, clear-cut, laid waste, paved over, eroded and defiled by greedy plunderers who have lost their patriotism and respect for God and Creation.

Please help us to establish a fund large enough to snatch from the edge of disaster, those parts of America the beautiful which are in imminent danger of destruction by the forces of greed which seems to have infected America.

Certainly, their mission suggests commitment to environmental quality, peace, and justice, although their website is not specific on those topics.

Overall, **we would likely have to search hard for a legitimate religion or credo that promotes the destruction of nature**. This understanding is in contrast to arguments that capitalism, socialism, and communism, as political-economic philosophies, view nature and ecosystems primarily as essential production feedstock to serve people's needs rather than critical, lifeway-sustaining and –enriching resources having intrinsic planetary and spiritual values.

Chapter 10: EDR and Management Styles

Autocratic management styles and communications may serve EDR well in crises; such managers often do not share power or include others in decision-making, and often communicate only in a one-way and incomplete manner; yet, in crises, the personal and public good may be well served by autocratic action

Cooperative management styles and communications serve EDR well at issues, full-blown conflict, and recovery stages; such managers share power and include others in decisions, and they communicate in a two-way and thorough manner

---

Chapter 9 discusses some of the commonly encountered participants in dispute resolution and some ethical and procedural considerations. This chapter delves more deeply into the effects of management styles on EDR process and success, particularly the styles of process managers and decision-makers.

Analytic Tools to Understand Management Style

Many training firms and management consultants offer books and training about the subject of managing people. For example, the U.S. Forest Service used the Kepner-Tregoe Managerial Grid (kepner-tregoe.com) training for many years, and more recently, the agency has used Myers-Briggs testing a great deal for orienting leadership teams.

It is not my intention to duplicate that valuable material in any way. Previously, in Chapter 6, I talked about autocratic behavior and effective power, specifically about the limitations on power that an autocratic manager or decision-maker, and the public working with them, might not understand. In this section, I move to a different discussion of how management and communications styles fit with best practices for EDR.

Autocratic Management Styles

Generally, **autocratic management styles**, characterized by urgent, controlling and sometimes threatening behaviors, **work best just prior to, in the midst of, and immediately following a crisis**. During a crisis, at some level, affected people expect, and sometimes even demand, autocratic management and leadership as long as autocratic leaders focus on sustaining the public good.

For example, during a wildfire emergency, people understand that Forest Service line officers and incident commanders will have to make decisions that may be uncomfortable or inconvenient for people. Managers may have to close roads, evacuate houses and businesses on short notice, and allow some properties to burn if the fire managers cannot protect them safely.

I led the firefighting effort on the Umpqua National Forest during the record fires of 2002. Working with cooperators like the Douglas County Sherriff's Office and the Oregon Department of Transportation, we closed many roads, choked other roads with firefighting equipment, and created a lot of smoke. We also stopped fires before they burned on to other properties, evacuated people, and cancelled public events. We tried to avoid inconveniencing the public, and we were generally effective, but, at times people were greatly inconvenienced. The public generally accepted the disruptions with little complaint.

Managers displaying autocratic behavior during EDR can be exercising appointed or tacit powers, or a blend of both. During natural or human-caused emergencies, fire crews and their supervisors make decisions regularly about whether to let a fire burn up a shelter, campground, or home. This power is as real as a bullet fired from a gun because it uses a natural phenomenon to make a physical change.

Government employees, including firefighters, emergency management staff, health officials and police, have appointed power for handling the emergency, such as making evacuations or placing diseased people or animals in quarantine. Often, we grant people tacit or positional powers if they possess special skills, knowledge, or equipment; these powers often exist for the duration of the emergency, such as timber fellers or blasters hired to eliminate hazards for the duration of the emergency.

People exercise these powers during emergencies, but they are also generally acceptable and effective in drills and practice efforts to prepare for emergencies. Citizens at large sometimes grumble about inconveniences during simulations and drills, but they are most often supportive.

When an **emergency or crisis is not yet manifest, autocratic management is usually acceptable in only a limited way: to prevent a crisis**. For example, labor unions and management may be required to enter a "cooling-off period" prior to a strike — an event that would cripple key services generally available to and important to the public. Airline and garbage-collection strike situations often call for such intervention.

However, note that the intervention is a temporary restructuring of the conflict, one that limits the escalation power of one opponent, and an imminent threat of unacceptable consequences. The intervention is limited. The strike may actually occur later because law and social forces support the union's power to strike when disputants reach an impasse.

Intervention temporarily affects the structure, but the composition and relationships have not changed. Once the cooling-off period is over, the initial structure is restored, and if resolution has not been found, the strike goes forward.

In the late 1960s, I rode a Greyhound bus through central Washington, DC when it was on fire. Soldiers in battle dress with bayonets fixed and rounds chambered stood on street corners, warily watching the downtrodden neighborhoods. Night curfews were in place.

136

The presence of the troops had changed all three aspects of the conflict. Structure was changed by introducing the brute force of law and order, and because the targets of violence (e.g., stores, vehicles, bars) had been partially eliminated. Composition changed by having soldiers present to enforce order against rioters, regardless of the rioters' intention. Relationships altered because the government had shown that it would not be passive in the face of social unrest that led to violence, which gave credibility and weight to neighborhood peacemakers.

Because Americans try to minimize unwanted and unwarranted uses of autocratic management and the arbitrary control of their property or persons, autocratic crisis control has to end as soon as leaders restore order; if it does not end promptly, followers will begin to suspect the leader's motives and reject the autocratic behavior.

History shows that, if autocratic control remains in place beyond what citizen's view as reasonable, **people may join an insurgency and seek an anarchic solution**. They act this way because of a values conflict. For example, in a protracted labor dispute, strikers might support actions to "free themselves from oppression by management" rather than act according to their initial desires for higher wages and better work conditions.

As an example, I once interviewed a former employee of the <u>Washington Star</u>. After a prolonged strike over wages and benefits, the Star had gone under and was sold to non-union management. The former employee told me he was delighted when the "bastards went down", referring to the newspaper's management, even though all the workers lost their jobs. The strike had begun over pay and benefits but the protracted and vocal conflicts led to labor invoking much higher-level values, an questioning the integrity of the newspaper's management and their perceived autocratic behavior. So, the guy I interviewed exulted in the loss of his job because it meant autocratic management "went down," too.

While the exercise of autocratic crisis control is limited, the threat of exercising it earlier, at the issue or conflict stage, is considerably less so. Sometimes, the mere threat of a government-imposed cooling-off period is enough to get opponents back to the bargaining table in good faith. Thus, resistance to "meddling" from outside the conflict can induce cooperation — the threat to impose peace can induce opponents to become peacemakers (or at least to behave more peacefully). Yet, the threat must represent effective power. If an authority chooses to threaten intervention and lacks the power or the will, the authority may lose appointed and tacit powers and frustrate the EDR effort.

Autocratic Management Styles and Communications

Communications experts speak of "single-tailed" and "two-tailed" communications — the communications from one person to another and between two people respectively. The quality, completeness, timeliness, and focus of communications are also important considerations. Autocratic managers tend to focus on single-tailed communications that may not be timely or complete for the receiving audiences. To be successful, autocratic managers should focus on two-tailed, complete and timely communications.

During times when the public supports or seeks autocratic management, communications that are timely, complete, and focused on key public issues best serve the EDR effort. During a wildfire emergency, for example, people concerned about natural resources, and how the fire and firefighting are affecting the resources, want to ask about (and have managers inform them about) the fire practices and effects. Therefore, if the protection and safety of elk habitat or nesting spotted owls are key issues, autocratic managers should mobilize the resource and communications expertise needed to inform and involve the public.

Managers should also inform and involve people concerned about economic, social or community effects. Information about fire threats to private property or evacuations must be prompt, accurate, and complete. Managers must likewise address present and future resource uses, such as campgrounds or fire-killed timber.

Because of our historic dislike and mistrust of autocratic behavior, even during emergencies, the more effort managers put into effective communications on issues important to the public, the more leaders will find EDR to be unnecessary and the better recovery can take place in the aftermath.

Communications objectives should include accurate descriptions of:
- authorities and activities
- means for articulation of key issues and how people will address them
- how credibility and trust will be developed with communities of interest, place, tradition, and fate

In one sense, the greater the chaos and threat to the quality of life, the greater and more thorough the communications effort has to be.

Cooperative Management Styles

In the EDR context, **cooperative or inclusive management styles have a broader applicability than autocratic styles**. They can be useful at every stage of the dispute. All disputes have rules, even if these are tacit, implied, or unstated. One of these unstated expectations is that escalation will follow a pattern. For example, people arguing about sports teams have the expectation that one opponent engaged in verbal conflict may escalate the conflict to a shoving match but will not suddenly call on a gang of armed fiends to kill their opponent. They may be wrong but they have the expectation; otherwise, instead of making a "fight" response, they might choose to "flee" or "hunker down".

Managers can handle disputes in an inclusive way using a "fishbowl" approach. This approach will work so long as the participants are a part of a situation that requires public disclosure, such as a National Environmental Policy Act process. The advantages of this approach to EDR are that agreements reached through the effort have public acknowledgement, and that the parties to any settlement have fewer means and reasons to breach the agreement. Divorce mediations normally take place behind closed doors, but their result, the settlement agreement and marriage dissolution, are public documents and provide public notification of crisis and some conditions of aftermath, such as parenting plans.

Environmental conflicts that concern public lands and resources, as well as public regulations applied to private lands and resources often have a public disclosure factor. The EDR practitioner who can get all parties to begin "fishbowl" behavior as early as possible in the process will find results are cleaner, clearer, and more supported by the public.

Cooperative Management Styles and Communications

Cooperative-style managers are likely to practice two-tailed communications, including considerable interpersonal communications. They have the same need to be complete and timely as autocratic managers. Where cooperative-style managers occasionally fall into error is to confuse the frequency and openness of communications with actually addressing the key issues most important to the affected segments of the public. In the intensity of the moment, cooperative manager can be off-topic, and this lack of focus causes interested publics to exit for lack of tangible, applicable knowledge and progress.

Teamwork and Dispute Work

Effective teams manage disputes rather than allowing conflict to overwhelm them. Teams manage risk differently than individuals do, drawing on the talents and group strengths to offset both perceived and real threats.

I have led high-performing teams in both emergency and routine situations. Emergencies do not require autocratic team leadership, but people tolerate and even request such behavior at those times. Routine situations tolerate autocratic team leadership less well. Autocratic leadership may result in reduced team performance and superficial teamwork, and diminished support for the autocratic leader against a background of performance resistance can lead to conditions of non-compliance or "malicious compliance."

To use the strength and wisdom of teams in conducting EDR, practitioners should create a cooperative and inclusive team environment. The higher the dispute level, the more imperative the dispute team is well managed and motivated, whether by an autocratic or an inclusive leader. To do otherwise is to invite the team to internalize the dispute issues and full-blown conflicts, paralyzing them as an effective dispute-resolution component.

When I took over the leadership of the Bridger-Teton Land and Resource Management Plan effort in 1987, the interdisciplinary team was in disarray. Both the interdisciplinary team and the forest management team had internalized external disputes over wildlife management, logging, oil and gas development, and potential Wilderness designation.

Only a few people were members of both teams, but each team had the disputes strongly embedded within.

I knew that the teams could only complete the Plan successfully if I strengthened both teams, but strengthening the interdisciplinary team presented the greatest urgency and importance for me. This was because the energy and focus of the team had to shift from battling other team member's positions and points of view to solving major natural resource and environmental problems in the public interest and for the long-term.

It took about a year to build a high-performing planning team. We met some milestones easily; others came hard. However, the day finally came when the team's passionate wildlife biologist said, "I don't have to be present [at a major and defining meeting] because Larry [the timber-development team member] will be there. He knows exactly what to say, and I trust him to say it." I smiled a secret smile, knowing our work was going to be successful. From then on, the team simply moved as one with common purpose, open to any public comment or advocacy without defensiveness or personal animus.

The critical EDR point is that **many EDR situations require similar teamwork that is high performing, open, professional, and resolution-oriented**. In this state, the verbal and non-verbal communications emanating from the team send clear signals to opponents and other participants about the team's commitments, strengths, intensions, and likely successes.

Some Related Personality Type Considerations

Myers-Briggs and other personality typologies make the distinction between **"maximizer" and "minimizer" personalities. Maximizers are generally extroverted people who are expressive, often exhibiting facial and other physical animation**. They tend to exhibit more and more animation when dealing with minimizers and are "present" and "emotionally available" during team and group events. They can be impulsive and manipulative.

Minimizers are generally introverted people who are low-expressive and provide little or very subtle signs of their thoughts and emotions. They tend to be more and more withdrawn when dealing with maximizers and may be "emotionally unavailable" when working in group settings. They can be compulsive and confrontational.

EDR practitioners should be aware of their own personal type, as well as those of the other participants, and understand their reactions to, and effects upon, other participants.

Although there may be only a partial connection between maximizer and minimizer types and autocratic and cooperative styles, it is worth noting that minimizers will have communication challenges similar to autocratic managers. This is because people will receive limited information and have a hard time understanding how managers have heard and acted on their comments.

Maximizers may have similar communication challenges to cooperative managers. Their communications may seem so expansive that people have a hard time understanding and figuring out what is later wanted.

Chapter 11: An EDR Method That Works

Because we know a great deal about the social and psychological causes of environmental disputes, about how disputes tend to progress, and about the ways tools work to resolve disputes, we can adopt a prescriptive model for addressing disputes

The best model for EDR is a holistic-medical one

Obviously, practitioners have to use methods or techniques conducive to transformation. While particular techniques (such as telephone trees) might be useful for some resolution efforts, and expertise (such as mediators) might be useful for others, practitioners have to apply them within an overall methodological structure that works. The method has to be focused enough to achieve resolution and flexible enough to cover the broad range of disputes and participant values.

This chapter presents a method that can work. Like other elements of this book, the method is simple but the application can be complex. Not to worry though; a little dispute resolution work often goes a long way. And as former Secretary of State Colin Powell said, "*A positive attitude is a force multiplier*." So, EDR leaders with the will and skills to be successful can prevail.

A Dispute-Resolution Method that Works

I like the **"allopathic" medical model** for framing and explaining a workable dispute-resolution method. Allopathic refers to using targeted counter-measures to defeat disease and bring about health. It's what we experience at most traditional doctor's offices and hospitals.

Other medical models, such as **"holistic" or "preventive"** medicine, also apply to dispute resolution. Holistic medicine seeks to treat the whole person, not simply a particular disease.   The EDR method presented in this book is holistic in concept because of its focus on the entire dispute community, its emphasis on flexibility and inclusivity, and its intention to prevent dispute re-occurrence over time. As it is when holistic-medicine patients accept social and spiritual healing along with disease treatment, this EDR method can be made even more effective when disputants and other participants take charge of and lead dispute-resolving actions.

Preventative medicine seeks to adjust unhealthy living into healthy living, asking patients to make changes in diet and exercise, for instance. As with holistic medicine, preventative dispute practices are most effective when opponents learn and apply effective dispute-resolution skills that give communities life-long dispute "resistance" and a means to prevent dispute escalation.

One of the "preventative" things society is doing right now is teaching children to understand dispute-resolution choices and to serve as mediators at school and at home. They are also being taught to work effectively in teams and to find satisfaction in both personal and shared group outcomes. Through such mediums as team problem-solving competitions and brainstorming/visioning innovation courses, students are gaining some valuable dispute-resolution abilities.

Because of these efforts, unfortunately still too few in numbers, many mid-21st century adults will move through society with basic dispute-resolution skills well in hand. Even though numbers of trained people are lower than we might wish, the effects of these increased skills on American society are already beneficial because they are present among younger employees in the workplace.

Aside from training in dispute resolution skills, certain people with a strong intuitive sense of how to achieve environmental dispute resolution — environmental peace and justice — can simply step into a dispute and achieve great results. This ability seems to be a manifestation of their charisma, experience, innate understanding of the basis for disputes, commitment to other people, trust in others, self-confidence, and self-trust.

The value of these charismatic interveners to practitioners and opponents cannot be underestimated. At the same time, if the charismatic interveners are unable to sustain their involvement, relying on them for long-term results may be a mistake. Therefore, practitioners should augment their impact using the EDR models to build opponent and community capacity for the long haul.

An EDR Model That Works

 First **"Do no harm."** The principle of "no-harm" has many aspects, but, as mentioned in Chapter 9's proposed EDR Code of Conduct, one of the most important is how an EDR practitioner and EDR leaders must conduct themselves.

In medicine, in order to objectively and effectively serve the patient, the physician must set aside personal biases and focus her professional judgment on the patient's disease and treatment options. Likewise in EDR work, environmental peace and justice cannot be achieved if EDR practitioners and sponsors approach a dispute with the intention of taking sides, forcing outcomes, or otherwise causing injury or modification to values held by opponents. Practitioners look to develop credibility for themselves and for participants, legitimacy for the EDR concepts and efforts, and a community understanding of the likely "nurturing" uses of power.

Second, consult the opponents to develop a dispute history and an understanding of current conditions. As a part of this step in the process, you develop a sense of trends and consequences.

Third, diagnose the dispute stage and factors contributing to it and share that diagnosis. You further orient yourself by summarizing the history of the dispute and recent diagnostics. You also validate the diagnosis of current conditions, and then, you adjust participant understanding if necessary. Peer consultation with other practitioners and checking in with caring onlookers can help here, too.

Fourth, prescribe some actions to address the dispute and gain <u>informed consent</u>[49] for those actions from the opponents, if possible, before beginning work. Informed consent is sought from opponents, caring onlookers, and other participants after it is clear they understand likely outcomes if no EDR actions are taken. Actions should permit both rational and rationalizing opponents and participants to "buy in" to long-term, complete resolution.

Fifth, apply preventive and holistic measures to address and eliminate dispute recycling. Look for techniques and create opportunities to build EDR capacity into communities, individuals, and businesses.

Sixth, monitor and adjust actions as warranted while communicating regularly with disputants and others. Checking in with peers and caring onlookers is a good idea here, too.

Seventh, let go and move on; check back if agreed to with participants and re-frame the dispute if necessary.

Considerations Before Starting Work

As I head into a dispute-resolution effort, I have a "mental map" of what key issues exist and generally how those might be resolved through structural, compositional, or functional and relationship changes. Once work begins, I have always found that my understanding of the situation changes considerably, and I have to adjust quickly as the individual or group works toward an effective resolution. Some elements of my "map" may be quite accurate, but those are quickly augmented and modified by the thinking, emotions, and past interactions of the disputants and any participating onlookers.

Regardless of the evolution of my mental map, as the work on the dispute ebbs and flows, I keep my focus on the goal of dispute resolution that will lead to long-term environmental peace and justice. Otherwise, the dispute work can break down into a narrow and limited series of compromises and slow, incremental changes. These may please some of the advocates but offend others and, as half-measures and slow progress often are, mostly be unsatisfying to participants.

Government officials are prone to engage in placation because of the intensity of the issues or the threats of reprisal through political processes. Consequently, they will often

---

[49] For good reviews of informed consent see www.socialpsychology.org/consent and www.ipmp-bleiker.com

accept far less than resolution. So, government officials also benefit if the longer-term issues are dealt with effectively by the community at large.

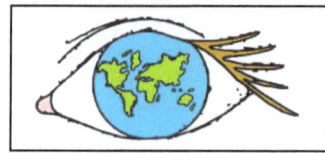

Completing the resolution process is not always a popular thing to do, and in our culture, the intentions of the resolution process may be misunderstood, but it is often far easier to achieve completion than people think. Rene Dubois' maxim, "*Think globally and act locally*," applies well in dispute-resolution work. As long as the localized, short-term components align towards the longer-term resolution and recovery outcomes, they will be far more effective and satisfying to the participants.

When dispute-resolution work has to be sustained for the long-term, there is always the question of whether institutions exist to follow through. Government is one obvious choice for sustaining an EDR resolution. And in fact, **when it comes to such structural issues as who will sustain wild lands for the long term, government and its partners are the preeminent choice**. When it comes to the sustaining cultural materials ("compositional" materials in the dispute sense), such as artifacts, books, and art, government and its partners may also play a role.

But when it comes to many less-formal elements, particularly inter-personal functions and relationships, government has less or no capacity. Personnel turnover, partisan politics, and changing program priorities make sustaining relationships difficult or impossible without structural support, and sustaining these relationships is challenging even when such support clearly exists in the form of laws, executive orders, charters, or treaties.

So, dispute-resolution communities may choose to **augment government efforts** with formal commissions or ad hoc committees to perpetuate compositional and functional or relationship commitments. These organizations can make sure the EDR agreements stay viable and actions proceed smoothly and long-term.

Organizational Leadership Considerations

Low Cost/ Single Issue Unpaid mediation over a fence-location issue	**Low Cost/Crisis** Red Cross volunteer relief effort after Haiti earthquake
High Cost/Single Issue Paid attorney intervention in fence-location issue	**High Cost/Crisis** FEMA/National Guard paid relief effort after hurricane Katrina

Once they adopt the medical model for EDR, people in top managerial and leadership roles have some dispute-management choices to make that directly affect organizational cost-efficiency and effectiveness.

In "quadratic" form, here is a simple way to think about dispute and cost considerations. As the "quadratic" figure shows, EDR leaders should think in terms of keeping costs minimized while making a measured and effective response to an environmental dispute. An issues-abatement effort such as the "fence-location" issue shown on the left side of the figure should not require a high-cost response, at least not initially. And as shown in the right side of the figure, even low-cost methods may serve for some responses in instances of full-blown conflicts and even crises.

For a broader overview on the efficacy of certain techniques, here is a more extensive representation of cost-benefit relationships previously shown in Chapter 1. This figure, which I've used for years in training and orientation sessions, shows the general relationship of satisfaction to cost by technique.

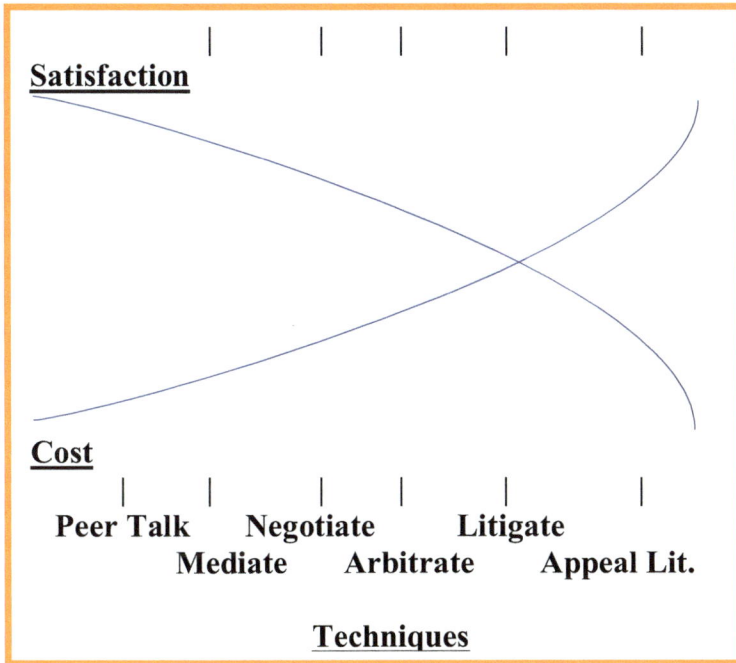

Satisfaction

Cost

| Peer Talk | Negotiate | Litigate |
| Mediate | Arbitrate | Appeal Lit. |

Techniques

EDR practitioners, public servants, and advocates should know that this relationship exists and understand that well-done EDR can minimize costs and increase likely satisfaction. The Practice book takes the basic allopathic-holistic model presented here and expands and details it so that managers can make appropriate selection of methods and means.

How Does Dispute Resolution Work Relate to Decision Making?

EDR is not explicitly a decision-making process, although it may lead to decisions or be incorporated into decision-making processes. Most decisions related to EDR will be process ones, particularly at the issues-abatement stage. At this stage, EDR may simply require fact-finding, improved communications, and relationship building. If environmental-policy or -management decisions are warranted to resolve disputes, two decision-making "moieties" exist for practitioners to consider: "**problem-solving/decision-making**" and "**visionary-opportunistic/decision-making**."

I have used Hans and Annemarie Bleiker's (IPMP) Augmentation Meta-Process for years because I was trained in it in graduate school, and although this process strongly promotes problem-solving as the basis for public decision making, it also permits visionary-opportunistic work as well. It is quite a good fit with implementations of National Forest Management Act and the Federal Land Planning and Management Act concepts, for example.

Other methods are more narrowly focused in one moiety or the other, including the National Environmental Policy Act (see Chapter 7) and state environmental analysis and clearance processes, which are primarily problem-solving in nature, whereas community

master planning, business-development plans, "zero-base" planning, and the Appreciative Inquiry (appreciativeinquiry.case.edu**) method are more focused on visionary-opportunistic decisions.**

EDR practitioners may consider whether a problem-solving, a visionary-opportunistic, or a combination approach will suffice to support any decisions to be made.

Problem-solving methods may have a more obvious value for work along the scandal pathway because they contribute more often to decisions that support the status quo. In other words, they tend to result in decisions that reflect incremental change from present conditions.

Problem-solving situations also represent real challenges because, as Paul Erdos (1913-1996) said, *"Problems worthy of attack prove their worth by fighting back."* Sometimes, problem-solving approaches are highly science- and data-dependent and may also be highly formalized. When this is the case, timeframes can be prolonged, and public participants sometimes exit because they are overwhelmed with data and process detail or, in their view, they cannot afford to invest enough time to make a difference.

Visionary-opportunistic methods tend to result in decisions that establish new conditions and can seek to promote utopian outcomes. Thus, these methods may have a more obvious value for the anarchy pathway because they help provide focus on the creation of a new social order or relationships.

Feasibility is a challenge for visionary-opportunistic methods. The founder of Federal Express, Fred Smith, was once told by a Yale professor regarding his student proposal for over-night delivery, *"The concept is interesting and well-formed, but in order to earn better than a "C", the idea must be feasible."* True. At some point, visionary-opportunistic ideas and decisions must meet this feasibility test. FedEx was a great idea and it works.

Sometimes, opponents and participants are wary of visionary-opportunistic work because it represents "pie-in-the-sky" thinking or threatening change. Practitioners should reassure folks with these concerns that all visionary or strategic ideas will eventually meet feasibility requirements through modeling, benchmarking to similar efforts completed by others, small-scale testing, or business planning.

Catastrophe pathway work tends to depend on pre-event problem-solving decisions for relief and response activities. Visionary-opportunistic methods may have been employed in advanced threat-response planning, for example, in conceiving and designing structures to prevent storm surge along a coastline as ocean levels rise driven by global warming.

Chapter 12: EDR Futures—Bringing EDR Mainstream

The world is filled with natural and human systems that exhibit both complexity and chaos, each working against and with the other

EDR structure, composition, and functions must be rethought and rebuilt by government and society if we are to save our planet and ourselves

---

Chapters 1-11 have given the reader an understanding of the origins of environmental disputes and some insights into how we might effectively resolve them. But really, as a society, we have just begun to define and understand EDR. One reason is that people rarely understand the social-political, psychological, ecological context for environmental disputes. Even more importantly, structural EDR elements, such as laws and regulations to require and govern EDR and ensure its effectiveness, are very basic or non-existent. These elements will appear in our government system only when Americans demand them.

For now, **the promise of EDR is clear, but the most effective ways to "mainstream" EDR is not**. As it was with ADR twenty-five years ago, some folks find the stated advantages of EDR speculative. Their "comfort" with the status quo and the advantages that zero-sum conflicts seem to hold for powerful people and organizations seem to make change unappealing.

Although it is not clear to us now, I believe that EDR will be very much a part of environmental management for the 21st Century. As Arthur Schopenhauer (1788-1860) said, *"All truth passes through three stages. First, it is ridiculed. Second, it is violently opposed. Third, it is accepted as being self-evident."*

We left the time of ridicule when Congress created the U.S. Institute for Environmental Conflict Resolution. We are still working with "violent opposition" in many forms now: censorship, active and persistent resistance from communities of place, tradition, interest, and fate, passive resistance by agency people, and open resistance from elected officials and media who based some of their political and business successes on engendering and perpetuating environmental conflicts..

This chapter helps define what future "self-evident" EDR policies and behaviors might look like — of what building a self-sustaining EDR culture at many scales might consist. Complex, adaptive, and relatively stable societies and cultures (versus degenerative, mal-adaptive, chaotic ones) exhibit beliefs that the attainment of environmental peace and justice enables their quality of physical and spiritual life. Moreover, they all accept the importance of defending their quality of life against threats to person, property, or individual rights.

Complex Systems and EDR

I pointed out in Chapter 4 that environmental disputes display many of the same characteristics as ecosystems, namely structure, composition, and functions or relationships. I also displayed how some of the aspects of environmental disputes at fit with ecological hierarchies.

I also find it useful to think of disputes and EDR in complexity and chaos terms. Instead of examples from nature, however, I prefer to keep this discussion simpler. So I will use concepts from Edgar Peters' work on complexity and chaos affecting financial markets[50] to help develop ideas for this chapter. The reason I chose Peters' work is that he has applied ecological concepts to human systems as I am doing in this book. And his ideas make a neat package for us to reflect on.

Complex systems have the following characteristics:

> Stability at global and other broad scales; potential chaos at site or local scales

> Apparent purpose, or a reason for being, including long-term survival

> Web of connections among system components – lots of communications and informal connections, but system "experiences," "knowledge," "values," and "choices" are decentralized and broadly shared

> Connections that allow for two-way communications and feedback

> Two-way communications and feedback that create potential and energy for change and adaptation

> Change and adaptation behaviors that are decentralized and compete with one another

> Competition combined with random events that allow one set of behaviors to succeed when others fail

> Rules that adaptively regulate behavior

Chaotic systems have the following characteristics:

> Instability at broad scales but stability at local scales

> No apparent purpose except control or change to suit one set of values

---

[50] *Complexity, Risk, and Financial Markets. Peters, Edgar E. John Wiley & Sons, NY, NY. 1999. and Fractal Market Analysis: Applying Chaos Theory to Investment and Economics.* Peters, Edgar E., John Wiley & Sons, Inc., NY, NY. 1994.

Centralized force or unified control of system components with connections and communications from the force or center outward

Connections that emphasize one-way communications and limited feedback if any

Change to increase control or the dominance of values and resist adaptation

Centralized change with competition suppressed or controlled and random events excluded as much as possible

Rules that rigidly regulate behavior

Complex systems manifest survival and allow for adaptive change at local and regional scales. National- or global-scale stability is an attribute of local adaptability. Complex systems accept risk, uncertainty, and random chaotic events as the necessary means to adapt and change through competition.

Chaotic systems manifest crisis and dispute recycling because they do not allow for adaptive change. National- or global-scale instability is a characteristic of local control and chaos. Chaotic systems attempt to control uncertainty, risk, and events and to create consistency and reliability at all scales, but because this control is impossible, they become brittle and break down.

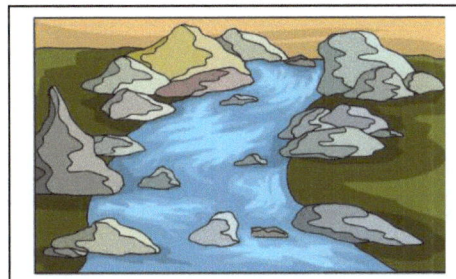

Think of a large rock in the middle of a river. The river roars and flows around the rock, sometimes more during spring runoff and sometimes lazily in the middle of winter. The rock appears to be stable, unmovable. However, as the Grand Canyon demonstrates, the river will eventually prevail as it wears rock down to sand or silt and carries the debris away.

It is perhaps counter-intuitive, but the river represents a complex system that is adaptable and survives over time. The rock represents a chaotic element that is mal-adaptive and fails over time. The river prevails in its strength, flexibility, and movement. The rock fails in its vulnerability, inflexibility, and rigidity.

To have a successful, adaptable EDR system, **we should design human EDR systems that emulate natural systems and develop EDR systems that are simultaneously complex, cooperative, adaptable, and intensely competitive**.

Why Current EDR Systems Must Be Rethought to Promote Adaptation or Eventually Die

Reflective of governmental laws and traditions, current, mostly tacit EDR systems are somewhat chaotic, displaying brittle and mal-adaptive characteristics. In the public-involvement sense, agencies and non-governmental organizations often have many choices of process and technique supported by law.

However, as regards formal or quasi-formal EDR processes, those same entities often have few choices and wind up instigating litigation or legislation.

So, because government entities are limited in what EDR they can do, citizens undertake EDR unilaterally. They may appeal to elected or appointed officials, petition the courts, or seek change through anarchy in some form. Informal means, such as finding a caring onlooker to serve as a mediator or developing collaborative groups, lack legitimacy and credibility for many people because resolutions, unless somehow legally sanctioned, are not enforceable. Thus people are forced to use zero-sum institutions in many cases that often lead them to higher-cost, lower-satisfaction outcomes.

The emergence and rise to prominence of mediation as a court-sanctioned dispute-resolution technique is an example of society and its institutions recognizing the potential (and the need) for adaptation. Mediation would never have emerged in this way except that processes that are more formal, like litigation, proved to be too chaotic — too often expensive, confusing, formulaic, ineffective, time consuming, and ultimately unsatisfying --for effective resolution work.

Alan Kay said, *"The best way to predict the future is to invent it."*

So, to move EDR work into a complex-system approach would be desirable. If we examine the characteristics of complex systems and adapt EDR to meet those characteristics, something like this broad description emerges:

Complex EDR systems would have the following characteristics:

Apparent purpose, or a reason for being, including long-term survival

> **Congress and state legislatures would give EDR a stated purpose and legal standing promoting environmental peace and justice, consistent with Constitutional imperatives for peace and justice overall**

Web of connections among system components – lots of communications and informal connections but system "experiences," "knowledge," "values," and "choices" are decentralized

> **EDR means and methods would be widely available to opponents and practitioners, with experiences, knowledge, values, and choices widely decentralized**

Connections that allow for two-way communications and feedback

Legislators, groups, and individuals involved with EDR would have several communications means and the potential to provide feedback about how things work and relative effectiveness

Two-way communications and feedback that create potential and energy for change and adaptation

Changes and adaptations in EDR, particularly at local levels, would be shared widely and celebrated and local communities would demand EDR from public officials

Change and adaptation behaviors that are decentralized and compete with one another

Local EDR efforts reflective of local values, choices, and knowledge would be available to other places, and one of the national rules would be that local EDR efforts could not be restricted to local preferences only

Competition combined with random events that allow one set of behaviors to succeed when others fail

The open competition of EDR ideas and behaviors combined with local circumstances and participants will create a model for successful adaptation and growth

Rules that adaptively regulate behavior

Along with a stated purpose for EDR, Congress, state legislatures, government agencies and non-governmental organizations promulgate rules and norms designed for flexibility and adaptation

Stability at global and other broad scales; potential chaos at site or local scales

New rules would not be promulgated if some local EDR efforts failed. EDR would be governed by general rules and norms nationally, and disputes would be settled at local levels using local methods that met the general rules and norms; local settlements could not be "elevated" but evaluations consistent with the rules and norms could be made for long-term adaptive purposes. EDR settlements would have to be consistent with existing environmental and other laws

This change would be an enormous shift towards an adaptive and successful approach – similar to what Pieter Glasbergen means when he refers to EDR as a part of "network management."[51] As local uncertainty went up and responsibility became localized, EDR practitioners would find engagement of dispute and dispute-resolution communities more energetic, focused, and effective.

Because national and state rules and norms would require the engagement of all affected interests, as well as maximum flexibility in selecting techniques to reflect local culture, the long-term potential for recycled value-based disputes would go down as local people implemented settlements with little delay.

Eventually, legislative bodies could rework many national and state environmental laws to reflect the same adaptive complex-systems approach. Decision makers could leave centralized, one-size-fits-all, command-and-control environmental laws behind and allow adaptive ideas to compete across America. Congress could replace currently chaotic and mal-adaptive laws, such as the Endangered Species Act and the Equal Access to Justice Act, with adaptive measures aimed at successful environmental management at all political scales and jurisdictions.

The authors of *Contemporary Conflict Resolution* make the point that an essential element to building any complex, adaptive system will be the development of an "ethical universalism."[52] In the EDR sense, this will mean that, in addition to more flexible dispute resolution laws, environmental dispute and dispute-resolution communities must establish an ethic that makes EDR a cornerstone of environmental decision-making, management, protection, and use.

What Would a Better-Defined and Effective Nationwide EDR System Look Like?

As in architecture, the **form** of a nationwide EDR system should follow its **function**. We should aim for a functionality that has high potential for bringing environmental peace and justice to environmental disputants at resolution-appropriate time and spatial scales. The optimum EDR system would allow dispute-resolution communities to form, to be successful, and then to dissolve, only to be replaced by a new dispute-resolution community if and when new disputes emerged – a system complex and adaptable enough to deal with disputes over any resource at any scale.

Moving to the more specific, I **have some pragmatic fixes** I believe Americans should consider:

- **Eliminate institutional supports for zero-sum behavior in environmental disputes**; for example, eliminate (or significantly limit access to) the courts and end the use of the Equal Access to Justice Act by environmental litigants

---

[51] *Managing Environmental Disputes*. Glasbergen, Pieter. Kluwer Academic Publishers, Boston, MA. 1995.
[52] *Contemporary Conflict Resolution: The prevention, management, and transformation of deadly conflicts, Second Edition*. Ramsbotham, Oliver, Woodhouse, Tom, and Miall, Hugh. Polity Press, Malden, MA. 2005. p.251.

- **Create institutional supports for positive-sum behavior towards environmental disputes**; for example, pass new (or amend existing) laws that promote the use of a broad spectrum of EDR techniques, including mediation, arbitration, and reconciliation-compensation at all scales. These laws would also promote effective experimentation and adaptation at appropriate time and geographic scales, and the sharing of information about EDR successes and failures worldwide.

- **Provide funding and other economic incentives for dispute resolutions that meet statutory timeframes**. For example, land- and resource-management agencies would receive increased funding if they conducted their business to achieve effective EDR. Advisory or resource boards working with them would be able to help guide the focus of the funding and resource management, to a greater or lesser degree, based on the effectiveness of their EDR efforts.

- **Create a single-focus "environmental" court system** (similar to the federal Court of Claims); make access possible but a last resort after less formal resolution efforts, undertaken in good faith, have failed; support the Environmental Courts with panels of agency and independent scientists and management experts to which the courts must defer in matters of environmental science and management, not law

- According to their respective ownership and authorities, **Congress and state legislatures combine existing environmental-regulation and land- and resource-management agencies and/or require co-management at all ecological scales**. They then create new agencies or management boards made up of existing agency representatives supported by cross-sectional resource advisory and governance boards at the eco-regional scale. Within eco-regional boundaries,[53] public-private partnerships and joint conservation agreements are encouraged but not required. Eco-regional partnerships are encouraged to participate in national and international agreements on production, protection, and mitigation, such as trading in carbon or wetland credits.

- **Create and train a cadre of EDR practitioners** (similar to the Federal Mediation and Conciliation Service) and develop a nationwide network of private EDR experts (an expansion of the U.S. Institute for Environmental Conflict Resolution's mediator/facilitator-focused registry)

- **Legislate that EDR be made a part of all federal, state, and local environmental managers' job descriptions and performance requirements**

- **Pass "sunshine" laws that require all natural resources agencies to operate their public decision-making efforts in a transparent, "fishbowl" manner**;

---

[53] In addition to other information on eco-regions, see also *Unified Ecoregions of Alaska: 2001*. Nowacki et al.USGS. 2001

allow agencies broad authority to determine how such transparency may be achieved

- **Support the development of EDR curricula in all natural resources schools nationwide**; provide incentives for conservation education partnerships that train EDR right along with elements that stress understanding natural systems

- **Offer citizen orientation and EDR "basic-training" opportunities nationwide through a consortium of colleges, universities, schools, government agencies, and supportive non-profit groups**

- **Create incentives for local EDR sponsorship through county commissioners, courts, chambers of commerce, or other concerned and caring onlookers**

- **Create guidelines and incentives for large-scale multi-jurisdictional EDR to deal with multi-state, national, and international disputes**

While honoring the environmental movement's first wave, making these changes would refine the second wave "legislate-regulate-watchdog-and-punish" model and move it away from its chaotic aspects. The changes would connect EDR and environmental management to the third and fourth waves of the environmental movement, specifically, emphasizing public-private partnerships and supporting interconnected and international performance.

Duty, Honor, Country, World

Builders of a strong EDR culture in the U.S would be well served to adopt a vision for a flexible, complex, adaptive system.

I am a former member of the "nuclear" Air Force, skilled in maintaining nuclear-tipped missiles to support the Mutually Assured Destruction doctrine during the Cold War. My work was scary, hard, and focused, but it was not always inspiring.

In doing that vital defense work, my resource management work for the Forest Service, and in contemplating EDR for the future, I found, and still find, inspiration in the words that General of the Army Douglas MacArthur delivered in his farewell address to the cadets at the U.S. Military Academy on May 12, 1962.

> *"Duty," "honor," "country" — those three hallowed words reverently dictate what you want to be, what you can be, what you will be. They are your rallying point to build courage when courage seems to fail, to regain faith when there seems to be little cause for faith, to create hope when hope becomes forlorn.*
>
> *Unhappily, I possess neither that eloquence of diction, that poetry of imagination, nor that brilliance of metaphor to tell you all that they mean.*

The unbelievers will say they are but words, but a slogan, but a flamboyant phrase. Every pedant, every demagogue, every cynic, every hypocrite, every troublemaker, and, I am sorry to say, some others of an entirely different character, will try to downgrade them even to the extent of mockery and ridicule.

But these are some of the things they build. They build your basic character. They mold you for your future roles as the custodians of the nation's defense. They make you strong enough to know when you are weak, and brave enough to face yourself when you are afraid.

They teach you to be proud and unbending in honest failure, but humble and gentle in success, not to substitute words for action, not to seek the path of comfort, but to face the stress and spur of difficulty and challenge; to learn to stand up in the storm, but to have compassion on those who fall; to master yourself before you seek to master others, to have a heart that is clean, a goal that is high; to learn to laugh, yet never forget how to weep; to reach into the future, yet never neglect the past; to be serious, yet never take yourself too seriously; to be modest so that you will remember the simplicity of true greatness; the open mind of true wisdom, the meekness of true strength.

They give you a temperate will, a quality of imagination, a vigor of the emotions, a freshness of the deep springs of life, a temperamental predominance of courage over timidity, an appetite for adventure over love of ease.

They create in your heart the sense of wonder, the unfailing hope of what next, and the joy and inspiration of life....

If you accept the duty and honor of doing EDR work for the country and the world, perhaps these words resonate for you and inspire you, too.

Chapter 13: Businesses and EDR

By incorporating EDR into strategic business plans and operations, businesses can achieve greater profitability over a longer time through greater market share and lowered costs

I have worked for retail, construction, service, and consulting businesses. I have owned and operated my own small businesses, met payroll, and developed and lost markets. So, I speak with some background in business management.

EDR makes **fundamental business sense for both "top line" and "bottom line" business considerations**. Top-line considerations affecting sales such as customer confidence, market acceptance, production volume, consumer targeting, and product quality benefit from successful EDR. Businesses that practice successful EDR have better public image and support, broader potential for joint ventures and partnerships, and greater potential for expansion even under tight environmental regulations and agency scrutiny. Timber mills using environmentally certified feedstock reflect this truth.

Businesses that prefer environmental "wars" and the communities that back them tend to lose market share and fail over the mid- and long-term.

EDR also benefits the bottom line, controlling costs in many aspects of product production or service provision. Cost control occurs in speed of production and to-market delivery, reduced or eliminated needs for advocacy, and reduced re-tooling and re-development cycles, among many considerations.

More cash flow and reduced costs throughout means increased profits and expansion potential.

Case Examples from Alaska

I had the privilege of working with several excellent mining companies and individual miners while working for the Forest Service in Alaska. Two stand out as examples of EDR and its relationship to business success.

Noranda Mining developed the Greens Creek property on Admiralty Island in Northern Southeast Alaska in the 1980's. The target mineral was zinc but the ore body contained massive amounts of silver and gold. In fact, the mine eventually became the biggest silver-producing mine in North America and one of their assays showed 56 ounces of gold to the ton.

Noranda Mining built EDR into their development plan from the outset. Not only did they determine to comply with or exceed every environmental quality law and regulation, they also sat down with the initial chief critics of the mine and worked out extra standards beyond statutory requirements, such as not creating a mine-mouth community and managing tailings extra carefully during production and then returning them underground at the end of production.

The Greens Creek mine went ahead with virtually no delays and benefitted the City and Borough of Juneau economically over three decades. When the day came in the 1990's that the ore body outside the Admiralty Island Wilderness had been developed and operators signaled that they might have to cease operations, Congress modified the Wilderness Act to permit the operators to mine the remainder of the ore beneath the Wilderness itself. The law passed with the support of Alaska Native and environmental groups.

In contrast, starting in the 1970's U.S. Borax, a subsidiary of Rio Tinto Corporation wanted to develop a molybdenum mine in southern Southeast Alaska near Ketchikan at Quartz Hill. The rich ore body contains about one-tenth of the potential world's supply (about 1.5 billion tons) of the mineral which is used in making high-strength steel. The proposed mine sits within, but is not a part of, the Misty Fiords National Monument. By the early 1990's U.S Borax had spent perhaps $100 million trying to develop the mine which, because of falling worldwide molybdenum prices, has ended, at least temporarily.

From the outset, U.S. Borax took an adversarial approach to working with environmental compliance agencies and the public, battling each in the media, in political arenas, and in the courts. The mine never opened and the people of Ketchikan, so hopeful of economic expansion and stability, were disappointed. The cost to Rio Tinto Corporation in unproductive private capital is huge. The cost in public funds, economic stability, and political energy is equally huge. Perhaps some of these costs can be turned to benefit and profits later—we just don't yet know.

I hope the Quartz Hill Mine eventually opens and provides all the benefits that it offers to Ketchikan, Alaska, and the world. But I predict that the mine will incur unnecessary operating costs due to public and agency scrutiny and environmental-compliance conflicts.

EDR and Business Plans

I recommend that all business involved in environmental-compliance issues or natural resource development build EDR into their business plans. Businesses should consider a step-by-step review of existing plans or the development of all-new plans.

Lately many companies have adopted "green" strategies for product development and delivery and for marketing. Greening refers to offering products or services with few or no negative environmental effects and often offer environmental enhancement opportunities related to sales such as planting a tree for each product sold.

Often these green business strategies do not go far enough to consider EDR aspects. Similar to the discussion of public policies and procedures in Chapter 12, businesses can look at potential EDR structure, composition, and function or relationships and craft corporate EDR policies and procedures to ensure long-term business success.

Complex EDR business systems would have the following characteristics:

Apparent purpose, or a reason for being, including long-term survival

> **Corporations and private companies would give EDR a stated purpose in their missions and business practices, going beyond ISO 14000 and LEED certifications**

Web of connections among system components – lots of communications and informal connections but system "experiences," "knowledge," "values," and "choices" are decentralized

> **EDR means and methods would be valued and discussed widely throughout the company, with experiences, knowledge, values, and choices widely decentralized**

Connections that allow for two-way communications and feedback

> **Owners and employees involved with EDR would have several communications means and the potential to provide feedback about how things work and relative effectiveness**

Two-way communications and feedback that create potential and energy for change and adaptation

> **Changes and adaptations in EDR, particularly at local levels, would be shared widely and celebrated and company owners and boards would require effective EDR from management**

Change and adaptation behaviors that are decentralized and compete with one another

> **Local EDR efforts reflective of local values, choices, and knowledge would be available to other places, and one of the company rules would be that local EDR efforts could not be restricted to local preference only**

Competition combined with random events that allow one set of behaviors to succeed when others fail

> **The open competition of EDR ideas and behaviors combined with**

local circumstances and participants will create a model for successful adaptation and growth within the company and its partners

Rules that adaptively regulate behavior

Along with a stated purpose for EDR, companies promulgate rules and norms designed for flexibility and adaptation

Stability at global and other broad scales; potential chaos at site or local scales

New rules would not be promulgated if some local EDR efforts failed. EDR would be governed by general rules and norms corporately, and disputes would be settled at local levels using local methods that met the general rules and norms; local settlements could not be "elevated" but evaluations consistent with the rules and norms could be made for long-term adaptive purposes. EDR settlements would have to be consistent with existing environmental and other laws and company guidelines

I believe companies can achieve ever-higher profitability by building EDR into business plans.

Appendix A -- National Hierarchical Framework of Ecological Units

By: David T. Cleland, Peter E. Avers, W. Henry McNab, Mark E. Jensen, Robert G. Bailey, Thomas King, and Walter E. Russell[54]

ECOLOGICAL UNIT DESIGN

The primary purpose for delineating ecological units is to identify land and water areas at different levels of resolution that have similar capabilities and potentials for management. Depending on scale, ecological units are designed to exhibit similar patterns in: (1) potential natural communities, (2) soils, (3) hydrologic function, (4) landform and topography, (5) lithology, (6) climate, and (7) natural processes such as nutrient cycling, productivity, succession, and natural disturbance regimes associated with flooding, wind, or fire.

It should be noted that climatic regime is an important boundary criterion for ecological units, particularly at broad scales. In fact, climate, as modified by topography, is the dominant criterion at upper levels. Other factors, such as geomorphic process, soils, and potential natural communities, take on equal or greater importance than climate at lower levels.

It follows, then, that ecological units are differentiated and maps designed by multiple components, including climate, physiography, geology, soils, water, and potential natural communities. These components may be analyzed individually, and then combined, or multiple factors may be simultaneously evaluated to classify ecological types, which are then used in ecological unit design. The first option may be increasingly used as geographic information systems (GIS) become more available. The interrelationships among independently defined components, however, will need to be carefully evaluated, and the results of layering component maps may need to be adjusted to identify units that are both ecologically significant and meaningful to management. When various disciplines cooperate in devising integrated ecological units, products from existing resource component maps can be modified, and integrated interpretations can be developed (Avers and Schlatterer, 1991).

Ecological unit inventories are generally designed and conducted in cooperation with the Natural Resource Conservation Service, Agricultural Experiment Stations of Land Grant Universities, Bureau of Land Management, and other appropriate state and federal agencies. Mapping conventions and soil classification meet standards of the National Cooperative Soil Survey.

---

[54]Ecosystem Management: Applications for Sustainable Forest and Wildlife Resources, Mark S. Boyce and Alan Haney, editors. Yale University Press, New Haven & London. 1997. pp 181-200. See also, Ecological Subregions of the United States: Section Descriptions, McNab, W. Henry and Avers, Peter E. USDA Forest Service. 1994

Table 1. National hierarchy of ecological units

Planning and analysis scale	Ecological Units	Purpose, objectives, and general use
Ecoregion Global Continental Regional	Domain Division Province	Broad applicability for modeling and sampling. Strategic planning and assessment. International planning.
Subregion	Section Subsection	Strategic, multi-forest, statewide, and multi-agency analysis and assessment.
Landscape	Landtype association	Forest or area-wide planning, and watershed analysis.
Land unit	Landtype Landtype phase	Project and management area planning and analysis.
Hierarchy can be expanded by user to smaller geographical areas and more detailed ecological units if needed.		Very detailed project planning.

CLASSIFICATION FRAMEWORK

The National Ecological Unit Hierarchy is presented in Tables 1, 2, and 3. The hierarchy is based on concepts and terminology developed by numerous scientists and resource managers (Hills 1952, Crowley 1967, Wertz and Arnold 1972, Rowe 1980, Allen and Starr 1982, Barnes et al. 1982, Forman and Godron 1986, Bailey 1987, Meentemeyer and Box 1987, Gallant et al. 1989, Cleland et al. 1992). The following is an overview of the differentiating criteria used in the development of the ecological units. Table 2 summarizes the principal criteria used at each level in the hierarchy.

Table 2. Principal map unit design criteria of ecological units.

Ecological unit	Principal map unit design criteria
Domain	Broad climatic zones or groups (e.g., dry, humid, tropical)
Division	Regional climatic types (Koppen 1931, Trewatha 1968) Vegetational affinities (e.g., prairie or forest) Soil order
Province	Dominant potential natural vegetation (Kuchler 1964) Highlands or mountains with complex vertical climate-vegetation-soil zonation
Section	Geomorphic province, geologic age, stratigaphy, lithology Regional climatic data Phases of soil orders, suborders, or great groups Potential natural vegetation Potential natural communities (PNC) (FSH 2090)
Subsection	Geomorphic process, surficial geology, lithology Phases of soil orders, suborders, or great groups Subregional climatic data PNC—formation or series
Landtype association	Geomorphic process, geologic formation, surficial geology, and elevation Phases of soil subgroups, families, or series Local climate PNC—series, subseries, plant associations
Landtype	Landform and topography (elevation, aspect, slope gradient, and position) Phases of soil subgroups, families, or series Rock type, geomorphic process PNC—plant associations

Landtype phase	Phases of soil subfamilies or series
	Landform and slope position
	PNC—plant associations or phases

Note: The criteria listed are broad categories of environmental and landscape components. The actual classes of components chosen for designing map units depends on conditions and relative importance of factors within respective geographic areas.

Table 3. Map scale and polygon size of ecological units.

Ecological unit	*Map scale range*	*General polygon size*
Domain	1:30,000,000 or smaller	1,000,000s of square miles
Division	1:30,000,000 to 1:7,500,000	100,000s of square miles
Province	1:15,000,000 to 1:5,000,000	10,000s of square miles
Section	1:7,500,000 to 1:3,500,000	1,000s of square miles
Subsection	1:3,500,000 to 1:250,000	10s to low 1,000s of square miles
Landtype association	1:250,000 to 1:60,000	1,000s to 10,000s of acres
Landtype	1:60,000 to 1:24,000	100s to 1,000s of acres
Landtype phase	1:24,000 or larger	<100 acres

Ecoregion Scale

At the Ecoregion scale, ecological units are recognized by differences in global, continental, and regional climatic regimes and gross physiography. The basic assumption is that climate governs energy and moisture gradients, thereby acting as the primary control over more localized ecosystems. Three levels of ecoregions, adapted from Bailey (1980), are identified in the hierarchy:

1. *Domains,* subcontinental divisions of broad climatic similarity, such as lands that have the dry climates defined by Koppen (1931), which are affected by latitude and global atmospheric conditions. For example, the climate of the Polar Domain is controlled by arctic air masses, which create cold, dry environments where summers are short. In contrast, the climate of the Humid Tropical Domain is influenced by equatorial air masses and there is no winter season. Domains are also characterized by broad

differences in annual precipitation, evapotranspiration, potential natural vegetation, and biologically significant drainage systems. The four Domains are named according to the principal climatic descriptive features: Polar, Dry, Humid Temperate, and Humid Tropical.

2. *Divisions,* subdivisions of domains determined by isolating areas of definite vegetational affinities (for example, prairie or forest) that fall within the same regional climate, generally at the level of the basic types of Koppen (1931) as modified by Trewartha (1968). Divisions are delineated according to: (a) the amount of water deficit (which subdivides the Dry Domain into semi-arid, steppe, or arid desert), and (b) the winter temperatures, which have an important influence on biological and physical processes and the duration of any snow cover. This temperature factor is the basis of distinction between temperate and tropical/subtropical dry regions. Divisions are named for the main climatic regions they delineate, such as steppe, savannah, desert, Mediterranean, marine, and tundra.

3. *Provinces,* climatic subzones, controlled primarily by continental weather patterns such as length of dry season and duration of cold temperatures. Provinces are also characterized by similar soil orders. The climatic subzones are evident as extensive areas of similar potential natural vegetation such as those mapped by Kuchler (1964). Provinces are named typically using a binomial system consisting of a geographic location and vegetative type such as Bering Tundra, California Dry-Steppe and Eastern Broadleaf Forests (Bailey et al. 1985).

Highland areas that exhibit altitudinal vegetation zonation and that have the climatic regime (seasonality of energy and moisture) of adjacent lowlands are classified as provinces (Bailey et al. 1985). The climatic regime of the surrounding lowlands can be used to infer the climate of the highlands. For example, in the Mediterranean division along the Pacific Coast, the seasonal pattern of precipitation is the same for the lowlands and highlands except that the mountains receive about twice the quantity. The provinces are named for the lower-elevation and upper-elevation (subnival) belts, for example, Rocky Mountain forest-alpine meadows.

Subregional Scale

Subregions are characterized by combinations of climate, geomorphic process, topography, and stratigraphy that influence moisture availability and exposure to radiant solar energy, which in turn directly control hydrologic function, soil-forming processes, and potential natural community distributions. Sections and Subsections are the two ecological units mapped at this scale.

*1. Section*s, broad areas of similar sub-regional climate, geomorphic process, stratigraphy, geologic origin, topography, and drainage networks. Such areas are often inferred by relating geologic maps to potential natural vegetation "series" groupings such as those mapped by Kuchler (1964). In recent years, numerical analyses of weather station and remotely sensed climatic information have assisted in determining Section boundaries. Boundaries of some sections approximate geormorphic provinces (for example, Blue Ridge) as recognized by geologists. Section names generally describe the predominant geomorphic type or feature upon which the ecological unit delineation is based, such as Flint Hills, Great Lakes Morainal, Bluegrass Hills, Appalachian Piedmont.

2. Subsections, smaller areas within Sections with similar surficial geology, lithology, geomorphic process, soil groups, subregional climate, and potential natural communities. Subsection boundaries usually correspond with discrete changes in geomorphology. Names of Subsections are usually derived from geologic features, such as Plainfield sand dune, Tipton till plain, and granite hills.

Landscape Scale

At the landscape scale, ecological units are defined by general topography, geomorphic process, surficial geology, associations of soil families, and potential natural communities, patterns, and local climates (Forman and Godron 1986). These factors affect biotic distributions, hydrologic function, natural disturbance regimes, and general land use. Local landform patterns become apparent at this level in the hierarchy, and differences among units are usually obvious to on-the-ground observers. At this level, terrestrial features and processes may also have a strong influence on ecological characteristics of aquatic habitats (Platts 1979, Ebert et al. 1991).

Landtype association ecological units represent this scale in the hierarchy. These are groupings of landtypes or subdivisions of subsections based on similarities in geomorphic process, geologic rock types, soil complexes, stream types, lakes, wetlands, subseries or plant association vegetation communities. Repeatable patterns of soil complexes and plant communities are useful in delineating map units at this level. Names of Landtype Associations are often derived from geomorphic history and vegetation community.

Land Unit Scale

At the basic land unit scale, ecological units are designed and mapped in the field based on properties of local topography, rock types, soils, and potential natural vegetation. These factors influence the structure and composition of plant communities, hydrologic function, and basic land capability. Landtypes and landtype phases are the ecological units mapped at this scale.

1. Landtypes, subdivisions of landtype associations or groupings of landtype phases based on similarities in soils, landform, rock type, geomorphic process, and plant associations. Land surface form that influences hydrologic function (for example, drainage density, dissection, and relief) is often used to delineate different landtypes in mountainous terrain. Valley bottom characteristics (for example, confinement) are commonly used in establishing riparian landtype map units. Names of landtypes include an abiotic and biotic component (USDA Forest Service Handbook 2090.11).

2. Landtype Phase, subdivisions of Landtypes based on topographic criteria (for example, slope-shape, steepness, aspect, position), hydrologic characteristics, associations and consociations of soil taxa, and plant associations and phases that influence or reflect the microclimate and productivity of a site. Landtype phases are often established based on interrelationships between soil characteristics and potential natural communities.In riparian mapping, landtype phases may be established to delineate different stream-type environments (Herrington and Dunham, 1967). Naming is similar to landtypes.

The Landtype Phase is the smallest ecological unit recognized in the hierarchy. However, even smaller units may need to be delineated for very detailed project planning at large scales (Table 1). Map design criteria depend on project objectives

Appendix B -- A Rationality Exercise and Discussion

Joe has inherited a lot of money and is willing to contribute that money to environmental causes. He is very passionate about these causes and is committed to funding them with his resources.

I am operating a fund-raising organization that represents several environmental and conservation groups. After talking to Joe and getting an understanding of his values, I find out Joe has the following preferences:

1. Joe will give me $100,000 more for "save-the-seals" causes than for "save-the whales" causes.
2. Joe will give me $100,000 more for "save-the-redwoods" causes than for "save-the-seals" causes.
3. Joe will give me $100,000 more for "save-the-whales" causes than for "save-the-redwoods" causes.

I know this is irrational because Joe's "scale" is actually "circular." He cannot articulate a "good," "better," "best" description for the causes. If I were unscrupulous, I could get all of Joe's money. Here is how:

1. I get Joe to give me $100,000 for saving whales.
2. Next, I point out to Joe that he wants to save seals more than he wants to save whales. He kindly gives me $200,000 more to save the seals, so I have $300,000 total.
3. Next, I point out to Joe that he wants to save redwoods more than he wants to save seals. He kindly gives me $300,000 more for saving redwoods, so I have $600,000 total.
4. I now point out to Joe that he prefers to save whales before saving redwoods. He kindly gives me $400,000 more for saving whales, and I now have $500,000 for the whales and $200,000 for seals and $300,000 for redwoods for a total of $1,000,000.
5. I continue this cycle until I have all of his money committed to the three causes by preying on his irrational preferences.

The circular nature of his preferences means he has no end to his "scale," no top or bottom, no beginning or end to his preference ranking. Knowing this, I can deprive him of all of his worldly resources; Joe is irrational and cannot cope with the world.

The sidebar offers an extreme example, but in dispute management, the notion of "irrational" refers to someone who cannot state their preferences in a manner that will allow them to adapt and survive — they are dysfunctional and maladaptive at some level. I have encountered a few such folks in almost 30 years of practice, and I have guided and guarded their rights and interests carefully.

*I submit that every party to a dispute who can scale their preferences is **rational**,* regardless of whether other people share their values and preference scales or not.

Groups display rational sets of values and preferences just as individuals do, consistent with their group mission and focus. In some respect, therefore, groups act like individuals, but because group members have their own unique values and preferences, groups can have a tendency to gridlock over stating a group position on complex issues.

Sometimes groups have to issue a preference based on a value held by the majority and also a "dissenting" preference based on a value held by a minority. This is also rational behavior because it states preference scales for sub-groups when a unanimous group position is not possible. The U.S. Supreme Court and other high courts often follow this pattern.

The concept of rationality rests on a person's or a group's ability to logically rank options using an internally consistent preference scale. This concept has three practical tests. The person or group must be able to rigorously:

1. If not perfectly, understand the consequences associated with each option as it is ranked or scaled according to preference,

2. Define the differences in preference between each option and all other options,

3. Rank each option on several different preference scales, evaluating several simultaneous relative differences and similarities.

Following this concept, Joe would have to:

1. Understand how contributing to each environmental cause (seals, whales, or redwoods) satisfies his desire to contribute to real conditions (i.e., more and healthier seals, whales, and redwoods); although not perfectly, Joe must understand all of the consequences of his contributions.

2. Define his relative preference for one cause compared to all others (ranking seals to both whales and redwoods, then whales to both seals and redwoods, then redwoods to both seals and whales) to arrive at an accurate scale ranking of preferences; Joe must rigorously compare all options to one another so that he can create an accurate preference scale.

3. Taking elements 1 and 2 together, compare consequences and scale rankings as well as evaluate related information about such items as his cash flow, effects from America's international money interest and currency-trade values, and the credibility of each "save-the…" group; if Joe creates a ranked set of preferences this way and does so without ties, he will have

accomplished a rational "forced ranking" of his preferences, displaying ordinal numbers (1st, 2nd, 3rd) and can act on that preference scale.

Forced ranking can be accomplished by an individual or a group. Because groups are apt to represent many diverse value preference scales, generating the forced ranked list will take quite a bit longer than for an individual.

Rationality implies an adequate level of analytic skill and rigorous application. In the example, Joe's apparent irrationality could be the result of a lack of these skills. Another reason could be that Joe may also be temporarily impaired by emotion, liquor or other influences.

Joe may also have a preference scale that is not clear or quite different than other people's preference scales. He may want to give his money away because he fears or dislikes the responsibility that having to manage it implies, and he may not be willing to share that set of values with us.

At the end of the day, rational people act in ways that maximally optimize attainment of their values and preference scales. This means that they understand what they value and can compare options to achieving those values.

Appendix C – Principal Publications by James Caplan

Unless otherwise noted, Caplan was sole author of the following publications:

- Umpqua National Forest Mission, Vision, Principles, and Management Guidelines 2001-2002 [co-author with forest management team, lead]

- Alaska Region Strategic Priorities, Alaska Natives Emphasis Item, December 2000 [co-author, lead]

- Alaska Region Strategies for "Collaborative Stewardship," "Budget," and "Integrated Information," August 1996-97, [co-author, lead]

- "New Perspectives for Sustainable Natural Resources Management", Ecological Applications, August 1992 [co-author]

- "Striding into Elephant Country: Exploring New Ground for Planning and Management in Protected Areas," The George Wright FORUM, Spring 1992

- "Sustaining Communities Through Sustained Ecosystems: Experience from the Bridger-Teton National Forest Land and Resource Management Plan in Northwestern Wyoming" to the Western Planners Conference, 1992

- "New Perspectives in Forest Management: Are We Going Over the Waterfall in the Same Canoe?" Proceedings of the Southern Forest Economics Workshop, Washington, D.C., February 1991

- "Fostering Credibility to Build Public Support", Journal of Soil and Water Conservation, Winter 1991

- "Some Thoughts on Bacteria, Planners, and Rumors of Mother Nature's Death" Environmental Planning Quarterly, Winter 1991

- Record of Decision, Bridger-Teton National Forest Land and Resource Management Plan Final Environmental Impact Statement, February, 1990

- Bridger-Teton National Forest Land and Resource Management Plan and Final Environmental Impact Statement, November 1989 [co-author and editor]

- "Point-Counterpoint," a response to a Readers Digest article about Alaska Region management, published and distributed to key groups and Congress, 1986

- Alaska Region Law Enforcement Plan, Approved 1984 [co-author, editor]

- Various Analyses of the Impacts of Pending Legislation on National Forest Management in Alaska, 1981-1984

- Assessments of Annual Legislative Programs for Congress, 1981-1984

- Public Comment Analyses and Narratives for Several Plans, Planning Reports, and Environmental Documents, including the Tongass Land Management Plan Evaluation Report {1984), the Alaska Region comments on the 1985 Draft RPA Program {1984), the Alaska Regional Guide {1983), the "Amendments 2,3 and 4" Environmental Impact Statement for the U.S. Borax Development at Quartz Hill {1983), and the Draft Regional Plan {1982) [co-author and editor]

- "Some Tips on Effective Coordination," Forest Service Internal Report, 1983

- "Seven Common Planning Errors and What to do About Them," Forest Planning, August, 1982

- The Eastern Region Draft Plan and Environmental Statement, "Issues" and "Public Comment" Sections, 1980-1981

- Conflict Management and Crisis Control: A Manager's Guide, unpublished manuscript. 1980

- "A Play Script of the Land Management Planning and Public Participation Process", 1980

- "Planners and Involvers," a weekly, informal newsletter for planners and information Specialists on the National Forests, 1980

- "Putting the Pieces Together," a Brochure on the Regional Planning Process, 1980

- The "Eastern Region Planner" Newsletter Series, 1979-80

- The Public Comment Portion of Alaska Region's <u>Final Environment Impact Statement: Withdrawal Request Under FLPMA Section 204 C for National Lands in Alaska</u>, 1980 co-author]

- <u>Wyoming Geothermal Institutional Handbook: A User's Guide of Agencies, Regulations, Permits, and Aids for Geothermal Development</u>, 1980

- <u>Big Horn Basin. Wyoming: Area Development Plan</u> (Geothermal), 1980

- <u>A Registry of Institutions Offering Services to Handicapped Wyomingites</u>, Published by the State of Wyoming, Division of Vocational Rehabilitation, 1979

- Master's Thesis: <u>Implementing Sexual Reorientation Services for Disabled Wyomingites</u>, An Institutional Plan Submitted to the State of Wyoming, 1979

- Report: "Some Suggestions for Effective Planning Coordination in Wyoming", Submitted to the State Planning Coordinator's Office, 1978

- Report: "Trends in Wyoming Voter Registration", Submitted to Representative Copenhaver, Wyoming State Legislature, 1977

Appendix D -- Definitions and Descriptions

EDR Definitions

This book explains EDR and introduces a number of key concepts that are further explored in Practices:

Crisis — an event (or series of related events) that results in a permanent, significant change in the structure, composition, or functions and relationships associated with a conflict; picture reaching a ridge between two watersheds: by crossing over, you enter a new watershed — a crisis is a "watershed" event. Loss of control by conflict participants is a characteristic of a crisis[55].

Dispute Escalation— increasing levels of strife usually exhibiting expanding numbers of issues and participants[56].

Dispute Progression—dispute escalation from issues to full-blown conflict to crisis to recovery in the aftermath of crisis.

Issue — a topic about which there is more than one opinion or position; usually a narrow, values-based dispute among two (or a few) parties leading, if unmanaged, to full-blown conflict. Dispute abatement at this stage is the most cost-efficient option, although abatement usually does not usually attempt to mitigate or eliminate the basic values conflict among parties[57].

Environmental Dispute — person-to-person, group-to-group, or nature-to-person/group strife marked by a power struggle between parties with well-defined opposing positions and different desired outcomes[58].

Environmental justice -- the equitable distribution of ecological services such as clean air and water, nutritious and safe food, and recreation while avoiding the inequitable imposition of environmental impacts such as pollutants, desertification, and disease.

Environmental peace – the condition of harmony between people and nature and among the people who live with nature.

Full-blown Conflict — a dispute with many issues and participants as well as complex interactions and communications; some conflicts exhibit accumulation of issues and participants that lead to crisis[59].

---

[55] IBID. Greek — "to decide"
[56] IBID. French — "to increase in extent, volume, number, amount, intensity of scope"
[57] IBID. French — "to come, go, or rise out of"
[58] *Webster's New Collegiate Dictionary,* G&C Merriam Co., Springfield, MA. 1979. Latin — "to discuss"
[59] IBID. Latin — "to strike together"

Recovery — the new structure, composition, and functions or relationships that exist after a crisis; if recovery is handled effectively, long-standing and recycling disputes may be reduced or eliminated[60].

Dispute Types

There are many ways to define disputes. Many of these derive from studies of war and international diplomacy practices and cannot be easily applied to civil disputes in America. Other definitions are driven by practitioners who advocate a particular method and try to apply it in every management context.

In the two books, I deliver a model focused on environmental disputes in America. More importantly, **the model allows EDR practitioners to select the right techniques for their specific situation**. No "cookie-cutter" approaches allowed. I focus on four broad "mental models," or "pathways," that I have found useful in my work over many years. These are:

> **Distress** – the internal struggles that individuals and small groups go through to resolve personal-values disputes.[61] EDR can help create positive outcomes, turning "distress" into "eustress.[62]"

> **Scandal*** – parties call for societal rejection of the values or behaviors of an individual or a group in order to create conformance with societal values or norms.[63]

> **Anarchy*** – individuals or groups reject a societal value or majority cultural view with the intention to re-order some commonly held values or behaviors or society as a whole.[64]

> **Catastrophe** – the undesirable and unacceptable effects of a natural event, or the breakdown of the built environment, on humans and society.[65]

> *I am broadening the meaning of the words "scandal" and "anarchy" in this book. My intention is to emphasize the commonalities of the concepts embodied in the pathways and reframe the readers' understanding of dispute progression.

The four pathways tend to mirror how most environmental disputes are structured, articulated, and fought out in our society. I find that the pathways approach allows participants to focus on acceptable outcomes and recovery more quickly and effectively. It is true that disputes along the four pathways may contain interdependent elements or

---

[60] IBID. Latin — "to receive or retain"

[61] *Webster's New Collegiate Dictionary,* G&C Merriam Co., Springfield, MA. 1979. Latin — "to bind or seize"

[62] www.eustress.com

[63] IBID. Latin — "stumbling block or offense"

[64] IBID. Greek — "having no ruler"

[65] IBID. Greek — "to overturn"

even overlap. However, a particular **dispute is usually characterized by one of the four pathways**, making the distinction valuable to people seeking resolution.

In short, using the pathways approach, a dispute can be effectively defined. The definition then makes resolution more efficient and focused.

www.ingramcontent.com/pod-product-compliance
Lightning Source LLC
Chambersburg PA
CBHW060814270326
41929CB00003B/30